THE MOUNTAIN BIKER'S GUIDE
TO CENTRAL APPALACHIA

Dennis Coello's America by Mountain Bike Series

THE MOUNTAIN BIKER'S GUIDE TO
CENTRAL APPALACHIA

Dennis Coello's America by
Mountain Bike Series

West Virginia
Western Maryland
Pennsylvania
New York

Joe Surkiewicz

Foreword and Introduction
by Dennis Coello, Series Editor

MENASHA
RIDGE
PRESS

FALCON PRESS®

Maps by Julie and David Taff
Cover photo by Dennis Coello

Menasha Ridge Press
3169 Cahaba Heights Road
Birmingham, Alabama 35243

Falcon Press
P.O. Box 1718
Helena, Montana 59624

Surkiewicz, Joe.
    The mountain biker's guide to Central Appalachia / Joe Surkiewicz.
        p.   cm. -- (America by mountain bike series)
    ISBN 1-56044-198-4
    1. All terrain cycling--Appalachian Region--Guidebooks.
2. Trails--Appalachian Region--Guidebooks. 3. Appalachian Region-
-Guidebooks. I. Title. II. Series.
GV1045.5.A55S87   1993   93-10696
796.6'4'0974--dc20   CIP

WARNING
   Outdoor recreation activities are by their very nature potentially hazardous. All
participants in such activities must assume the responsibility for their own action and
safety. The information contained in this guidebook cannot replace sound judgment
and good decision-making skills, which help reduce risk exposure, nor does the scope
of this book allow for disclosure of all the potential hazards and risks involved in
such activities.
   Learn as much as possible about the outdoor recreation activities you participate
in, prepare for the unexpected, and be safe and cautious. The reward will be a safer
and more enjoyable experience.

I thought all the wilderness of America was in the West till the ghost of the Susquehanna showed me different. No, there is a wilderness in the East; it's the same wilderness Ben Franklin plodded in the ox-cart days when he was postmaster, the same as it was when George Washington was a wildbuck Indian-fighter, when Daniel Boone told stories by Pennsylvania lamps and promised to find the Gap, when Bradford built his road and men whooped her up in log cabins. There were not great Arizona spaces for the little man, just the bushy wilderness of eastern Pennsylvania, Maryland, and Virginia, the backroads, the black-tar roads that curve among the mournful rivers like Susquehanna, Monongahela, old Potomac and Monocacy.

From *On the Road*, Jack Kerouac

Table of Contents

List of Maps

MAP LEGEND

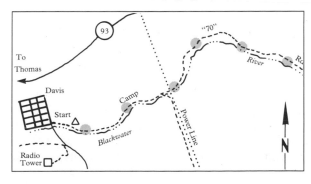

Start   △
Ride   ● ● ● ●
Landmarks   ☐
Trails   --------
Roads   ——○——
Creeks   · · · —— · · ·

Foreword

Welcome to *America by Mountain Bike*, a twenty-book series designed to provide all-terrain bikers with the information necessary to find and ride the very best trails everywhere in the mainland United States. Whether you're new to the sport and don't know where to pedal, or an experienced mountain biker who wants to learn the classic trails in another region, this series is for you. Drop a few bucks for the book, spend an hour with the detailed maps and route descriptions, and you're prepared for the finest in off-road cycling.

My role as editor of this series was simple: First, find a mountain biker who knows the area and loves to ride. Second, ask that person to spend a year researching the most popular and very best rides around. And third, have that rider describe each trail in terms of difficulty, scenery, condition, elevation change, and all other categories of information which are important to trail riders. "Pretend you've just completed a ride and met up with fellow mountain bikers at the trailhead," I told each author. "Imagine their questions, be clear in your answers."

As I said, the *editorial* process—that of sending out riders and reading the submitted chapters—is a snap. But the work involved in finding, riding, and writing about each trail is enormous. In some instances our authors' tasks are made easier by the information contributed by local bike shops or cycling clubs, or even by the writers of local "where-to" guides. Credit for these contributions is provided in each chapter, and our sincere thanks go to all who have helped.

But the overwhelming majority of trails are discovered and pedaled by our authors themselves, then compared with dozens of other routes to determine if they qualify as "classic"—that area's best in scenery and cycling fun. If you've ever had the experience of pioneering a route from outdated topographic maps, or entering a bike shop to request information from local riders who would much prefer to keep their favorite trails secret, or know how it is to double- and triple-check data to be positive your trail info is correct, then you have an idea of how each of our authors has labored to bring about these books. You and I, and all the mountain bikers of America, are the richer for their efforts.

Dennis Coello
Salt Lake City

P.S. You'll get more out of this book if you take a moment to read the next few pages explaining the "Trail Description Outline." Newcomers to mountain biking might want to spend a minute as well with the Glossary, so that terms like *hardpack, single-track,* and *windfall* won't throw you when you come across them in the text. "Topographic Maps" will help you understand a biker's need for topos, and tell you where to find them. And the section titled "Land-Use Controversy" might help us all enjoy the trails a little more. Finally, though this is a "where-to," not a "how-to" guide, those of you who have not traveled the backcountry might find "Hitting the Trail" of particular value. All the best.

Preface

For the first 200 years after the Eastern Seaboard was settled, the central Appalachian Mountains formed a natural barrier that deterred pioneers from moving west. But the population of youthful America grew steadily. Around 1800 that barrier finally burst, and thousands of settlers surged west through the mountain passes into the Ohio Valley and beyond.

During the tumultuous years that followed, the West was won. And most people began to think of the East as a tame, settled world, inhabited by big-city slickers and sedentary bankers in bowler hats.

According to the myth, the *real* outdoor action had moved West, to the rugged frontier where the intrepid explorer could vanish at will into wild mountain terrain that promised both exhilarating opportunities and no small amount of physical risk.

That was the myth, anyway.

But this antiquated view has been shattered in recent years by a hardy new breed of recreational pioneers—mountain bikers—and their rediscovery of America's eastern wilderness.

Outfitted with the latest in lightweight, high-tech equipment, this new generation of cyclists can be found cruising along wooded ridges and plunging through mountain hollows from the Potomac Highlands of West Virginia to New York's Catskills.

As they climb old forest roads and descend on twisting single-track trails, mountain bikers are discovering that Jack Kerouac was right when he suggested that the mountains of the East contained wilderness aplenty for adventurers who know where to look.

This book is designed to help mountain bikers in their search for exciting wilderness rides. The trails it describes range in difficulty from easy rambles along rivers and canals to all-day treks through rugged mountains.

My survey of Central Appalachia's best rides begins in the high mountains of southeastern West Virginia and follows the ridges northeast through western Maryland and central Pennsylvania and into upstate New York. The terrain varies from Canadian-like tundra on the Allegheny Front in West Virginia to gentle paths along old railway routes in Pennsylvania's Poconos.

The southernmost rides, in Pocahontas County, West Virginia, are the highest, most rugged and remote—nearly six hours by car from any major city. Continuing northeast, the mountains get a little lower, and a lot closer to major highways. Davis, West Virginia, an increasingly popular destination for mid-Atlantic mountain bikers, is four hours from Washington, DC.

Who says biking in the mountains has to be hard? As this West Virginia rail trail shows, there's lots of easy riding in the Central Appalachians. *Photo by Steve Shaluta, Jr.*

In western Maryland the Appalachians are only a couple of hours from Washington, Baltimore, and Pittsburgh, while the trailheads are often only minutes from Interstate 68. Traveling farther to the northeast into Pennsylvania, you'll find highways that provide good access to state forests and gamelands which offer virtually unlimited opportunities for mountain biking.

Huge river valleys near Olean and Corning in western New York evoke images of Vermont, while in the Finger Lakes region of central New York state forests offer challenging mountain biking opportunities. Only a few hours north of New York City, the Shawangunk Mountains and Catskill Park are earning a national reputation among fat-tired cyclists. Some say the scenery rivals that of Colorado. And in Adirondack Park there are thousands of square miles of wilderness to explore.

And now a few words about riding in the Appalachians. These ancient, heavily forested mountains are often wet, especially in spring. Riding through creeks and wading small rivers with your bike hoisted on your shoulder is a common experience. Sinking in bogs up to your hubs is, alas, another.

Steep uphill climbs are a reality that can't be ignored. Many of the roads and trails were laid out by hardy pioneers with oxen-pulled carts who denied themselves the luxury of switchbacks. The short, steep, straight-to-the-top climbs can be a bear.

While mountain biking in the Appalachians is often challenging, the rewards are almost always worth the effort. In spring and summer the forests are green and explode with life. The sounds of birds fill the air, and it's not unusual to surprise a browsing deer, or a young black bear ambling up the trail ahead of you.

In winter, bare trees change the views dramatically. Trails along ridges, which in summer are often just narrow green tunnels through trees, open up to reveal dramatic views of neighboring mountains and valleys.

Yet many local riders say the best time to mountain bike the Appalachians is in fall. The leaves turn from dull green to brilliant red, orange, and yellow, and the air is crisp and cool. Fall is also the driest season of the year, making the roads and trails hard-packed and fast.

This book, however, is more than a collection of top-notch bike rides. It also contains numerous tributes to a great American institution—the bike shop.

As I did my research, it was bike shop owners and the people who work in them who took their time and drew on their love of cycling to show me their favorite rides, trace routes on maps, and at times even fix my bike. In many ways, therefore, this book is as much about America's dedicated bike shop professionals as it is about wilderness riding.

For most of us mountain biking is more than just a way to spin the cranks and get a good workout—it's our *favorite* way of exploring the backcountry.

And as we cruise these mountains day after day, we're confronted with some intriguing questions: What's on the other side of that ridge? Where does that single-track go? What's the view from the summit?

Armed with this guide, a knobby-tired bike, and a sense of adventure, you're ready to begin finding the answers.

Joe Surkiewicz

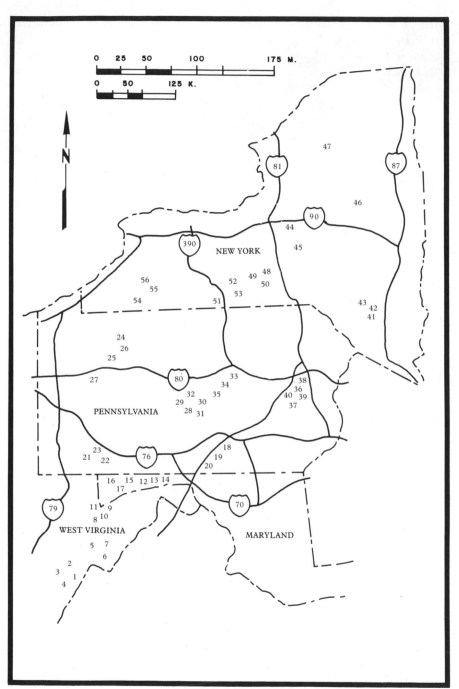

RIDE LOCATIONS

Introduction

TRAIL DESCRIPTION OUTLINE

Information on each trail in this book begins with a general description which includes length, configuration, scenery, highlights, trail conditions, and difficulty. Additional description is contained in eleven individual categories. The following will help you to understand all of the information provided.

Trail name: Trail names are as designated on USGS (United States Geological Survey) or Forest Service or other maps, and/or by local custom.

Length: The overall length of a trail is described in miles, unless stated otherwise.

Configuration: This is a description of the shape of each trail—whether the trail is a loop, out-and-back (that is, along the same route), figure-eight, trapezoid, isosceles triangle . . . , or if it connects with another trail described in the book.

Difficulty: This provides at a glance a description of the degree of physical exertion required to complete the ride, and the technical skill required to pedal it. Authors were asked to keep in mind the fact that all riders are not equal, and thus to gauge the trail in terms of how the middle-of-the-road rider—someone between the newcomer and Ned Overend—could handle the route. Comments about the trail's length, condition, and elevation change will also assist you in determining the difficulty of any trail relative to your own abilities.

Condition: Trails are described in terms of being paved, unpaved, sandy, hardpacked, washboarded, two- or four-wheel-drive, single-track or double-track. All terms that might be unfamiliar to the first-time mountain biker are defined in the Glossary.

Scenery: Here you will find a general description of the natural surroundings during the seasons most riders pedal the trail, and a suggestion of what is to be found at special times (like great fall foliage or cactus in bloom).

Highlights: Towns, major water crossings, historical sites, etc., are listed.

General location: This category describes where the trail is located in reference to a nearby town or other landmark.

Elevation change: Unless stated otherwise, the figure provided is the total gain and loss of elevation along the trail. In regions where the elevation variation is not extreme, the route is described in a more general manner of flat, rolling, or possessing short steep climbs or descents.

1

Season: This is the best time of year to pedal the route, taking into account trail condition (for example, when it will not be muddy), riding comfort (when the weather is too hot, cold, or wet), and local hunting seasons.

Note: Because the exact opening and closing dates of deer, elk, moose, and antelope seasons often change from year to year, it is suggested that riders check with the local Fish and Game department, or call a sporting goods store (or any place that sells hunting licenses) in a nearby town. Wear bright clothes in fall, and don't wear suede jackets while in the saddle. Hunter's-orange tape on the helmet is also a good idea.

Services: This category is of primary importance in guides for paved-road tourers, but is far less crucial to most mountain bike trail descriptions because there are usually no services whatsoever to be found. Authors have noted when water is available on desert or long mountain routes, and have listed the availability of food, lodging, campgrounds, and bike shops. If all these services are present, you will find only the words "All services available in. . . ."

Hazards: Special hazards like steep cliffs, great amounts of deadfall, or barbed-wire fences very close to the trail are noted here.

Rescue index: Determining how far one is from help on any particular trail can be difficult due to the backcountry nature of most mountain bike rides. Authors therefore state the proximity of homes or Forest Service outposts, nearby roads where one might hitch a ride, or the likelihood of other bikers being encountered on the trail. Phone numbers of local sheriff departments or hospitals have not been provided because, again, phones are almost never available. Besides, if a phone is reached the local operator will connect you with emergency services.

Land status: This category provides information as to whether the trail crosses land operated by the Forest Service, Bureau of Land Management, a city, state, or national park, whether it crosses private land whose owner (at the time the author did the research) allowed mountain bikers right of passage, and so on.

Note: Authors have been extremely careful to offer only those routes that are open to bikers and are legal to ride. However, because land ownership changes over time, and because the land-use controversy created by mountain bikes still has not subsided totally, it is the duty of each cyclist to look for and to heed signs warning against trail use. Don't expect this book to get you off the hook when you're facing some small-town judge for pedaling past a "Biking Prohibited" sign erected the day before. Look for these signs, read them, and heed the advice. And remember there's always another trail.

Maps: The maps in this book have been produced with great care, and in conjunction with the trail-following suggestions will help you stay on course. But as every experienced mountain biker knows, things can get tricky in the backcountry. It is therefore strongly suggested that you avail yourself of the detailed information found in the 7.5 minute series USGS (United States Geological Survey) topographic maps. In some cases, authors have found that specific Forest Service or other maps may be more useful than the USGS quads, and tell how to obtain them.

Finding the trail: Detailed information on how to reach the trailhead, and where to park your car is provided here.

Sources of additional information: Here you will find the address and/or phone number of a bike shop, governmental agency, or other source from which trail information can be obtained.

Notes on the trail: This is where you are stepped carefully through any portions of the trail that are particularly difficult to follow. The author also may add information about the route that does not fit easily into the other categories.

ABBREVIATIONS

The following road-designation abbreviations are used in the *America by Mountain Bike* series:

CR   County Road
FR   Farm Route
FS   Forest Service road
I-   Interstate
IR   Indian Route
US   United States highway

State highways are designated with the appropriate two-letter state abbreviation, followed by the road number. *Example:* UT 6 = Utah State Highway 6.

Postal Service two-letter state code

AL	Alabama	MT	Montana
AK	Alaska	NE	Nebraska
AZ	Arizona	NV	Nevada
AR	Arkansas	NH	New Hampshire
CA	California	NJ	New Jersey
CO	Colorado	NM	New Mexico
CT	Connecticut	NY	New York
DE	Delaware	NC	North Carolina
DC	District of Columbia	ND	North Dakota
FL	Florida	OH	Ohio
GA	Georgia	OK	Oklahoma
HI	Hawaii	OR	Oregon

ID	Idaho	PA	Pennsylvania
IL	Illinois	RI	Rhode Island
IN	Indiana	SC	South Carolina
IA	Iowa	SD	South Dakota
KS	Kansas	TN	Tennessee
KY	Kentucky	TX	Texas
LA	Louisiana	UT	Utah
ME	Maine	VT	Vermont
MD	Maryland	VA	Virginia
MA	Massachusetts	WA	Washington
MI	Michigan	WV	West Virginia
MN	Minnesota	WI	Wisconsin
MS	Mississippi	WY	Wyoming
MO	Missouri		

TOPOGRAPHIC MAPS

The maps in this book, when used in conjunction with the route directions present in each chapter, will in most instances be sufficient to get you to the trail and keep you on it. However, these maps cannot begin to provide the detailed information found in the 7.5 minute series USGS (United States Geological Survey) topographic maps. Recognizing how indispensable these are to bikers and hikers alike, many bike shops and sporting goods stores now carry topos of the local area.

But if you're brand new to mountain biking you might be wondering "What's a topographic map?" In short, these differ from standard "flat" maps because they indicate not only linear distance, but elevation as well. One glance at a topo will show you the difference, for "contour lines" are spread across the map like dozens of intricate spider webs. Each contour line represents a particular elevation, and each topo has written at its base a particular "contour interval" designation. Yes, it sounds confusing if you're new to the lingo, but it truly is a simple and wonderfully helpful system. Keep reading.

Let's assume that the 7.5 minute series topo before us says "Contour Interval 40 feet." And that the short trail we'll be pedaling is two inches in length on the map, and crosses five contour lines between its beginning and end. What do we know? Well, because the linear scale of this series is two thousand feet to the inch (roughly 2¾ inches representing a mile), we know our trail is approximately four-fifths of a mile long (2″ × 2,000′). But we also know we'll be climbing or descending two hundred vertical feet (5 contour lines × 40 feet each) over that distance. And the elevation designations written on occasional contour lines will tell us if we're heading up or down.

The authors of this series warn their readers of upcoming terrain, but only a detailed topo gives you the information that enables you to pinpoint your position exactly on a map, steer you toward optional trails and roads nearby, plus let you know at a glance if you'll be pedaling hard to take them. It's a lot of information for a very low cost. In fact, the only drawback with topos is their size—several feet square. I've tried rolling them into tubes, folding them carefully, even cutting them into blocks and photocopying the pieces. Any of these systems is a pain, but no matter how you pack the maps you'll be happy they're along (you'll want to take a compass, too).

Major universities and some public libraries also carry topos; you might try photocopying the ones you need to avoid the cost of buying them. But if you want your own and can't find them locally, write to:

USGS Map Sales
Box 25286
Denver, Colorado 80225

Ask for an index while you're at it, plus a price list and a copy of the booklet *Topographic Maps*. In minutes you'll be reading them like a pro.

A second excellent series of maps available to mountain bikers is that put out by the United States Forest Service. If your trail runs through an area designated as a national forest, look in the phone book (white pages) under the United States Government listings, find the Department of Agriculture heading, and then run your finger through that section until you find the Forest Service. Give them a call and they'll provide the address of the regional Forest Service office, from which you can obtain the appropriate map.

LAND-USE CONTROVERSY

A few years ago I wrote a long piece on this issue for *Sierra Magazine*, and called literally dozens of government land managers, game wardens, mountain bikers, and local officials, to get a feeling for how ATBs were being welcomed on the trails. All that I've seen personally since, and heard from my authors, indicates there hasn't been much change. Which means we're still considered the new kid on the block, that we have less right to the trails than horses and hikers, and that we're excluded from many areas including:

a) wilderness areas
b) national parks (except on roads, and those paths specifically marked "bike path")
c) national monuments (except on roads open to the public)
d) most state parks and monuments (except on roads, and those paths specifically marked "bike path")

e) an increasing number of urban and county parks, especially in California (except on roads, and those areas specifically marked "bike path")

Frankly, I have little difficulty with these exclusions, and would in fact restrict our presence from some trails I've ridden (one time) due to the environmental damage and chance of blind-siding the many walkers and hikers I met up with along the way. But these are my personal views. They should not be interpreted as those of the authors, and are mentioned here only as a way to introduce the land-use problem and the varying positions on it which even mountain bikers hold.

You can do your part in keeping us from being excluded from even more trails by riding responsibly. Many local and national off-road bicycle organizations have been formed with exactly this in mind, and one of the largest—NORBA, the National Off-Road Bicycle Association—offers the following code of behavior for mountain bikers:

1. I will yield the right of way to other non-motorized recreationists. I realize that people judge all cyclists by my actions.
2. I will slow down and use caution when approaching or overtaking another and will make my presence known well in advance.
3. I will maintain control of my speed at all times and will approach turns in anticipation of someone around the bend.
4. I will stay on designated trails to avoid trampling native vegetation and minimize potential erosion to trails by not using muddy trails or short-cutting switchbacks.
5. I will not disturb wildlife or livestock.
6. I will not litter. I will pack out what I pack in, and pack out more than my share whenever possible.
7. I will respect public and private property, including trail use signs, no trespassing signs, and I will leave gates as I have found them.
8. I will always be self-sufficient and my destination and travel speed will be determined by my ability, my equipment, the terrain, the present and potential weather conditions.
9. I will not travel solo when bikepacking in remote areas. I will leave word of my destination, and when I plan to return.
10. I will observe the practice of minimum impact bicycling by "taking only pictures and memories and leaving only waffle prints."
11. I will always wear a helmet whenever I ride.

Now, I have a problem with some of these—number nine, for instance. The most enjoyable mountain biking I've ever done has been solo. And as to leaving word of destination and time of return, I've enjoyed living in such a way as to say, "I'm off to pedal Colorado. See you in the fall." Of course it's senseless to take needless risks, and I plan a ride and pack my gear with this in mind. But for me number nine smacks too much of the "never-out-of-touch" mentality. And getting away from civilization, deep into the wilds, is for many people what mountain biking's all about.

All in all, however, theirs is a good list, and surely we mountain bikers would be liked more, and excluded less, if we followed the suggestions. But let me offer a "code of ethics" I much prefer, one given cyclists by Utah's Wasatch-Cache National Forest office.

Study a Forest Map Before You Ride
Currently, bicycles are permitted on roads and developed trails within the Wasatch-Cache National Forest except in designated Wilderness. If your route crosses private land, it is your responsibility to obtain right of way permission from the land owner.

Keep Groups Small
Riding in large groups degrades the outdoor experience for others, can disturb wildlife and usually leads to greater resource damage.

Avoid Riding on Wet Trails
Bicycle tires leave ruts in wet trails. These ruts concentrate runoff and accelerate erosion. Postponing a ride when the trails are wet will preserve the trails for future use.

Stay on Roads and Trails
Riding cross-country destroys vegetation and damages the soil.

Always Yield to Others
Trails are shared by hikers, horses and bicycles. Move off the trail to allow horses to pass and stop to allow hikers adequate room to share the trail. Simply yelling "Bicycle!" is not acceptable.

Control Your Speed
Excessive speed endangers yourself and other forest users.

Avoid Wheel Lock-up and Spin-out
Steep terrain is especially vulnerable to trail wear. Locking brakes on steep descents or when stopping needlessly damages trails. If a slope is steep enough to require locking wheels and skidding, dismount and walk your bicycle. Likewise, if an ascent is so steep your rear wheel slips and spins, dismount and walk your bicycle.

Protect Waterbars and Switchbacks
Waterbars, the rock and log drains built to direct water off trails, protect trails from erosion. When you encounter a waterbar, ride directly over the top or dismount and walk your bicycle. Riding around the ends of waterbars destroys them and speeds erosion. Skidding around switch-

back corners shortens trail life. Slow down for switchback corners and keep your wheels rolling.

If You Abuse It, You Lose It

Mountain bikes are relative newcomers to the forest and must prove themselves responsible trail users. By following the guidelines above, and by participating in trail maintenance service projects, bicyclists can help avoid closures which would prevent them from using trails.

I've never seen a better trail-etiquette list for mountain bikers. So have fun. Be careful. And don't screw up things for the next guy.

HITTING THE TRAIL

Once again, because this is a "where-to," not a "how-to" guide, the following will be brief. If you're a veteran trail rider these suggestions might serve to remind you of something you've forgotten to pack. If you're a newcomer, they might convince you to think twice before hitting the backcountry unprepared. **Water:** I've heard the questions dozens of times. "How much is enough? One bottle? Two? Three?! But think of all that extra weight!" Well, one simple physiological fact should convince you to err on the side of excess when it comes to determining how much water to pack: a human working hard in ninety-degree temperature needs approximately ten quarts of fluids every day. Ten quarts. That's two and a half gallons—*twelve* large water bottles, or *sixteen* small ones. And with water weighing in at approximately eight pounds per gallon, a one-day supply comes to a whopping twenty pounds.

In other words, pack along two or three bottles even for short rides. And make sure you can purify the water found along the trail on longer routes. When writing of those routes where this could be of critical importance, each author has provided information on where water can be found near the trail— if it can be found at all. But drink it untreated and you run the risk of disease. [See *Giardia* in the Glossary.]

One sure way to kill both the bacteria and viruses in water is to boil it for ten minutes, plus one minute more for each one thousand feet of elevation above sea level. Right. That's just how you want to spend your time on a bike ride. Besides, who wants to carry a stove, or denude the countryside stoking bonfires to boil water?

Luckily, there is a better way. Many riders pack along the effective, inexpensive, and only slightly distasteful tetraglycine hydroperiodide tablets (sold under the names of Potable Aqua, Globaline, Coughlan's, and others). Some invest in portable, lightweight purifiers that filter out the crud. Yes, purifying water with tablets or filters is a bother. But catch a case of Giardia sometime and you'll understand why it's worth the trouble.

Tools: Ever since my first cross-country tour in '65 I've been kidded about the number of tools I pack on the trail. And so I will exit entirely from this discussion by providing a list compiled by two mechanic (and mountain biker) friends of mine. After all, since they make their livings fixing bikes, and get their kicks by riding them, who could be a better source?

The following is suggested as an absolute minimum:

tire levers
spare tube and patch kit
air pump
allen wrenches (3, 4, 5, and 6 mm)
six-inch crescent (adjustable-end) wrench
small flat-blade screwdriver
chain rivet tool
spoke wrench

But their personal tool pouches carried on the trail contain, in addition to the above:

channel locks (small)
air gauge
tire valve cap (the metal kind, with a valve-stem remover)
baling wire (ten or so inches, for temporary repairs)
duct tape (small roll for temporary repairs or tire boot)
boot material (small piece of old tire or a large tube patch)
spare chain link
rear derailleur pulley
spare nuts and bolts
paper towel and tube of waterless hand cleaner

First-aid kit: My personal kit contains the following, sealed inside double zip-lock bags:

sunshade
aspirin
butterfly closure bandages
band-aids
gauze compress pads (a half-dozen 4″×4″)
gauze (one roll)
ace bandages or Spenco joint wraps
Benadryl (an antihistamine to guard against possible allergic reactions)
water purification tablets
moleskin/Spenco "Second Skin"

hydrogen peroxide/iodine/Mercurochrome (some kind of antiseptic)
snakebite kit

Final considerations: The authors of this series have done a good job in suggesting that specific items be packed for certain trails—like raingear in particular seasons, a hat and gloves for mountain passes, or shades for desert jaunts. Heed their warnings, and think ahead. Good luck.

Dennis Coello
Salt Lake City

WEST VIRGINIA

Pocahontas County

For mountain bikers who like riding in wilderness—and lots of it—Pocahontas County is arguably the best mountain biking destination in the East. Consider: This county in southeastern West Virginia boasts a major chunk of the 830,000-acre Monongahela National Forest, where the rugged Allegheny Mountains soar toward 5,000 feet. Here too are the headwaters of eight rivers: the Greenbrier, Cherry, Elk, Cheat, Gauley, Tygart Valley, Williams, and Cranberry. With 330,000 acres of state and national forests to explore in Pocahontas County alone, it's not stretching the point to call this place "Mountain Bike Heaven."

Additional high-quality wilderness attractions include the Cranberry Glades Wilderness Area (closed to mountain bikes, but open to mountain *bikers* who don't mind hiking for a while), which features 35,000 acres of bogs and forests that evoke visions of Alaskan tundra. Underground erosion created over 96 significant caverns in the county. The Cass Scenic Railroad, a steam locomotive–pulled train that climbs Bald Knob (the state's second-highest peak), is a spectacular trip that should not be missed. The Highland Scenic Highway extends 22 miles at altitudes reaching over 4,000 feet, and has views of wilderness stretching in all directions to the horizon.

So what's the mountain biking like in Pocahontas County? The answer is scenic, varied, and virtually unlimited. While many trails are surprisingly easy (the Greenbrier River Trail, for example, is 75 miles long and virtually flat), the region is renowned for its steep and rugged trails. Be warned: Mountain biking on foot trails in the mountains often means negotiating wet, steep, rocky, boggy, and root-tangled obstacle courses. If this isn't your idea of fun, stick to the many Forest Service roads that lace the mountains. But if mile after mile of technical single-track turns you on, this is the place.

A word of warning to intrepid backcountry trekkers: The weather in the high mountains of Pocahontas County matches the terrain for severity and unpredictability. Mountain bikers embarking on an all-day ride should carry rain gear and extra clothes, food, water, first-aid items, tools, a topo map, and compass.

Mountain bike headquarters in Pocahontas County is the Elk River Touring Center in Slatyfork, a small village about 20 miles north of Marlinton. Owners Gil and Mary Willis started guiding mountain bike tours in 1984 and are the resident mountain biking experts for this vast area. On your visit to Pocahontas County, be sure to visit Slatyfork for the latest information on trail conditions. Elk River also offers lodging, an excellent restaurant, a mountain bike shop and rentals, and touring services (both guided and self-guided). Gil and Mary want to help visiting mountain bikers have a good time, and thereby spread the word about "Mountain Bike Heaven."

RIDE 1 GREENBRIER RIVER TRAIL / MARLINTON TO SHARP'S TUNNEL

The Greenbrier River Trail winds through a remote mountain valley along a clean, fast-flowing river that has been involved in wild and scenic river studies. Old Appalachian farms, many of them deserted and overgrown, overlook the river. On this section of the trail you can explore the 511′-long Sharp's Tunnel. And if the weather's warm, check out the swimming hole at the base of the trestle leading to the tunnel. The wildflower blossoms in late May and early June are spectacular.

This 8.5-mile (one-way), out-and-back ride takes you along some of the best scenery in Pocahontas County. And being virtually flat, it's a perfect introductory ride to the area. The trail, formerly a railroad right-of-way, is mostly hard-packed gravel. There are short sections of loose gravel, and washouts occasionally occur where streams and creeks empty into the river.

General location: The ride starts in Marlinton, West Virginia, located on US 219 between Lewisburg and Elkins.

Elevation change: With a virtually flat grade, the change in elevation along the trail is nominal.

Season: The trail can be ridden from late March through late October. Spring can be muddy and cold, and expect snow from November through March. Avoid riding in deer hunting season, in the late fall.

Services: All services are available in Marlinton. Water is available at the restored railroad depot in town. Two primitive camping areas ideal for cyclists are located above and below Sharp's Tunnel. Elk River Touring Center, 20 miles north of Marlinton in Slatyfork, has a mountain bike shop.

Hazards: Sharp's Tunnel is littered with rocks; carrying a flashlight is a good idea, although not absolutely necessary. Watch for washouts along the trail where creeks flow into the river.

Rescue index: The trail runs through isolated country. While there are farms in the area, many are remote and hard to reach.

Land status: West Virginia state park.

Maps: A map of the Greenbrier River Trail is available at the restored railroad depot in Marlinton. The USGS 7.5 minute topo maps for this section of the Greenbrier River Trail are Marlinton and Edray.

Finding the trail: Marlinton is located at the intersection of WV 39 and US 219, between Lewisburg and Elkins, West Virginia. Park at the Old Train

GREENBRIER RIVER TRAIL/
MARLINTON TO SHARP'S TUNNEL

To 92   To Dunmore

Stony Bottom   Clover Lick

SNOWSHOE SKI AREA

1

Greenbrier

28

To Elkins

9

SHARP'S TUNNEL

Greenbrier River Trail

To Minnehaha Springs

River

15

River

Trail

39

Slatyfork

219

Edray

Campbelltown

Marlinton

I 0 I 2 3 4 5 M.

I 0 I 2 3 4 5 K.

To Buckeye

Depot on Main Street (WV 39), which serves as Marlinton's Visitor Center. The trail starts behind the building.

Sources of additional information:

Superintendent
Greenbrier River Trail
Star Route
Box 125
Caldwell, West Virginia 24925
(304) 536-1944

Pocahontas County Tourism Commission
P.O. Box 275
Marlinton, West Virginia 24954
(800) 336-7009

Elk River Touring Center
Slatyfork, West Virginia 26291
(304) 572-3771

Easy pedaling along the Greenbrier River. *Photo by Ron Snow*

Notes on the trail: From the Old Train Depot, pedal out 4th Avenue for a half mile to the sign for the trail on the left. This stretch of the Greenbrier River Trail north of Marlinton is probably the most scenic and remote on the trail's 75-mile length. As it winds its way through the river valley, the trail passes through many villages and traverses 35 bridges and 2 tunnels.

RIDE 2 *PROP'S RUN*

Here's a ride for the serious off-road enthusiast that shows what West Virginia mountain biking is all about. Strictly for experienced, well-conditioned cyclists, Prop's Run is a 16-mile loop that climbs for 2,000' on a well-main-

PROP'S RUN

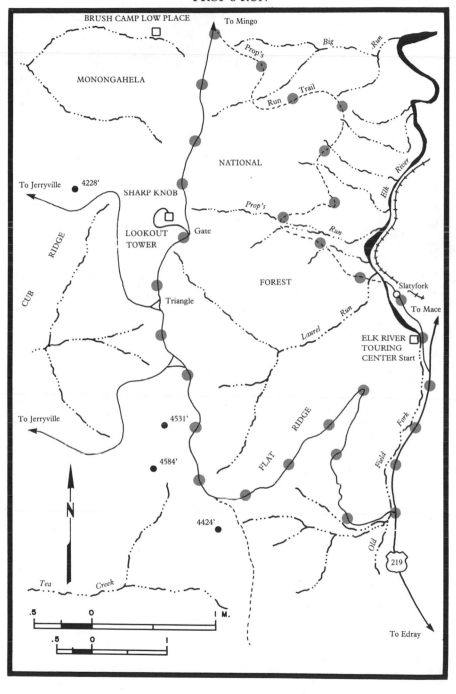

tained Forest Service road, followed by 6 miles of steep, wet, and rocky downhill single-track that only expert riders will "clean."

From the lookout tower on Sharp Knob, spectacular wilderness views in all directions are your reward for the long climb. But for the truly hard-core, it's the 6 intense miles of downhill single-track on Prop's Run that make this ride memorable. After the hammering descent, the final spin along the Elk River is quiet and peaceful, and affords a nice place to wash off your bike. It'll need it.

General location: Monongahela National Forest, near the village of Slaty-fork, 20 miles north of Marlinton, West Virginia.

Elevation change: The ride starts at 2,735' of elevation in Slatyfork and climbs to 4,532' at the lookout tower on Sharp Knob. Next comes approximately 2 miles of roller-coaster Forest Service road. At the trailhead to Prop's Run, the elevation is 4,216' and drops to 2,671'. The total elevation gain is around 2,000'.

Season: The best riding is from mid-May through early October. Spring is wet and usually cold. Expect snow from late October through April. Avoid riding in deer hunting season, in the late fall.

Services: Water, bicycle equipment and repairs, a restaurant and lodging are available at Elk River Touring Center. All other services are available in Marlinton to the south and in Linwood to the north. Camping is available at Tea Creek Campground and Handley Public Hunting and Fishing Area.

Hazards: You can get seriously lost in this wilderness, so be sure to carry a topo map and compass. The weather in these mountains can change dramatically. Carry raingear, extra clothing, food, water, first-aid items, and tools. The single-track is intense; don't exceed your abilities.

Rescue index: Mountain bikers won't see a soul on this ride. There are no residences, very little traffic on the Forest Service road, no farms, no *nothing*.

Land status: Monongahela National Forest.

Maps: The USGS 7.5 minute topo is Sharp Knob.

Finding the trail: The ride starts at Elk River Touring Center on US 219 in Slatyfork, about 20 miles north of Marlinton. Park in the lot past the wooden bridge.

Sources of additional information:

District Ranger
Monongahela National Forest
Cemetery Road
Marlinton, West Virginia 24954
(304) 799-4334

Elk River Touring Center
Slatyfork, West Virginia 26291
(304) 572-3771

Notes on the trail: Riding from the Touring Center in Slatyfork, turn right on US 219 and go 1.5 miles to Forest Service Road 24; turn right. Stay on this road, climbing past several trailheads and roads on the left, to the big intersection with the triangle in the middle of the road (look for pine trees growing inside the triangle) and bear right. Pass through a gate past the lookout tower on Sharp Knob, then look for the Prop's Run Trail sign on the right.

At the end of the trail, cross Laurel Run, a small stream. Ride 50 yards to a "T" intersection and turn left to reach the Elk River. Wade through the river; the old ford turns into a double-track trail. Follow it across the railroad tracks, bear right and pedal about .2 miles to US 219, which is paved. Turn right for the short return spin to Elk River Touring Center.

RIDE 3   *RED RUN*

While only a 7-mile loop ride, this stretch of single-track is demanding. Though fairly level, the technical riding requirements make up for the lack of climbing. Most of the trail surfaces are spongy and mossy—and wet. Rocks, wet roots, bogs, deep mud, and stream crossings make for low-speed, technical riding. The trails are frequently littered with deadfalls. Yet intermediate- and advanced-level riders will be delighted by the challenges of the trails and the natural beauty of the area.

The ride starts in lush hardwood forests, progresses through red spruce groves, and then ends in a mixed hardwood and spruce forest. From the overlook at the start, the view is of cranberry bogs and the headwaters of the Williams River. Hawks soar at eye level. This is subtle, beautiful, rugged West Virginia at its best.

General location: Monongahela National Forest, off the Highland Scenic Highway, about 10 miles from Marlinton, West Virginia.

Elevation change: The ride starts at 4,200' of elevation and varies only a few hundred feet or so over its length.

Season: The trail is usually rideable from mid-May through early October. Avoid riding in deer hunting season, in the late fall. Expect snow from late October through March.

Services: Most services are available in Marlinton, about 10 miles from the intersection of US 219 and the Scenic Highway. Bike supplies, repairs, a restaurant and lodging are available at Elk River Touring Center in Slatyfork, about 9 miles north on US 219.

Hazards: The single-track is technical, with lots of slick rocks and tree roots. The weather at this altitude changes fast, so carry raingear, extra clothes, food, water, first-aid items, and tools.

RED RUN

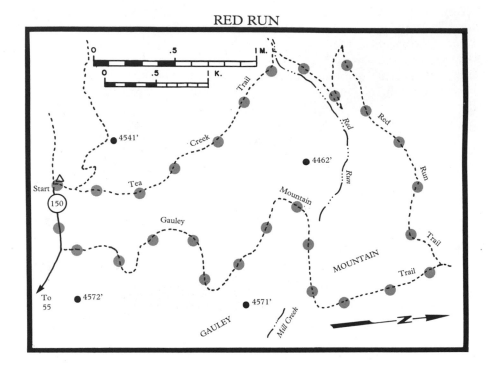

Rescue index: This ride goes deep into the national forest; there are no farms or residences on the loop. Cars can be flagged down on the Scenic Highway where the ride starts.

Land status: Monongahela National Forest.

Maps: The USGS 7.5 minute topo is Woodrow.

Finding the trail: From Marlinton, drive north on US 219 to the intersection with WV 150, the Highland Scenic Highway. Drive 4 miles to the second overlook (Little Laurel Overlook), and park. The trailhead is across the road and through the large field.

Sources of additional information:

District Ranger
Monongahela National Forest
Cemetery Road
Marlinton, West Virginia 24954
(304) 799-4334

Elk River Touring Center
Slatyfork, West Virginia 26291
(304) 572-3771

Riders cross an open field to begin the Red Run—a demanding 7-mile stretch of single track. *Photo by Ron Snow*

Notes on the trail: To start the loop, turn right out of the overlook parking lot and ride down the Scenic Highway a short distance to the Gauley Mountain Trail on the left.

Red Run Trail is significantly more gnarly than Gauley Mountain Trail; if it gets too intense, turn back and continue on Gauley Mountain Trail to do an easier out-and-back ride. All the trails in this area are signed, so it's an easy area to explore.

RIDE 4   *WILLIAMS RIVER LOOP*

While this 12-mile loop begins and ends at the same location as the Red Run ride, it's completely different in character. Technically, it's easy, but requires good endurance for the long climbs. The loop begins on the paved Highland Scenic Highway, then changes to a gravel road, then to a dirt road, and then

WILLIAMS RIVER LOOP

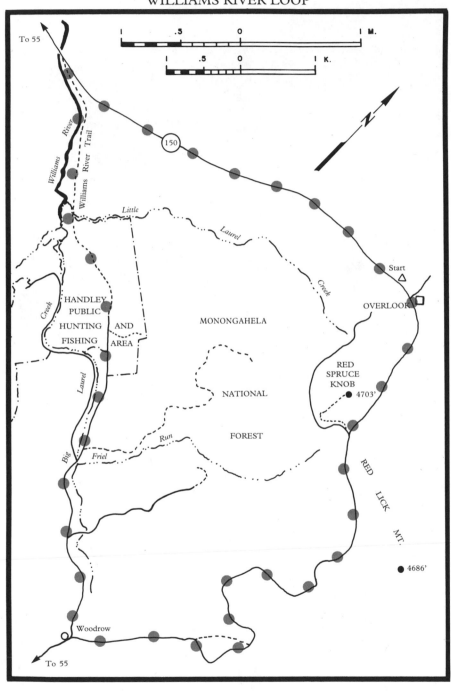

to a wide, grassy single-track. The ride finishes with a long climb on the paved Scenic Highway.

This ride is an energetic blast through huge mountains and isolated alpine valleys. At the beginning of the loop, the descent on the gravel road into Woodrow seems like it goes forever. Then it continues through the Handley Public Hunting and Fishing Area, with views of ponds and lakes, ducks and geese, and the Williams River. On the climb back to the start the vista gets better and better, which helps take your mind off your legs.

At the beginning of the ride there are majestic views from the Highland Scenic Highway. After the descent into the Williams River Valley the loop winds through sheep farms, old homesteads, meadows, and forests with a backdrop of 5,000' mountains. Along the headwaters of the Williams River, the views from the trail look down through mixed pine and hardwood forests to the river below.

General location: Monongahela National Forest and Handley Public Hunting and Fishing Area, off the Highland Scenic Highway near Marlinton, West Virginia.

Elevation change: The ride starts at 4,200' of elevation and drops to 3,200' at Woodrow. This is followed by some roller coaster riding that drops to 3,022'. The ride ends with a 1,200' climb back to the overlook on the Scenic Highway. The total elevation gain is around 1,400'.

Season: This route is rideable from late May through early October. Expect snow from late October through April. Avoid riding in deer hunting season, in late November.

Services: Most services are available in Marlinton, about 10 miles from the intersection of US 219 and the Highland Scenic Highway. Bike supplies, repairs, a restaurant and lodging are available at Elk River Touring Center in Slatyfork, about 9 miles north on US 219.

Hazards: The descent on the gravel road from the overlook is long and steep; watch for metal cattle grates, which should be crossed at right-angles.

Rescue index: There is light traffic on all the roads on this loop. You will find a forest ranger residence at the Handley Public Hunting and Fishing Area.

Land status: Monongahela National Forest, state game lands, state and county roads.

Maps: The USGS 7.5 minute topo is Woodrow.

Finding the trail: From Marlinton, drive north on US 219 to the intersection with WV 150, the Highland Scenic Highway. Drive 4 miles to the second pulloff (Little Laurel Overlook), and park.

Sources of additional information:

District Ranger
Monongahela National Forest
Cemetery Road

Marlinton, West Virginia 24954
(304) 799-4334

Elk River Touring Center
Slatyfork, West Virginia 26291
(304) 572-3771

Notes on the trail: From the overlook, turn right and continue on the Scenic Highway past the head of the Gauley Mountain Trail on the left. At the next intersection turn right, ride about 60 yards, and turn left onto Williams River Road (a gravel road that starts to drop rapidly). The gravel road ends at a "T" intersection; turn right onto the paved road and ride into Woodrow. Follow the signs into the Handley Public Hunting and Fishing Area. At the lake, the road turns to gravel. Ride toward the houses and through the gate; the road will begin to narrow into single-track (the Williams River Trail). Turn right onto a small footpath that leads to a parking lot at the Scenic Highway; if you reach a cement highway overpass, you've gone too far. Turn right at the Scenic Highway and climb back to the overlook.

Gil Willis of Elk River Touring Center calls this ride "a confidence builder": a ride so scenic—yet non-technical—that it converts novice mountain bikers into fanatics.

Spruce Knob / Monongahela National Forest

God knows it's a long drive. This mountain bike destination is about six hours from Washington, and the last 12-mile segment snakes up a mountain on a narrow dirt road. But it seems only natural that some of the best mountain biking in West Virginia is in the middle of nowhere.

"Nowhere," in this case, happens to be Spruce Knob (the highest point in West Virginia—elevation 4,861 feet), and the mountains surrounding it. Located near the center of Monongahela National Forest, the Spruce Knob area has a well-earned reputation for ruggedness. Don't be put off by that, however, if you're a strong rider. For mountain bikers the area really isn't too formidable, since the terrain around Spruce Knob features meadows, open woods uncluttered by underbrush, and easy-to-follow streams and ridges.

But this is still West Virginia. Much of the single-track is incredibly technical, with long obstacle courses full of rocks, roots, mud, and flowing water. Yet the area contains enough Forest Service roads, off-road-vehicle trails, and well-graded hiking paths to make Spruce Knob attractive to all mountain bikers, regardless of their skill level.

Spruce Knob rates four stars in backcountry ambience. The area's remoteness, high altitude, and mature forests create a pristine wilderness setting. After all, these remote mountains contain the headwaters of three major river systems—the Cheat, Potomac, and Greenbrier Rivers. The wildlife species range from the shy black bear to wild turkey. Mosses and ferns grow in great variety on the forest floor. Rhododendron and mountain laurel add their waxy green beauty to the scene. Because of a wide variety of trees, the fall foliage is particularly riotous in these mountains.

The mountain biking possibilities around Spruce Knob are nearly endless. The Seneca Creek Trail System, just north of Spruce Knob, contains more than 60 miles of hiking trails. Using Spruce Knob Lake Campground as a base, it would take weeks to explore all the trails and Forest Service roads in the area. For multi-day treks, ride west to Middle Mountain (west of Spruce Knob), to link up with Canaan Valley and Dolly Sods to the north and Shavers Fork and the Williams River region to the south. It's no exaggeration to say that Monongahela National Forest represents a lifetime of mountain biking opportunities.

But if you can't quit your job to spend a few weeks exploring this fascinating area, at least plan a long weekend. The three rides that follow are an excellent introduction to the mountain biking around Spruce Knob. Set up a base camp at Spruce Knob Campground, and get ready for one of the best mountain biking experiences this side of Colorado.

RIDE 5   *GRANTS BRANCH TO GANDY CREEK LOOP*

Mountain biking doesn't get easier than this fun ride in the mountains around Spruce Knob. This 5-mile loop starts with a gentle descent on an abandoned railroad grade that's been converted to a wide, grassy off-road-vehicle trail. The return follows a well-maintained dirt Forest Service road with a gentle uphill grade.

It's a loop with a little of everything. The descent on Grants Branch Trail is through a mature hardwood forest. At WV 29 the ride is along Gandy Branch, a fast-moving mountain stream. On Forest Service Road 1, the trail leaves the stream and begins a gentle ascent. On the climb, the views of the mountains just get better and better.

General location: Spruce Knob, located in Monongahela National Forest, is about 40 miles southwest of Petersburg, West Virginia.

Elevation change: The loop starts at Spruce Knob campground at an elevation around 3,800', and descends to about 3,400' at Gandy Creek. The altitude is recovered on the return leg along Narrow Ridge. The total elevation gain is around 400'.

Season: Mid-summer through fall are the best seasons to ride around Spruce Knob. Spring and early summer can be cold and wet. Expect snow from November through March. Avoid riding in deer hunting season, in the late fall.

Services: The nearest town is Petersburg. Limited services—motels, small grocery stores, and gas—are available in the villages of Seneca Rocks and Riverton. The nearest bike shop is Blackwater Bikes in Davis.

Hazards: On this easy ride, the biggest hazard is the weather. It can change rapidly, so carry raingear and extra clothes.

Rescue index: This is an isolated area, so the closest help is at Spruce Knob Lake Campground. Cars can be flagged down on WV 29, but traffic is very light.

Land status: National forest.

Maps: The USGS 7.5 minute topo is Spruce Knob. In addition, the Seneca Creek Trail System, Spruce Knob Unit map complements the topo by showing more trail details.

Finding the trail: From WV 28, turn onto FS 112, 3 miles south of Riverton. (There is a sign for Spruce Knob.) Follow the road about 13 miles to the camp-

GRANTS BRANCH TO
GANDY CREEK LOOP

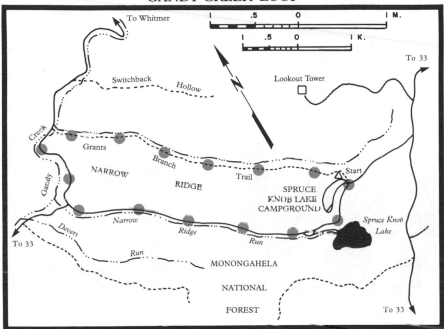

ground or to Spruce Knob Lake and park. The Grants Branch trailhead is at the entrance to the campground.

Sources of additional information:

U.S. Forest Service
Monongahela National Forest
Route 3 Box 240
Petersburg, West Virginia 26847
(304) 257-4488

Blackwater Bikes
West Virginia Highway 32
Davis, West Virginia 26260
(304) 259-5286

Photo by Ron Snow

RIDE 6 *BIG RUN LOOP*

This ride is for dedicated hammerheads. While most of the riding is on Forest Service roads, the route's technical single-track (featuring rocks, wet roots, bogs, mud, and streams) requires good bike handling skills and endurance. But without a lot of steep climbing to wear you down, this ride is considered moderate by rugged West Virginia standards. The high elevation, remoteness, and varied terrain make Big Run Loop challenging and beautiful.

The 8-mile loop features excellent views of Spruce Knob (at 4,861 feet, the highest point in West Virginia) to the east and into Big Run Valley. Much of the trail passes through huge, grassy meadows on the ridges. Big Run is an excellent trout-fishing stream and is lined with beaver ponds. The single-track near the beginning of the ride is intense, with an amazing tangle of tree roots along a line of spruce trees that will challenge expert riders. More railroad grade follows, leading you through open meadows and over a couple of high fences. The last half of the ride follows a dirt Forest Service (FS) road.

BIG RUN LOOP

General location: Spruce Knob, located in Monongahela National Forest, is about 40 miles southwest of Petersburg, West Virginia.

Elevation change: The ride starts around 4,000' of elevation, descends to about 3,700', and then slowly returns to 4,000' at the end of the ride.

Season: The best riding is from mid-summer through the fall. Spring and early summer tend to be wet and cool. Expect snow from November through March. Avoid riding in deer hunting season, in the late fall.

Services: The nearest town is Petersburg. Limited services—motels, small grocery stores, and gas—are available in the villages of Seneca Rocks and Riverton. The nearest bike shop is Blackwater Bikes in Davis.

Hazards: This is remote country, so carry a topo map and a compass. Be prepared for severe weather and carry extra food, water, and bike tools.

Rescue index: Mountain bikers venturing into this wilderness rarely meet other people. A vehicle could be flagged down on lightly traveled FS 103.

Land status: National forest.

Maps: The USGS 7.5 minute topo is Spruce Knob. In addition, the Seneca Creek Trail System, Spruce Knob Unit map complements the topo by showing more trail details.

Finding the trail: From WV 28, turn onto FS 112, 3 miles south of Riverton. (There is a sign for Spruce Knob.) Follow the road about 13 miles to the campground or to Spruce Knob Lake and park.

Sources of additional information:

> U.S. Forest Service
> Monongahela National Forest
> Route 3 Box 240
> Petersburg, West Virginia 26847
> (304) 257-4488

> Blackwater Bikes
> West Virginia Highway 32
> Davis, West Virginia 26260
> (304) 259-5286

Notes on the trail: Start the ride on the Short Trail, a narrow, technical single-track that begins near the campground entrance. Turn left at FS 103 and ride a short distance to the hiking trail on the right at the intersection with FS 1.

This loop can be tricky to follow. Good map and compass skills are a must. Often the trail is obscured, especially when crossing fields and meadows. Check the map and compass regularly.

RIDE 7   *ALLEGHENY MOUNTAIN / SENECA CREEK LOOP*

For a great variety of terrain and views, this 15-mile loop can't be beat. It starts with the Allegheny Trail, a wide, grassy double-track that's an easy ramble along a forested mountain ridge. Bear Hunter Trail, a challenging single-track, drops through a mature forest along a small stream. Next, the loop follows Seneca Creek on a gentle path through a forest that is rapidly returning to wilderness after being logged at the turn of the century. The ride ends on well-maintained, dirt Forest Service roads.

The single-track on Bear Hunter Trail is white-knuckle all the way, so good bike handling skills are a must. Also, this is a long ride requiring good endurance. But most of the trails are well-maintained, wide and smooth, and are a joy to ride.

General location: Spruce Knob, located in Monongahela National Forest, is about 40 miles southwest of Petersburg, West Virginia.

Elevation change: The ride starts at 3,900' of elevation and follows the Allegheny Trail along a mountain ridge. The steep descent on Bear Hunter Trail

ALLEGHENY MOUNTAIN/
SENECA CREEK LOOP

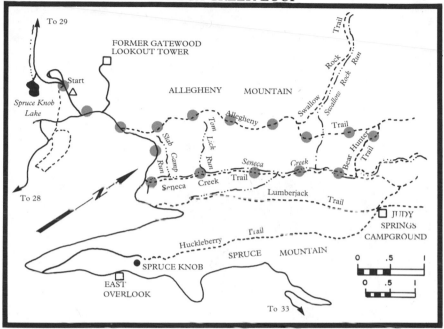

drops over 500' in just over 1 mile. The elevation is regained slowly on the return along Seneca Creek Trail.

Season: The best riding is from mid-summer through fall. Spring and early summer tend to be wet and cool. Expect snow from November through March. Avoid riding in deer hunting season, in the late fall.

Services: The nearest town is Petersburg. Limited services—motels, small grocery stores, and gas—are available in the villages of Seneca Rocks and Riverton. The nearest bike shop is Blackwater Bikes in Davis.

Hazards: Bear Hunter Trail, with its steep and rocky descent, offers a high potential for "unscheduled dismounts" (crashes). Also, be prepared for rapid changes in the weather.

Rescue index: Judy Springs Campground, on Seneca Creek Trail, is a camping area that is popular in the summer months. There is light traffic on FS 112.

Land status: National forest.

Maps: The USGS 7.5 minute topo maps are Spruce Knob and Whitmer. In addition, the Seneca Creek Trail System, Spruce Knob Unit map complements the topo maps by showing more trail details.

Finding the trail: From WV 28, turn onto FS 112, 3 miles south of River-

Photo by Ron Snow

ton. (There is a sign for Spruce Knob.) Follow the road about 13 miles to the campground or to Spruce Knob Lake and park. The entrance to the Allegheny Trail is on the left-hand side of FS 112, past the entrance to the Gatewood Lookout Tower.

Sources of additional information:

U.S. Forest Service
Monongahela National Forest
Route 3 Box 240
Petersburg, West Virginia 26847
(304) 257-4488

Blackwater Bikes
West Virginia Highway 32
Davis, West Virginia 26260
(304) 259-5286

Davis

While most of West Virginia was settled by pioneers in the late eighteenth and early nineteenth centuries, the region around the Allegheny Front—a huge geologic fault that runs north and south through Pennsylvania, Maryland, and West Virginia—wasn't settled until the 1840s and later. Pioneers avoided this region of rugged mountains, dense forests, and severe weather as they surged west into Ohio, Indiana, Illinois and beyond. The early explorers saw the neighborhood as dark and forbidding, and originally named the upper plateaus along the Allegheny Front "Canada."

Two unique geological features in this part of northeastern West Virginia are Dolly Sods and Canaan (k'NANE) Valley. Wedged between the Allegheny Front to the east and Canaan Valley to the west, Dolly Sods is a high plateau of spruce and hemlock stands, sphagnum moss bogs, and beaver ponds. Renowned for its harsh weather—snow in July, and a lowest recorded winter temperature of −48 degrees—the region is the unique result of heavy deforestation in the late nineteenth and early twentieth centuries, followed by fires that burned away the topsoil. What remains is a unique blend of second-growth forests, open spaces dominated by bogs and beaver ponds, and gently rolling ridges.

Canaan Valley, too, was heavily deforested and is now a mixture of small farms, second-growth forests, and vacation homes. At 3,200 feet of elevation, this is the highest alpine valley of its size east of the Mississippi River. Surrounded by 4,300-foot ridges, the valley is considered to be "a bit of Canada gone astray." The climate and plant life are more common to northern regions than to the southern Appalachians.

The northern end of Canaan Valley is 6,000 acres of wetlands, a wildlife habitat for an abundance of animals: white-tailed deer, black bear, bobcat, fisher, fox, mink, beaver, and cottontail rabbit. Over 160 species of birds and waterfowl have been identified here, including great blue heron, Canada goose, black duck, woodcock, turkey, and grouse. The goshawk and common snipe have their southernmost nesting sites in the valley.

Dolly Sods and Canaan Valley are popular destinations for hikers, backpackers, birders, skiers, and, increasingly, mountain bikers. Davis, an old logging town located over the mountain from Canaan Valley, is well situated for mountain biking. Off-road cyclists can ride in virtually any direction from town to the best mountain biking in the state: flat or mountainous, single-track or Forest Service road, old strip mines or bogs, and, for the energetic, all of the above. As a result, Davis is one of the most popular mountain biking destinations in the East.

The Canaan Mountain Series of mountain bike races, held every summer in Davis, is the oldest race series in the United States and has introduced thousands of cyclists to the area. The ramshackle old town even boasts its own mountain bike shop, Blackwater Bikes. When visiting Davis, stop in and ask owners Gary and Matt for the latest trail information. The shop also sells maps and the latest in bike components, offers expert repairs, and sells and rents mountain bikes.

The trail descriptions that follow, written with the help of former Blackwater Bikes employee Mary Morningstar, are the most popular rides around Canaan Valley. Yet they represent only a fraction of the riding in this large and fascinating section of West Virginia. Let the experts at Blackwater Bikes turn you on to other great rides in this beautiful and rugged region.

RIDE 8 *PLANTATION TRAIL*

The Plantation Trail got its name in the 1930s when clear-cut Canaan Mountain was replanted with spruce trees. Rhododendron thickets grow rampant throughout this area, creating a glorious sight on a spring day when the bushes are in bloom and dripping with moisture from a rain shower. That's one reason why this 12-mile loop, which has a shorter 9-mile option, is legendary among knowledgeable East Coast mountain bikers. As the trails wind through these forests, the trees drop suddenly away and the trail crosses through the peat bogs that Canaan is so famous for. Just as quickly, the trail dives back into the thick underbrush and wooded canopy of the spruce forest. When riding around corners keep a sharp lookout for the mother bear and cubs seen often in these parts.

The majority of this ride is on rugged hiking trails, and good technical riding skill is required. Expect to encounter wet roots, windfall, mountain streams, short steep hills, and peat bogs. Canaan Loop Road is a graded Forest Service road of hard-packed rock and gravel. Warning: Don't be deceived by the low mileages. Only highly skilled mountain bikers will be able to ride all the single-track without dismounting. This is a low-speed, *very* technical ride.
General location: Monongahela National Forest, near Davis, West Virginia.
Elevation change: The ride starts in Davis at 3,080' of elevation and climbs 2.5 miles on the paved road to 3,600', a climb of 520'. Plantation Trail rolls along the ridge of Canaan Mountain through creeks and ravines, creating short, steep climbs and descents but losing only 300' in elevation over 5 miles. Davis Trail drops 400' in elevation over 1.5 miles. Lindy Trail drops 300' in elevation in about a mile.
Season: The best riding conditions are from mid-summer through fall. Fall has the best surface conditions and inspiring foliage. Late May through early

PLANTATION TRAIL

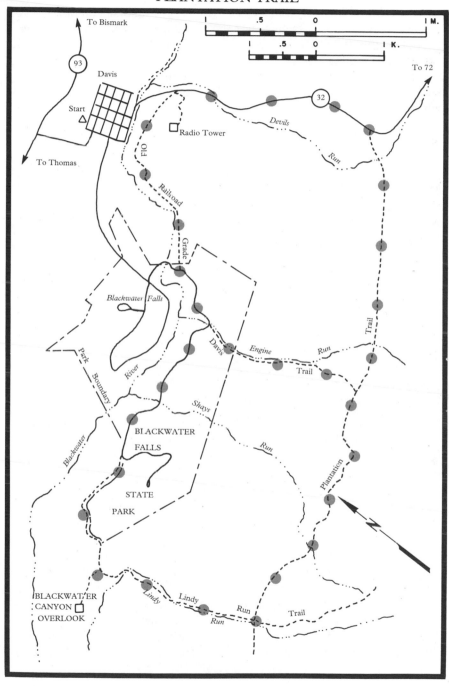

June, although wet and often cold, offer huge thickets of rhododendrons in bloom.

Services: All services are available in Davis, West Virginia. Additional lodging and restaurants are available over the mountain in Canaan Valley. Camping is available at Blackwater Falls State Park from spring through fall and at Canaan Valley State Park year-round.

Hazards: This is rugged terrain over rocks, roots, and bogs. There are steep and unexpected dropoffs and descents. Water crossings can be waist-deep when high and the water is always cold.

Rescue index: Blackwater Falls State Park is staffed and has phones. It is unusual to encounter anyone on the trails; occasionally four-wheel-drive vehicles can be spotted on Canaan Loop Road.

Land status: Monongahela National Forest and Blackwater Falls State Park.

Maps: The USGS 7.5 minute topos for this ride are Mozark Mountain and Blackwater Falls. A detailed mileage guide and maps are available at Blackwater Bikes in Davis. A small map of the hiking trails is available at Blackwater Falls State Park.

Finding the trail: The ride starts in Davis, West Virginia. Blackwater Bikes on WV 32 is a good starting point, or park anywhere in town. Ride south on WV 32 and cross the Blue Bridge.

Sources of additional information:

U.S. Forest Service
Cheat Ranger District
Nursery Bottom
Parsons, West Virginia 26287
(304) 478-3183

Blackwater Bikes
West Virginia Highway 32
Davis, West Virginia 26260
(304) 259-5286

Blackwater Falls State Park
Davis, West Virginia 26260
(304) 259-5216 or
(800) CALL WVA

Notes on the trail: From Davis, ride south on WV 32 (Williams Avenue, the main street) and follow it as it bears right at the convenience store/motel. Cross over the Blue Bridge and continue on WV 32 up Canaan Mountain for about 2.5 miles. The trailhead is on the right and is well marked with a sign. After turning onto the Plantation Trail from WV 32, there are two options. The 9-mile ride turns right onto the Davis Trail (2.5 miles from the start of

Plantation Trail). It descends 1.5 miles into Blackwater Falls State Park. The other option (12 miles) is to continue another 2.5 miles to the intersection with the Lindy Run Trail and turn right. This is a tricky, technical trail with a steep, treacherous hill.

Both these trails end at Canaan Loop Road. Turn right and follow the dirt road into Blackwater Falls State Park. Turn left onto the paved road and ride about 2 miles to Falls View Gentle Trail (on the left). Turn right onto a maintenance road, then take an immediate left onto an old railroad grade. This leads to a settling pond on the left. Skirt around the edge of the pond and follow the railroad grade back to the Blue Bridge and into Davis.

RIDE 9   CANAAN LOOP ROAD (FOREST SERVICE ROAD 13)

While definitely not a technical ride—virtually the entire 25-mile loop follows a well-maintained Forest Service road and paved road—the Canaan Loop Road requires stamina. Although most of the route is along rolling hills, the last 7 miles are all up. But the rewards are worth the effort. The road passes through magnificent spruce and hardwood forests and accesses trails leading to breathtaking overlooks.

Look for spectacular rhododendron blooms in late May or early June. For a view of the Blackwater Canyon, take a short spur trail at about the 5.5-mile mark. (Look for a small wooden post, no sign.) Although technical, the trail is only a half-mile long and leads to a limestone outcropping overlooking the Blackwater River 860 feet below. A tougher option, but worth the effort, is the spur leading to Table Rock Overlook. There is a well-marked sign at about the 10.5-mile mark. It's a brutal 1.5-mile trail (all but the most advanced riders will portage most of it) leading to an overlook of the Dry Fork River 1,635 feet below.

General location: Blackwater Falls State Park and Monongahela National Forest, near Davis, West Virginia.

Elevation change: The ride starts at 3,080' in Davis and is fairly level for the first 4 miles. Then the Loop Road gradually climbs 280' in elevation with several roller-coaster dips and rises through creeks and ravines. It crosses the mountain ridge at 3,360'. Here, a fast 425' descent begins with a drop to the low point on the ride of 2,935'. A long uphill climb (7 miles) starts with a steep hill. It evens out and starts to roll along until reaching the high point of 3,800', ending an 825' elevation gain. The remainder of the ride is mostly downhill, a descent of 720' in elevation on pavement. The total elevation gain is around 1,100'.

CANAAN LOOP ROAD
(FOREST SERVICE ROAD 13)

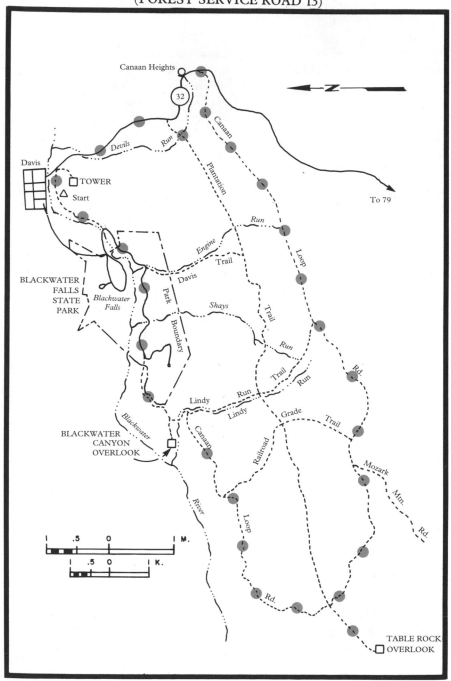

Photo by Larry Belcher

Season: The best seasons for riding this loop are from mid-summer through fall. The water crossings can be high in spring and winter. In all seasons, be prepared with raingear and warm clothes. The summer climate is typified by Canadian-like weather and cool temperatures.

Services: All services are available in Davis, West Virginia. Additional motels, restaurants, and camping are in nearby Canaan Valley.

Hazards: The biggest hazards are changes in the weather—which can be sudden and brutal—leading to hypothermia, wet feet, and darkness. Watch for traffic on the roads, especially WV 32.

Rescue index: The Loop Road is accessible to two-wheel-drive, high-clearance vehicles and is a popular camping spot, so traffic can be flagged down. Blackwater Falls State Park is fully staffed.

Land status: Monongahela National Forest and Blackwater Falls State Park.

Maps: The USGS 7.5 minute topos for this ride are Mozark Mountain and Blackwater Falls. A detailed mileage guide and maps are available at Blackwater Bikes in Davis. A small map of the Canaan Loop Road and interconnecting trails is available at Blackwater Falls State Park.

Finding the trail: The ride begins in Davis, West Virginia. Park near Blackwater Bikes on WV 32 or anywhere else in town. Ride south on WV 32, cross the Blue Bridge and immediately turn right onto an old dirt road to begin the loop.

Sources of additional information:

U.S. Forest Service
Cheat Ranger District
Nursery Bottom
Parsons, West Virginia 26287
(304) 478-3183

Blackwater Bikes
West Virginia Highway 32
Davis, West Virginia 26260
(304) 259-5286

Blackwater Falls State Park
Davis, West Virginia 26260
(304) 259-5216 or
(800) CALL WVA

Notes on the trail: To start the ride, pedal south on WV 32 (Williams Avenue, the main street in Davis) toward the convenience store/motel on the right. Bear right, cross the Blue Bridge, and take an immediate right onto a dirt road (an old railroad grade). This follows the river, then bears left; look for a settling pond on the right. Follow the railroad grade to the far end of the pond, where the road forks. Turn right onto a rocky double-track that follows the fence line of the pond. The railroad grade will continue through a stream crossing and will end at the intersection of a maintenance road and a paved road.

Turn left onto the paved road and continue about 2.5 miles. When the road bears left, turn right onto the dirt road marked with a wooden sign for Sled Run. This is the beginning of Canaan Loop Road. Canaan Loop Road ends at WV 32, a paved road with heavy traffic. Turn left and descend into Davis.

RIDE 10 *CAMP 70 ROAD TO CANAAN VALLEY OVERLOOK*

Camp 70 Road is a virtually flat dirt road that starts in Davis, follows the Blackwater River, and then heads out into the northern end of Canaan Valley. At the start of this very easy 9.5-mile, out-and-back ride, Northern hardwoods line the road. Expect to see cherry, beech, birch, and sugar maple, making this

CAMP 70 ROAD TO
CANAAN VALLEY OVERLOOK

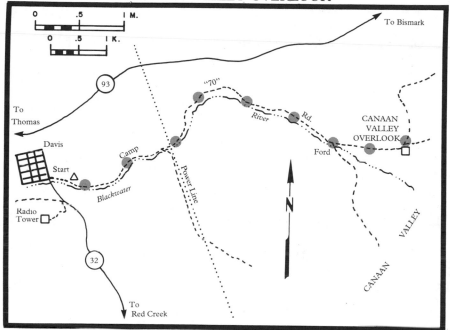

an especially enjoyable trip in the fall. Interspersed among the hardwoods are aspen groves, hemlock, spruce, and balsam fir stands. Note: unfortunately, mountain bikers aren't permitted in the woods along Camp 70 Road.

About .75 miles from Davis on the right are the remains of an old dam, a great place to swim and sun. At the 3.5-mile mark, look for a spring on the left side of the road surrounded by blueberries. At the 4-mile mark, bear left at a fork in the road to ride out into Canaan Valley. The road will begin to deteriorate and become rocky and increasingly narrow, but still easy to ride.

To reach a swinging bridge over the Blackwater River that leads out into a beautiful section of Canaan Valley, look for all-terrain-vehicle tracks going to the right from a point less than a quarter mile past the fork. Follow these tracks down a gully (toward the river), bear right through a hemlock grove and follow the river about 150 yards to the bridge. Park your bike. Cross the bridge, turn left, and hike along an old railroad grade that leads out across the valley floor. On all sides look for peat bogs, shrub swamps, and beaver ponds. The railroad grade may be muddy and there are always puddles. In a couple of spots, the beaver dams have flooded the trail. But it's one of the most unique places in all of West Virginia.

General location: Davis, West Virginia.

Elevation change: The road starts at 3,079' of elevation and then winds its way along the banks of the Blackwater River. It never climbs more than 40' in any one spot. The total elevation gain is 80'.

Season: The road can be ridden year-round. Mid-summer is best for berry picking. In winter and early spring, the road can get very muddy.

Services: All services are available in Davis. Additional motels and restaurants are in nearby Canaan Valley.

Hazards: Look and listen for four-wheel-drive vehicles and four-wheel all-terrain vehicles.

Rescue index: Most of camp 70 Road is accessible to high-clearance, two-wheel-drive vehicles, so it's easy to flag down traffic.

Land status: Private. Owned by Monongahela Power Company and open for recreational use. Mountain bikes are not allowed in woods bordering Camp 70 Road.

Maps: The USGS 7.5 minute topo is Davis, West Virginia.

Finding the trail: The ride starts in Davis. Blackwater Bikes on WV 32 is a convenient place to begin. Park near the shop or anywhere else in town. With a high-clearance, two-wheel-drive or four-wheel-drive vehicle you can drive directly onto Camp 70 Road and park anywhere. Ride south on WV 32 (Williams Avenue, the main street in Davis). When the road bears right at the convenience store/motel continue straight onto a rough paved road, which quickly turns to dirt. Cross the bridge over Beaver Creek; this is the beginning of Camp 70 Road. It follows the Blackwater River on the right upstream.

In spring of 1994, Monongahela Power Company banned all vehicles (including mountain bikes) from its property along Camp 70 Road. State and local officials are working with the utility to reopen access to mountain bikes. Contact Blackwater Bikes in Davis for updated information about access to this area.

Sources of additional information:

Tucker County Chamber of Commerce Visitor Center
West Virginia Highway 32
Davis, West Virginia 26260
(304) 259-5315

Blackwater Bikes
West Virginia Highway 32
Davis, West Virginia 26260
(304) 259-5286

RIDE 11 OLSON FIRE TOWER

For spectacular West Virginia scenery, this is a hard ride to beat. Simply pedal on a well-maintained fire road to the top of a mountain and you're rewarded with a 360-degree view of all the mountains surrounding Canaan Valley, the highest alpine valley in the East. On a clear day you can see as far away as Spruce Knob, the highest point in West Virginia.

This 18-mile, out-and-back ride doesn't require any technical riding skills —just the endurance to pedal 9 miles uphill to the top. The reward, of course, is that it's all downhill on the return.

Make sure to make some stops on the ascent. About 5 miles up the road, look for an overlook blazed with a yellow dot on a boulder on the left. From this point you can see the Blackwater Canyon to the left and Big Run heading down to the river on your right. The entire mountainside is covered with rhododendron, an amazing sight when in bloom. At the 6.5-mile mark, look carefully for a trail to the left that leads to high elevation marshlands and a bird sanctuary. An elevated boardwalk leads out to the middle of the wetlands, where there is a beaver pond and several bird houses.

General location: The ride starts near Thomas, West Virginia, about 4.5 miles from Davis.

Elevation change: The ride starts at an elevation of 2,820' and climbs steadily along the rim of the Blackwater Canyon for 7.3 miles to an elevation of 3,355' at the left turn onto Forest Service Road 717. Here the road becomes steeper for the short climb to the tower at an elevation of 3,736'. The total elevation gain is 920'.

Season: This ride is excellent all year. Each season has its special attractions. When the leaves are down in winter there are dramatic views of the canyon. In spring the road isn't as muddy as other areas, and the rhododendron are blooming. In summer the majority of the ride is in the shade. There are pockets of hemlock groves and cold mountain streams to cool off in. And in fall the colors are the best in all of Canaan.

Services: All services are available in Davis. There is a water pump near the fire tower.

Hazards: Avoid excessive speed on the return trip. Watch for blind corners, for the roads are open to traffic.

Rescue index: Canyon Rim Road is accessible to two-wheel-drive vehicles and is a popular spot in the summer months. But, as is the case with most of Canaan Valley, its remoteness can lead to problems when help is needed.

Land status: Monongahela National Forest.

OLSON FIRE TOWER

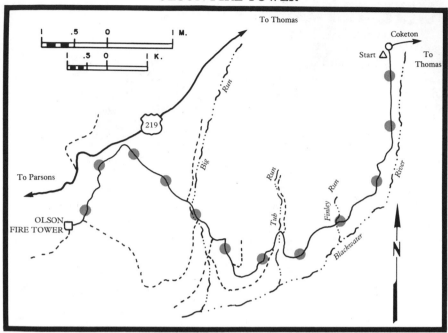

Maps: The USGS 7.5 minute topos are Lead Mine and Mozark Mountain. A detailed mileage log and trail guide are available at Blackwater Bikes in Davis.
Finding the trail: The ride starts at Canyon Rim Road (FS 18). From Davis drive north on WV 32 toward the town of Thomas. A quarter mile past the Mountain Top Market on the left, turn left onto Douglas Road. Drive 2.5 miles, crossing over 2 bridges. Park on the right immediately after the second bridge. At this point Douglas Road turns to dirt and becomes Canyon Rim Road.

Sources of additional information:

> Monongahela National Forest
> Cheat River District
> Nursery Bottom
> Parsons, West Virginia 26287
> (304) 478-3183

> Blackwater Bikes
> West Virginia Highway 32
> Davis, West Virginia 26260
> (304) 259-5286

Notes on the trail: The scenery on this ride is spectacular and shouldn't be missed. The view from Olson Fire Tower includes the entire western rim of Dolly Sods and its northern drainage.

This ride can be lengthened to 28.5 miles by riding from Davis. Check with Blackwater Bikes about the route that parallels WV 32 through the woods (and away from traffic).

MARYLAND

Green Ridge State Forest

Mountain bikers living in the Washington and Baltimore areas are lucky. When they get bored riding the same old trails over and over, relief is only two hours away.

A half hour west of Hancock, Maryland (where the state narrows down to a stone's throw between West Virginia and Pennsylvania), lies a series of mountain ridges running north and south. It's all state forest land, and it's Maryland's best-kept mountain biking secret.

Little-known and seldom visited, Green Ridge State Forest features 28,000 acres of mountain ridges and valleys. The forest is laced with dirt roads, jeep trails, and single-track hiking trails. It's also a crazy quilt of campsites, private hunting shacks, vacation homes, overlooks, power line cuts, and logging operations strewn over several low mountains that border the Paw Paw Bends of the Potomac River.

To be blunt: Colorado it ain't. These mountains have been heavily deforested in the past, and the poor soil doesn't yield the lush kind of scenery you associate with, say, Shenandoah National Park in Virginia. Yet in some respects this is an advantage to mountain bikers. The area doesn't draw crowds or traffic, and on a mountain bike the less scenic areas are quickly bypassed. But there are beautiful views of mountains, forests, and the Paw Paw Bends of the Potomac River.

Camping and mountain biking are a great combination at Green Ridge. Campsites are scattered throughout the forest, and many are secluded. Some are ideally located for the mountain biker bent on exploration, and the many circuit rides mean you won't have to move your car. Camping is free (register at the park headquarters) and the only major drawback is the lack of drinking water at campsites. Just bring lots of water jugs and a sun shower, and fill up at the park headquarters. Some campsites offer picnic tables (it's nice to have one on a multi-day visit), but otherwise they are completely primitive.

Getting to Green Ridge State Forest is easy, because it's interstate all the way from either Washington or Baltimore. Head out Interstate 70 (from Baltimore) or I-270 (from D.C.) to Hancock, Maryland, where you bear left onto the new I-68 (formerly US 40/48) toward Cumberland. From the top of Sideling Hill (where there is a Visitor Center and rest area) Green Ridge State Forest is visible to the left.

Continue on I-68 over Town Hill to the next ridge, Green Ridge Mountain, and take Exit 64 (M.V. Smith Road) to the park headquarters. Stop here to pick up a free map and, if you're camping, to register your campsite.

RIDE 12 *MERTENS AVENUE AREA*

The attractions of this area are low-key. There are miles and miles of roads twisting through mountain hollows and second-growth forest, the luxury of camping in one spot for days while mountain biking different trails every day, and solitude. This area is a maze of small roads and trails which are great for exploration by mountain bike; rides lasting from an hour to all day are possible. The roads are well-maintained, but watch out for the steep climbs that go up to the ridges. Switchbacks are rare.

Loop rides are easy to design. Here's some help. The easiest roads are Gordon, Railroad Hollow (an old railroad right-of-way), and Mertens Avenues (heading west, away from Green Ridge Mountain). More challenging roads are Jacobs, Twigg, Piclic, and Sugar Bottom. This area can be linked to the area north of I-68 by going out Fifteen Mile Creek Road. (Piclic Road is a good choice to reach it.) To get to the Stafford–East Valley Roads ride, take Fifteen Mile Creek Road over Green Ridge Mountain to Stafford Road.

The roads are well maintained for county residents who live on private land inside the boundaries of the state forest. Railroad Hollow is a single-track that requires some scrambling over small streams, but is virtually flat. Piclic Road has a steep and rocky drop as it approaches Fifteen Mile Creek Road. It has the best descent (fast, and verging on the technical) and Gordon Road is the prettiest ride in the area. Pedal Railroad Hollow in the late afternoon and you may see wild turkey.

General location: Fifteen miles west of Hancock, Maryland.

Elevation change: Your climb is up to 500′ if you decide to ride to the top of Green Ridge Mountain. Smaller climbs are still nasty since there's little or no switchbacking to ease your pain. The climbing can be minimized by staying inside the area defined by Gordon Road, Railroad Hollow, Jacobs Road, and Williams Road.

Season: Summers here are as hot, humid, and buggy as in the nearby cities, so try to start your ride early in the day to beat the worst heat. Spring, the wettest season of the year (and discouraging for all but the most intrepid mountain bikers), is a good time to visit this area, since the well-maintained roads are usually less muddy than the forest trails at home. Winter is good, too, if you like cold-weather riding; snow is rare. Fall is probably the best time to ride Green Ridge State Forest because of the cool weather and fall foliage. Stay out of the woods during deer hunting season, which starts the Saturday after Thanksgiving.

Services: There are small grocery stores on Orleans Road north of I-68 and

MERTENS AVENUE AREA

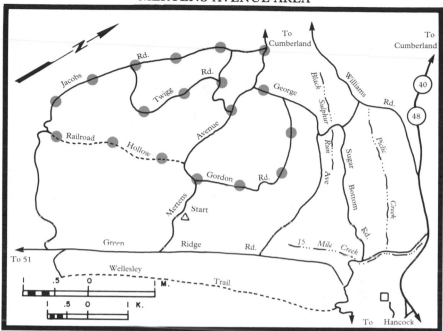

in Flintstone. The nearest bike shop is in Cumberland. All other services are available in Hancock and Cumberland.

Hazards: Water is scarce in these mountains, so be sure to carry enough. Watch out for traffic on the steep descents.

Rescue index: Farms and private residences are scattered throughout this part of the forest.

Land status: State forest.

Maps: A map of the roads and trails is free at Green Ridge State Forest headquarters on M.V. Smith Road (Exit 64 off I-68).

Finding the trail: From I-68 get off at Exit 62, Fifteen Mile Creek Road (1 mile west of M.V. Smith Road). Turn left at the stop sign, cross back over the highway and follow the road about a mile (it runs alongside its namesake on the left). After crossing Fifteen Mile Creek the road begins climbing up Green Ridge Mountain. Just before the top there's an intersection; continue straight (the road's name changes to Green Ridge Road). Go about 2 miles to the second right (Mertens Avenue), and turn. You'll begin to see campsites (where you can park your car) after the descent from the ridge.

Sources of additional information:

> Green Ridge State Forest
> Star Route
> Flintstone, Maryland 21530
> (301) 777-2345

Notes on the trail: While Green Ridge State Forest does have its drawbacks—it's a weird mix of forests, hunting shacks, power line cuts, logging operations, even a juvenile detention center—the area's pluses outweigh the minuses. It's close to major population centers, yet is located in a sparsely populated area and is largely ignored by everyone but hunters (and you'll only see them in the fall).

Stake out a campsite, set up a tent, and do a loop ride before lunch and another after. Or start with your lunch in the morning and ride all day, returning to your campsite before dinner. Come to Green Ridge for the kind of riding usually associated with the western United States—long rides over mountain ridges. The scenery's not the same, but your quads won't know the difference.

RIDE 13 *NORTH OF I-68*

This section of Green Ridge State Forest is less visited than the areas below I-68, so it's even more secluded. And with fewer campsites and private cabins (none on Treasure Road), it has more of a wilderness feel. The scenery is of low mountains and mixed hardwood forests, and some rolling farmland on Old Cumberland Road. The ride along Fifteen Mile Creek—a narrow dirt road that follows the falling mountain stream—is beautiful.

This 8-mile loop follows well-maintained dirt roads and requires no technical skills, except for a short, steep, rocky descent on Treasure Road. The challenges lie in the long climbs, especially on Old Cumberland Road. To connect with the other rides in the area, take Fifteen Mile Creek Road south into the main body of the forest. A left on Sugar Bottom Road (great name) is the easiest way to ride into the Mertens Avenue Area. To get to Stafford–East Valley Roads, stay on Fifteen Mile Creek Road, turning left as you approach the ridge on Green Ridge Mountain. Then, after passing the Wellesley Trail parking area, turn right onto Stafford Road.

General location: Fifteen miles west of Hancock, Maryland.

Elevation change: About 400′ total. The ride starts with a stiff climb up Big Ridge Road, which is paved for a short stretch. Most of the elevation loss is on Old Cumberland Road as you descend to Fifteen Mile Creek Road.

Season: This trail is good riding year-round, with the exception of deer

NORTH OF I-68

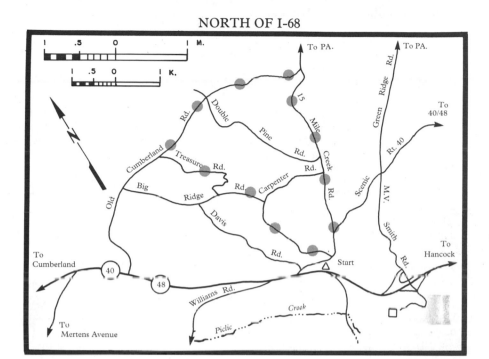

hunting season (which starts the Saturday after Thanksgiving). Summers are usually hot, humid, and buggy, so plan your rides to start and finish early in the day. The area usually doesn't get much snow, so winter riding is good. Spring and fall are the best seasons. Spring offers relatively mud-free riding on these hard-packed roads, and fall provides cool weather and beautiful foliage when the leaves are changing.

Services: There are small grocery stores on Orleans Road north of I-68 and in Flintstone. The nearest bike shop is in Cumberland. All other services are available in Hancock and Cumberland.

Hazards: Be careful on the steep descents.

Rescue index: You're never more than a couple of miles from a private residence or farm.

Land status: State forest.

Maps: Free maps are available at Green Ridge State Forest headquarters off Exit 64 (M.V. Smith Road) on I-68.

Finding the trail: Leave I-68 at Exit 62 (Fifteen Mile Creek Road). Turn right at the stop sign and park your car at the pulloff a quarter of a mile on the right. Start the ride on Big Ridge Road, the paved road on the left. (It turns to dirt at the top of the hill.)

Sources of additional information:

Green Ridge State Forest
Star Route
Flintstone, Maryland 21530
(301) 777-2345

Notes on the trail: While this area isn't as easy to link up with other rides (you must cross over I-68 on Fifteen Mile Creek Road—hardly a wilderness experience), it's worth a visit on its own. The highway isolates it from the rest of the forest, and once you start your ride you probably won't see anyone else.

RIDE 14 *STAFFORD–EAST VALLEY ROADS*

The demands of this 9-mile loop ride are strictly cardiovascular, not technical. The ride starts with a stiff climb up Stafford Road to the ridge of Town Hill Mountain and ends with another steep climb just before you return to your car. Only really well-conditioned cyclists will be able to ride these; lesser mortals will push their bikes up the steep (but relatively short) hills. Stafford Road is a well-maintained dirt road; East Valley Road is a jeep road—essentially, a double-track—that's closed to motor traffic.

The rewards of this ride? No Name Overlook on Stafford Road and Banner's Overlook (at the intersection of Stafford and Mertens Avenue) offer grand views of the Paw Paw Bends, the Potomac River's meandering course between Maryland and West Virginia. The C&O Canal, stretching from Cumberland to Washington, follows the river on the Maryland side. And both Stafford and East Valley Roads are roller-coaster romps through hardwood forests.

General location: Twenty miles west of Hancock, Maryland.

Elevation change: From your car it's a stiff climb (a couple of hundred feet of elevation gain) to the top of Town Hill. There's a big descent on Mertens Avenue to East Valley Road, which ends with a steep climb back to your car. But most of this ride is along a ridge. The total elevation change is about 500'.

Season: Good year-round, with the exception of deer hunting season (which starts the Saturday after Thanksgiving). Summers are usually hot, humid, and buggy, so plan your rides to start and finish early in the day. Green Ridge usually doesn't get much snow, so winter riding is good. Spring and fall are the best seasons. Spring offers relatively mud-free riding on these hard-packed roads, and fall offers cool weather and beautiful foliage when the leaves are changing.

Services: There are small grocery stores on Orleans Road north of I-68 and

STAFFORD-EAST VALLEY ROADS

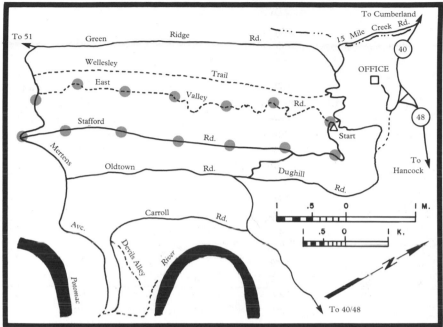

in Flintstone. The nearest bike shop is in Cumberland. All other services are available in Hancock and Cumberland.

Hazards: The descent from Banner's Overlook on Mertens Avenue is very steep; be on the lookout for traffic. The intersection with East Valley Road comes up very fast and it's easy to blow past it. (You want to turn right there.)

Rescue index: All of the route except East Valley Road carries light traffic.

Land status: State forest.

Maps: Free at Green Ridge State Forest headquarters on M.V. Smith Road (Exit 64 off I-68).

Finding the trail: From I-68 get off at Exit 62, Fifteen Mile Creek Road. Turn left at the stop sign, cross back over the highway, and follow the road about 2 miles. After crossing Fifteen Mile Creek the road ascends Green Ridge Mountain. Just before the top turn left at the intersection (straight becomes Green Ridge Road). Continue past the parking area for the Wellesley Trail, then turn right onto Stafford Road. Park at the intersection with East Valley Road (look for the gate on the right).

Sources of additional information:

Green Ridge State Forest
Star Route
Flintstone, Maryland 21530
(301) 777-2345

Notes on the trail: This part of Green Ridge State Forest has spectacular views of the Potomac River as it snakes between Maryland and West Virginia. Also, the rides along Stafford and East Valley Roads are a blast to ride—a series of undulating hills that let momentum do most of the hard work.

Garrett County / Savage River State Forest

Driving from the east, dramatic changes occur about a half hour west of Cumberland, Maryland, as you crest Big Savage Mountain on Interstate 68. In summer the temperature drops, and in winter the weather can turn near-Arctic in intensity. The character of the mountains changes here, too. They're higher, wetter, and not as steep as the ridges to the east. Wide, rolling valleys dominated by hemlock forests separate the mountains. You've reached the Appalachian Plateau.

Welcome to Garrett County, Maryland, the state's most isolated county. Located entirely on the Appalachian Plateau, Garrett County averages 2,300 feet in elevation. Although farming, coal mining and timbering dominate the county's economy, outdoor recreation is big business. Because of cool, bug-free summers and dependable snow (or at least snow-making) conditions for skiing, Garrett County draws vacationers from Pittsburgh, Washington, and Baltimore.

Deep Creek Lake, a 3,900-acre reservoir, is the major tourist hub, with many vacation homes littering its 65-mile shoreline. The county also has two major whitewater attractions, the Youghiogheny (Yock-uh-ganey) and Savage rivers, which draw paddlers and rafters literally from around the world. In 1989 the World Whitewater Canoe/Kayak Championships were held on the rapids of the Savage River.

As befits an isolated corner of the Appalachian Mountains, there are 70,000 acres of state forests and parks in Garrett County, creating a mecca for mountain bikers. The largest (and most accessible) tract of state-owned land is Savage River State Forest, which straddles Big Savage Mountain to the east and Meadow Mountain to the west. Its 53,000 acres contain two state parks (New Germany and Big Run), the 350-acre Savage River Reservoir, and many lakes, rivers, and streams. Camping, swimming, fishing, and even rental cabins make the forest an attractive destination for mountain bikers. And there are many miles of forest trails and woods roads to explore by bike.

New Germany State Park is a great place to set up a base camp for exploring the forest. The park is easy to reach (only five miles from I-68, the county's major highway), and all the rides in this chapter start there. It has the basic amenities—camping, hot showers, and a lake for swimming (perfect after a ride). *Après*-ride, nearby Frostburg is a college town with restaurants ranging from French and Italian to Greek. For breakfast drive to Grantsville, where you can stoke up on buckwheat pancakes at the Casselman Restaurant (circa 1824). For details on camping call New Germany State Park at (301) 895-5453.

RIDE 15   *MEADOW MOUNTAIN SNOWMOBILE / OFF-ROAD-VEHICLE TRAIL*

Meadow Mountain O.R.V. Trail, a 10-mile, out-and-back ride, follows the ridge of the mountain through beautiful mature hemlock and hardwood forest, interspersed with views of Big Savage Mountain, surrounding valleys, and small farms. This ride requires almost no technical skill, since most of the trail is along a well-maintained woods road. Yet the dirt road is punctuated by climbs, bogs, and rough sections that make the ride challenging. Flatlanders will breathe a little harder—and do some pushing—on the half-mile climb that starts the ride up Meadow Mountain. The rest of the trail follows the ridge of Meadow Mountain.

Starting from parking lot #5 in New Germany State Park, the first half mile is along paved road to the trailhead in the park maintenance area. (Or you can park in front of the park office and skip the paved road.) The trail is a well-maintained, 10-foot-wide forest road. However, plenty of boggy and rocky sections will keep your attention riveted to the 100 square inches in front of your wheel. The optional trail to the Meadow Mountain Overlook at the end of the O.R.V. Trail is narrower and littered with deadfalls. The reward for your efforts is a spectacular, down-the-throat view of Monroe Run with Big Savage Mountain in the background.

While riding, stay alert for wildlife. The mountains are home to a great diversity of animal species, ranging from black bear to brook trout, and great horned owls to long-tailed salamanders. Mammals include deer, bobcat, raccoon, squirrel, beaver, and bats. There are over 100 species of birds, including hawks, owls, turkey, grouse, and warblers. Snakes, turtles, salamanders, frogs, and fish complete the long list of animals you may encounter on your Meadow Mountain ramble.

General location: Savage River State Forest. The ride starts at New Germany State Park, 5 miles southeast of Grantsville, Maryland.

Elevation change: The narrow road climbs from 2,468' of elevation at New Germany to 2,900' on Meadow Mountain. The balance of the trail follows the ridge with little change in elevation. The overlook (an option at the end of the O.R.V. Trail) brings you to 2,959'.

Season: The best riding conditions are from June through October. The summer climate on the Appalachian Plateau is pleasant. It's much cooler than in big cities to the east and has no mosquitoes or ticks. Early spring can be very muddy. Snow is possible from October through April. Avoid riding

MEADOW MOUNTAIN SNOWMOBILE/
OFF-ROAD-VEHICLE TRAIL

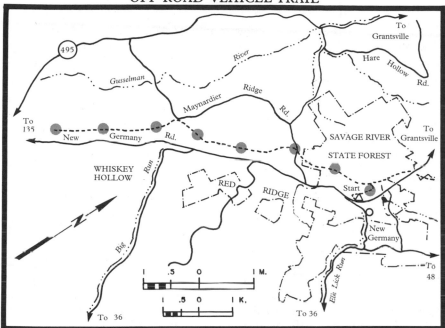

during deer hunting season (after Thanksgiving). In mid-June the mountain laurel along the ridge blooms. The spectacular fall foliage is at its best in late September and early October.

Services: The nearest restaurants, lodging, and grocery stores are in Grantsville, north of I-68. Frostburg, about a half-hour drive east of New Germany, has a great selection of restaurants and lodging. The nearest bike shop is in Cumberland.

Hazards: The woods road is well maintained. However, be alert for downed trees. Use caution at all road crossings. You may come across timber rattlesnakes, especially on the ridge—be alert and give them plenty of room.

Rescue index: The O.R.V. Trail parallels New Germany Road, which carries a fair amount of traffic. Residences can be reached from Otto Lane, Maynardier Ridge Road, and Frank Brenneman Road.

Land status: Maryland state forest and parks, and short sections of county road.

Maps: Maps of the trail are available at the State Forest Administrative Office on New Germany Road. The Grantsville and Bittinger quadrangles of the USGS topo series and the Garrett County topo map (available at the administrative office) are also good.

Finding the trail: Take Exit 24 from I-68; follow the signs for New Germany State Park/Savage River State Forest. The Administrative Office and the trailhead are located on the right side of New Germany Road, where you may park. Or turn left into New Germany State Park and park in lot #5 (across from the lake). Ride your bike back to the park entrance and cross New Germany Road to the trailhead, which is just past the park office. (No overnight parking is allowed.)

Sources of additional information:

Savage River State Forest
Route #2, Box 63-A
Grantsville, Maryland 21536
(301) 895-5759

Notes on the trail: The ride starts with a .7-mile climb to a "T" intersection; turn left. (To the right the O.R.V. Trail continues 4.5 miles north toward I-68.) After a couple of miles the trail reaches another "T" intersection. Turn left and ride a short distance to the intersection of 2 dirt roads (Otto Lane and West Shale Roads). From here you can see the O.R.V. Trail to the right.

When the trail ends at Frank Brenneman Road (the trail to Meadow Mountain Overlook is across the road), you have the option of creating a loop ride by returning to the park via New Germany Road (which is paved and has a wide shoulder). To ride the loop, turn left and descend to the intersection. Turn left for the 5-mile spin back to the park.

RIDE 16 *POPLAR LICK / ELK LICK LOOP*

Here's a great ride for the beginning mountain biker—just don't tell him or her that all mountain biking is this easy. It starts with 5 miles of gentle downhill through a gorgeous forest beside a fast-flowing mountain stream. While lacking spectacular views of the surrounding mountains, this ride shows off the intrinsic beauty of the Appalachian Plateau. Be on the lookout for wildlife—bear, deer, bobcat, raccoon, great horned owls, beaver, and bats are abundant here. Also, the rhododendrons along the streams bloom in early July, and the fall foliage peaks in late September or early October.

The ride begins in a hemlock forest and follows a beautiful mountain stream, Poplar Lick Run. The forest changes to second-growth hardwood as you descend. The O.R.V. Trail ends in a wide, grassy meadow where Poplar Lick Run flows into the Savage River. There are a few short stretches of easy

POPLAR LICK/ELK LICK LOOP

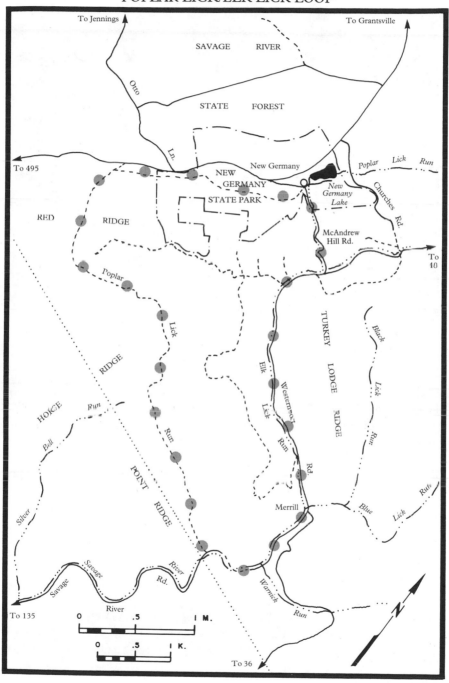

Photo by author

single-track. The return trip (on paved road) follows Elk Lick Run. A note to purists: Don't let the paved road put you off. This is a very pretty ride.

The trail requires no technical skills except for the five stream crossings along Poplar Lick (which can be walked). Expect to get your feet wet; in the spring or after rain you may have to carry your bike and wade through calf-deep water. Last but not least, there's a stiff climb on McAndrew Hill Road just before the finish.

General location: Savage River State Forest. The ride begins at New Germany State Park, 5 miles southeast of Grantsville, Maryland.

Elevation change: There's a gentle slope downstream along Poplar Lick dropping from 2,468′ of elevation to 1,686′, followed by a gentle rise along the Savage River and Elk Lick up to 2,300′. The short, steep climb on McAndrew Hill Road (about a 300′ elevation gain) is followed by a short descent back to the start.

Season: The best biking conditions are from June through October. Earlier in the spring the dirt roads and trails can be extremely muddy, and the stream crossings deep. (This may not be the best choice for a cold-weather ride.)

Snow is possible from October through April. Avoid riding in deer hunting season (late fall).

Services: The nearest restaurants, lodging, and grocery stores are in Grantsville, north of I-68. Frostburg, about a half-hour drive distant, has a great selection of restaurants and lodging. The nearest bike shop is in Cumberland.

Hazards: Use caution on county roads and the O.R.V. Trail; traffic is minimal, but keep alert. Slippery rocks can make stream crossings hazardous. Extreme care should be exercised during periods of high water (usually in the spring).

Rescue index: You can flag down motorists on New Germany Road (follow the O.R.V. Trail uphill from the intersection of the 3 Bridges Trail) and other roads along the loop. There are residences along the paved and unpaved roads on the second half of the ride.

Land status: State forest and park; county roads.

Maps: Ask for a map of the Poplar Lick O.R.V. Trail and the New Germany Hiking Trails at the park office, which is across from the park entrance on New Germany Road. You can also purchase a Garrett County topo map there.

Finding the trail: Take Exit 24 from I-68 (Grantsville) and follow signs for New Germany State Park/Savage River State Forest. Park in lot #5 at New Germany State Park.

Sources of additional information:

Savage River State Forest
Route #2, Box 63-A
Grantsville, Maryland 21536
(301) 895-5759

Notes on the trail: The trailhead is near the end of parking lot #5. The key to reaching the Poplar Lick O.R.V. Trail is to stay with the stream. (Don't climb any hills.) Look for the gate that marks the entrance to the O.R.V. Trail and follow it downstream for about 5 miles. The O.R.V. Trail ends at the intersection with Savage River Road; turn left and go 1.5 miles to the stop sign. Turn left onto the paved Westernport Road where you cross a rail and concrete bridge over the Savage River. Follow this county road (traffic is light) for almost 3 miles along Elk Lick Run. After crossing the third wooden bridge, turn left onto the second road (McAndrew Hill Road). Follow this unpaved road back to New Germany State Park.

RIDE 17

MEADOW MOUNTAIN / MONROE RUN / POPLAR LICK LOOP

This is a ride for the well-conditioned cyclist, for it's a long and strenuous 20-mile loop. There are rough riding surfaces (mud, rocks, gravel, logs) and many stream crossings. Start early in the day and pack a lunch. Although the trails are well marked, it's a good idea to carry a topo map and compass.

The ride along Meadow Mountain is on a woods road featuring views of the surrounding mountains. The fast descent on Big Run Road is through beautiful forests and ends at Big Run State Park, with views of Savage River Reservoir—an uncluttered jewel ringed by cliffs and forested hills. The Poplar Lick O.R.V. Trail is a woods road about 5 miles long and has 5 stream crossings. The 3 Bridges Trail is a single-track that connects with the Green Trail, an easy woods road that returns you to New Germany State Park. Warning: This ride could induce sensory overload during peak fall foliage in late September or early October.

General location: Five miles southeast of Grantsville, Maryland.

Elevation change: The loop climbs from 2,468′ at New Germany State Park to 2,900′ on Meadow Mountain. There's little change in elevation along the ridge until the descent to Big Run Road (2,525′). A gentle descent along the Big Run Road drops you to 1,500′ at Savage River Road, followed by a gentle rise up the Savage River and Poplar Lick Run to the starting point in New Germany State Park.

Season: June through October offer the best riding conditions. The summer climate is very pleasant, with no mosquitoes or ticks. Early spring can be extremely muddy. From October through April snow is possible. Avoid riding in deer hunting season (late fall). Mountain laurel blooms peak along the ridges in mid-June; rhododendron blooms peak along the streams in early July.

Services: The nearest restaurants, lodging, and grocery stores are in Grantsville, north of I-68. Frostburg, about a half-hour drive distant, has a good selection of restaurants and lodging. The nearest bike shop is in Cumberland.

Hazards: Use caution on county roads and the O.R.V. Trail; traffic is usually light, but keep alert. Slippery rocks make stream crossings hazardous—use care during periods of high water (usually in the spring.) And keep an eye peeled for rattlesnakes, especially along the ridges.

Rescue index: Meadow Mountain O.R.V. Trail parallels New Germany Road, which carries a lot of traffic. There is a phone at B.J.'s Store, a small grocery store on Savage River Road 1 mile upstream from Big Run State Park.

Land status: Maryland State Forest and Parks; county roads.

Maps: A hiking map of the loop is available at the New Germany Park office. A topo map of Garrett County is also available there.

MEADOW MOUNTAIN/MONROE RUN/
POPLAR LICK LOOP

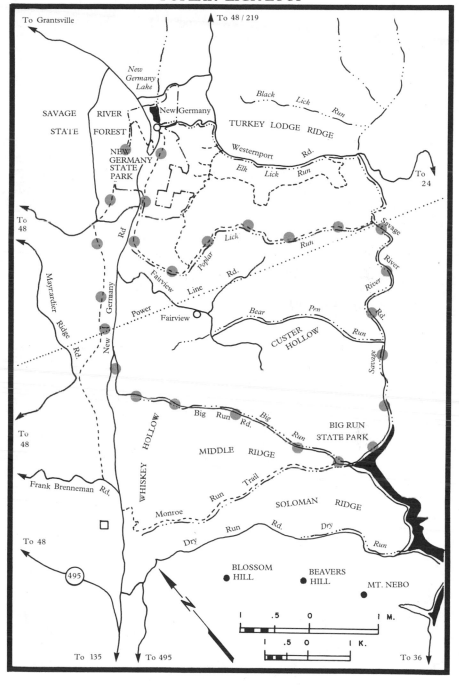

To Grantsville

To 48 / 219

New
Germany
Lake

New Germany

SAVAGE

STATE

RIVER

FOREST

TURKEY LODGE RIDGE

Black   Lick   Run

NEW
GERMANY
STATE
PARK

Westernport   Rd.

Elk   Lick   Run

To
48

To
24

Savage

Rd

Lick   Run

River

River

Poplar

Fairview   Line   Rd.

Mayrardier

Power

Fairview

Bear   Pen   Run

Ridge

CUSTER
HOLLOW

New Germany

Rd.

Savage

Rd.

To
48

Big   Run   Rd.   Big

Run

BIG RUN
STATE PARK

WHISKEY   HOLLOW

MIDDLE   RIDGE

Frank Brenneman Rd.

Monroe   Run   Trail

SOLOMAN   RIDGE

To 48

Dry   Run   Rd.   Dry

Run

495

BLOSSOM
● HILL

BEAVERS
● HILL

MT. NEBO
●

To 135

To 495

1   .5   0   1 M.

1   .5   0   1 K.

To 36

Finding the trail: Take Exit 24 from I-68 and follow the signs to New Germany State Park/Savage River State Forest. Turn left into the Park and park at lot #5, or turn right and park at the administrative office. The trailhead (Meadow Mountain O.R.V. Trail) is on the right, just past the office.

Sources of additional information:

Savage River State Forest
Route #2, Box 63-A
Grantsville, Maryland 21536
(301) 895-5759

Notes on the trail: On Meadow Mountain O.R.V. Trail, which starts this loop, look for an old woods road that makes a sharp left immediately before the power lines. This trail is marked with a sign that says "No Snowmobiling." Follow this steep woods road to a yellow-pole gate on New Germany Road; turn right for a quarter mile and turn left onto Big Run Road, which descends to Big Run State Park.

Turn left onto Savage River Road (which parallels its namesake) to the Poplar Lick O.R.V. Trail on the left (there's a sign). Follow this trail to the gate and pick up the blue-blazed 3 Bridges Trail, which continues upstream along Poplar Lick Run. Turn left at the end and follow the Green Trail (a woods road) back to New Germany State Park.

PENNSYLVANIA

Michaux State Forest

Located between Gettysburg to the east and Chambersburg to the west, Michaux State Forest encompasses over 82,000 acres of Pennsylvania forests and mountains. With a well-defined system of roads, snowmobile trails, and foot trails, Michaux (me-SHOW) is an increasingly popular destination for mountain bikers.

The prominent geographic feature in the forest is South Mountain, a long ridge that runs north out of nearby Maryland into Pennsylvania. Forty miles of the Appalachian Trail, the 2,000-mile foot trail running from Maine to Georgia, follow the ridge of South Mountain the length of the forest. The Appalachian Trail is closed to mountain bikes, as are most trails in the state parks located inside the forest.

Only a few hours away from large metropolitan areas such as Baltimore, Washington, and Philadelphia, Michaux is convenient to many mountain bikers hankering for a weekend of exploration. With its extensive trail and road system, Michaux offers a wide variety of interesting and scenic rides.

Jes Stith, owner of Gettysburg Schwinn bike shop, has raced mountain bikes for five years and trains in Michaux regularly. Michaux, he says, offers hard-core riders and racers looking for difficult training rides lots of technical single-track and numerous long climbs. Yet, Jes points out, there are also miles of moderate trails and roads for non-expert riders. "Plus," he adds, "it's so darned beautiful up there." With a knowledgeable staff dedicated to mountain biking, Gettysburg Schwinn is headquarters for off-road enthusiasts in south-central Pennsylvania. Be sure to stop by for information on other great places to ride.

RIDE 18   *SLATE ROAD, PINEY RIDGE ROAD TO POLE STEEPLE LOOP*

The geologic centerpiece of this 11-mile loop ride is Pole Steeple, a rock feature composed of 60- to 80-foot-high cliffs at the top of a ridge. Pole Steeple provides great views of nearby mountains. Without trees in the way the vista is impressive in any season. More attractions on this difficult ride include steep climbs and descents through dense forest, which provide plenty of opportunities to glimpse wildlife. Pine Grove Furnace Park, at the start of the loop, features hiking and nature trails, as well as some interesting historical features and two large lakes for swimming.

Most of the route is on all-terrain-vehicle trails covered with loose scree.

SLATE ROAD, PINEY RIDGE ROAD TO POLE STEEPLE LOOP

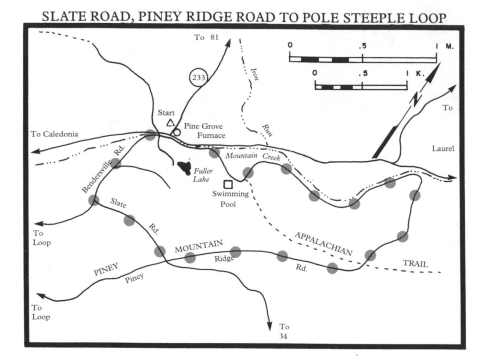

Good bike handling skills are a must for the descents. Some sections on Piney Ridge Road are fast descents on a loose, irregular surface. The final descent is on a deeply rutted trail that frequently has water flowing on it. A cinder trail completes the loop.

General location: Six miles east of Chambersburg, Pennsylvania.

Elevation change: The initial climb up Slate Road to the top of the ridge on Piney Ridge Road involves approximately 500' of vertical gain in under 3 miles. Piney Ridge Road to Pole Steeple undulates between 100' gains and losses. After Pole Steeple it's all downhill.

Season: The loop is usually rideable from late spring through the fall. Spring can be wet and summer is usually hot, humid, and buggy. Fall, with its foliage, is probably the best time of year to ride this loop. Avoid riding in deer hunting season, which starts in the late fall.

Services: Water and toilet facilities are available in Pine Grove Furnace State Park. The park has a general store, youth hostel, and overnight camping.

Hazards: The trails are used by all-terrain vehicles. Use caution if clambering on the boulders of Pole Steeple.

Rescue index: Return to Pine Grove Furnace or Bendersville Road, which is paved and carries light traffic.

Land status: Pennsylvania state forest and park. Trails are not open to moun-

tain bikes in the state park, so return through the park on the bike/hike trail.
Maps: The USGS topo is the Dickinson quad. The Pennsylvania State Park's
Pine Grove Furnace map features additional trail detail.
Finding the trail: From Interstate 81 take either US 30 or Route 94 to PA 233
and Pine Grove Furnace State Park. Park near the furnace.

Sources of additional information:

> District Forester
> Michaux State Forest
> 10099 Lincoln Way East
> Fayetteville, Pennsylvania 17222
> (717) 352-2211

> Gettysburg Schwinn
> 100A Buford Avenue
> Gettysburg, Pennsylvania 17325
> (717) 334-7791

Notes on the trail: After parking, pedal south on Bendersville Road approximately a half mile to Slate Road and turn left. Climb to Piney Ridge Road and turn left. Cross the Appalachian Trail and pick up the blue-blazed trail to Pole Steeple. (The dead-end spur trail on the left leads to a cliff overlook.) Drop down the ravine to Laurel Forge Pond, then follow the cinder path to Pine Grove Furnace.

RIDE 19 *ALL-TERRAIN-VEHICLE TRAIL TO LOG SLED TRAIL VIA PINEY RIDGE ROAD*

This 12-mile loop follows a combination of paved roads, two-wheel-drive roads, hard-packed dirt roads, all-terrain-vehicle trails, and multiple-use trails. While there are some steep sections, this ride is not very technical. However, since the ride features some steep climbing and fast descents on loose rock and dirt, it requires a good fitness level and good bike handling skills.

The trail passes through second-growth mixed coniferous and deciduous forest. There are excellent views from Piney Ridge Road. The descent on Log Sled Trail is through a beautiful wooded hollow along a mountain stream. Pine Grove Furnace State Park features hiking and nature trails, and two large lakes for swimming.

General location: Six miles east of Chambersburg, Pennsylvania.
Elevation change: The ride starts at about 900' of elevation and climbs gradually to over 1,500' on Piney Mountain. The elevation drops sharply along Log Sled Trail to 1,049' and then gradually to around 900' along paved PA 233. The total elevation gain is about 800'.

ATV TRAIL TO LOG SLED TRAIL VIA PINEY RIDGE ROAD

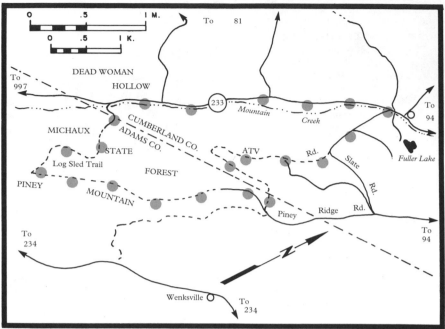

Season: The best riding is between late spring and fall. Spring can be wet and summer can be hot, humid, and buggy. Fall is the best time to ride, but avoid riding in deer hunting season, which starts in the late fall.

Services: Water and toilet facilities are available in Pine Grove Furnace State Park. The park has a general store and youth hostel, and overnight camping is permitted.

Hazards: Watch out for hikers and all-terrain vehicles on the fast descent on Log Sled Trail.

Rescue index: For help, return to Pine Grove Furnace or wave down traffic on PA 233.

Land status: State forest and state park.

Maps: The USGS 7.5 minute topos are Pine Grove Furnace and Arentsville.

Finding the trail: From I-81, take either US 30 or Route 94 to PA 233 and Pine Grove Furnace State Park. Park near the furnace.

Sources of additional information:

District Forester
Michaux State Forest
10099 Lincoln Way East

Fayetteville, Pennsylvania 17222
(717) 352-2211

Gettysburg Schwinn
100A Buford Avenue
Gettysburg, Pennsylvania 17325
(717) 334-7791

Notes on the trail: Ride out Bendersville Road past Slate Road to the orange-signed all-terrain-vehicle trail on the left. At the end of the climb, turn right onto Piney Ridge Road. Ride for 4 miles to Log Sled Trail on the right. Descend to PA 233, turn right, and return to Pine Grove Furnace.

RIDE 20   *LONG PINE RESERVOIR LOOP*

The major attraction of this 12-mile loop ride is a chance to explore a vast, undeveloped forest. The geography features long ridges called "flats," due to their flat-top profiles. Another nice aspect to this ride is Long Pine Reservoir, a large, beautiful lake nestled in the hills that's also a popular destination for anglers. The hollows and valleys between the flats are heavily wooded, mostly with conifers. The views of the surrounding valleys and mountains from the ridges are striking in any season.

Steep climbs on loose rock and dirt require good fitness and bike-handling skills. However, this ride isn't very technical. The trail follows hard-packed dirt roads (some sections with washboarded surface), rough double-track covered with loose rock, and single-track that varies from packed dirt with a pine-humus surface to football-sized rock scree.

General location: Six miles east of Chambersburg, Pennsylvania.

Elevation change: The first 3 miles gain about 600' in elevation, followed by a ridge traverse with slight undulations. A single-track drops 300' in a half mile, which is followed by a 100' climb and a 300' drop on a dirt road. A 400' climb over 1 mile on a double-track is followed by a 400' drop over 1 mile, then a gradual descent and a final 200' climb over a quarter mile. The total elevation gain is around 1,500'.

Season: The best riding is between late spring and fall. Spring can be wet and summer can be hot, humid, and buggy. Fall is the best season to ride, but avoid riding in deer hunting season, which starts in the late fall.

Services: Water, rest rooms, and camping are available in Caledonia State Park on PA 233. All other services are available in Chambersburg, Pennsylvania.

Hazards: Aside from all-terrain vehicles and blind curves on single-track de-

LONG PINE RESERVOIR LOOP

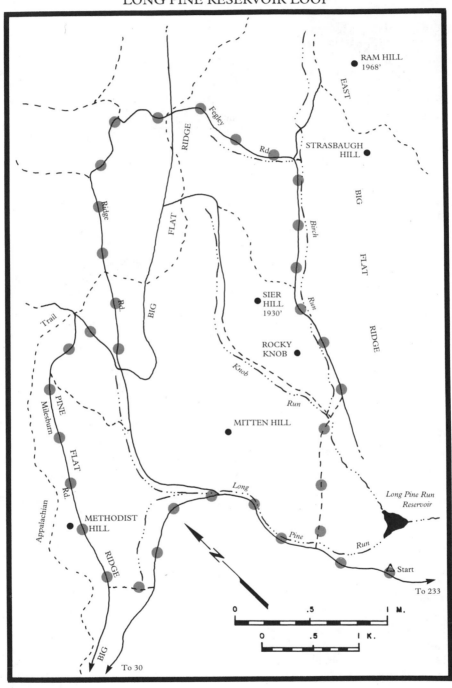

RAM HILL
1968'

EAST

Fegley

Rd.

STRASBAUGH
HILL

RIDGE

BIG

FLAT

Ridge

FLAT

Birch

RIDGE

Rd.

BIG

Run

SIER
HILL
1930'

Trail

ROCKY
KNOB

PINE

Knob

Milesburn

Run

FLAT

Rd.

MITTEN HILL

Run

Appalachian

Long

Long Pine Run
Reservoir

METHODIST
HILL

Pine

Run

RIDGE

Start

To 233

BIG

To 30

0   .5   1 M.

0   .5   1 K.

scents, the biggest hazard in the area is getting lost. There are many roads, unmarked trails, and a sameness to the topography, so it's easy to get confused. Carry a map and compass.

Rescue index: The area is closed to motorized vehicles; the closest help is traffic on PA 233.

Land status: State forest.

Maps: The USGS 7.5 minute topo is Caledonia Park.

Finding the trail: From I-81, take either US 30 or PA 94 to PA 233. Look for a dirt road on the north side of PA 233 at the Chambersburg Reservoir pull-out. Take this road approximately 3 miles to Long Pine Reservoir and park in the parking area.

Sources of additional information:

District Forester
Michaux State Forest
10099 Lincoln Way East
Fayetteville, Pennsylvania 17222
(717) 352-2211

Gettysburg Schwinn
100A Buford Avenue
Gettysburg, Pennsylvania 17325
(717) 334-7791

Notes on the trail: From the parking area, ride north on the dirt road and pass the first road on the right of the fork. At the next fork, bear left and climb to the top of Big Pine Flat. Turn right along the power line right-of-way and then turn right onto the dirt road. After 2 miles or so take the fourth trail on the right. (All 4 trails drop down the south side of the mountain to a road in the valley.) Turn right onto the road at the bottom of the descent and go straight at the next intersection. Take the rough dirt road a mile later and climb to a partially clear-cut meadow. Bear right at the next trail intersection. Continue to climb to the top of Big Flat. Cross the road and take the trail for the descent. At the dirt road turn right toward the reservoir. Bear right at the fork and then turn left at the dirt road and return to the parking area.

Confused? Even mountain bikers that ride the area regularly get disoriented on occasion. Carry a map and compass, and give yourself enough time so that you're not racing against a setting sun.

Laurel Highlands

Two hundred fifty miles west of Philadelphia, the Laurel Highlands of southwestern Pennsylvania stretch over a five-county region dominated by two large mountain ridges, the Laurel and the Chestnut, both carved by the Youghiogheny River and the Conemaugh Gorges. These mountains offer virtually unlimited possibilities for rugged, scenic mountain biking.

Historically, a lot happened in the hills, valleys, and deep forests located in the Laurel Highlands. Major skirmishes in the French and Indian War were fought here, and George Washington suffered his only military defeat at Fort Necessity. The Whiskey Rebellion, the United States' first constitutional crisis, was crushed here by federal troops under the command of General "Mad" Anthony Wayne. We've been paying taxes ever since.

The nineteenth century brought coal mining, steel making, and coke production into the Laurel Highlands. Railroads and canals linked the region with Pittsburgh to the west and Cumberland, Maryland, to the south. Following the decline of the steel industry, tourism became increasingly important to the region. The hills and mountains of the Laurel Highlands attract hikers, skiers, and whitewater enthusiasts. The Youghiogheny (YOCK-uh-ganey) River, which defines the southwest corner of the Highlands, is considered the best whitewater river east of the Mississippi.

Hikers can trek the Laurel Highlands Hiking Trail, which stretches for 70 miles between Ohiopyle and Youngstown. The Connellsville-Cumberland Trail, a proposed 70-mile hiking and biking route along the old Western Maryland Railroad right-of-way, will eventually link up with the C&O Canal (which extends to Washington, D.C.).

The Laurel Highlands are characterized by beautiful vistas, tidy farms, and tens of thousands of acres of wilderness. Because of its relatively high altitude (Mt. Davis, the state's highest point at 3,213 feet, is nearby), the region's climate is significantly colder and snowier in winter and cooler in summer than are the cities to the west and east.

The following rides start from Hidden Valley Resort, 12 miles west of Somerset, Pennsylvania. Hidden Valley is a vacation-home resort and ski area (both downhill and cross-country). Taking advantage of its beautiful setting (it's surrounded by 25,000 acres of state wilderness lands), the resort began renting mountain bikes in the mid-1980s. Hidden Valley made a financial commitment to mountain biking largely because of one of its employees, Jim Sota.

"I suggested we look into offering mountain bikes after I got my first bike six years ago," recalled Sota, who manages the bike shop in summer and the cross-country skiing facilities in the winter. "We started small, with only ten rental bikes, but it's proven popular. Now we've got a rental stable of 35 bikes, a bike shop, and we sponsor a race every fall."

All the trails from Hidden Valley lead to state forests. Where they cross private land Hidden Valley has permission for users to pass. Mountain bikers may park at the Ski Lodge or behind The Barn, the cross-country ski center on PA 31. Jim Sota asks that bikers check in at the shop (located at the Ski Lodge) to inquire about trail conditions, pick up a map, and let them know when you're returning.

RIDE 21 *RACE LOOP RIDE*

This is a moderately hilly 10-mile loop that will give experienced mountain bikers a good workout. The ride requires some technical skill due to short sections of rocky single-track. The first climb is long and steep, but the rest of the climbs are easier. The trail surface varies from mud to paved road, but most is packed dirt. At the higher elevations there are excellent views of the mountains to the west and of the Jones Mill Run Valley. The fall foliage in mid-October is spectacular. This area contains abundant wildlife (white-tailed deer, bear, rabbit, pheasant, turkey, squirrel, grouse) and a wide variety of plant species. The clear mountain streams and beautiful western Pennsylvania scenery attract visitors from all over the country.

The first part of the loop is paved road leading to a dirt-and-grass trail. Roots and rocks make for a bumpy ride on Lookout Trail. The pipeline adjacent to Fire Tower Road is smooth dirt with some muddy sections. Cherry Trail has some rocky and muddy portions. Timberhaul Road is a hard-packed and gravel double-track.

After the first climb you're rewarded with a delightful single-track through a mature white-pine forest. The rest of the loop is almost as enjoyable. Vistas of the mountains to the west are visible as you ride through a variety of settings, ranging from deciduous hardwood and coniferous forests to open meadows.

General location: Twelve miles west of Somerset, Pennsylvania.

Elevation change: The ride begins at 2,500' of elevation and climbs to 2,800' in the first mile. The highest point is 2,900', at 3.5 miles. You descend to 2,300', then climb for 2 miles to 2,800' on Timber Haul Road. There's a quick descent to the ski area parking lot. The total elevation gain is 1,000'.

Season: Fall riding is the best. In summer, start the ride early in the day to avoid the mugginess. From November through March expect snow. In spring the trails are very muddy. Avoid riding during deer hunting season, which begins in late November.

RACE LOOP RIDE

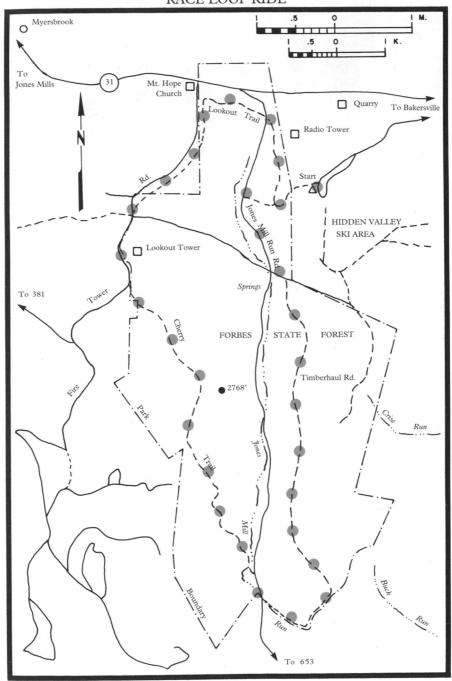

Services: All services are available at Hidden Valley Resort. Camp at Kooser State Park, 2 miles east of Hidden Valley on PA 31.

Hazards: Rocky areas approach very quickly on fast descents, so look ahead. Watch out for a sharp left turn on Cherry Trail that has a surface of large loose gravel.

Rescue index: Jones Mill Run Road carries light traffic that can be flagged down.

Land status: Private (Hidden Valley Resort) and state forest.

Maps: Bakersville quads of the USGS series. The Seven Springs Department of Forestry Snowmobile Trail Maps are also helpful, and are available from Hidden Valley Resort.

Finding the trail: Hidden Valley Resort is located off PA 31 between Somerset and Donegal, PA. From points north and west take the Pennsylvania Turnpike to Exit 9/Donegal. Continue 8 miles east on PA 31 to Hidden Valley. From Washington, DC, and points south and east, take the Pennsylvania Turnpike to Exit 10/Somerset. Continue 12 miles west on PA 31 to Hidden Valley. Follow the signs to the Lodge to start the ride.

Sources of additional information:

Mountain Bike Shop
Hidden Valley Resort
One Craighead Drive
Somerset, Pennsylvania 15501
(800) 458-0175, ext. 473

District Forester
Forbes State Forest
P.O. Box 519
Laughlintown, Pennsylvania 15655
(412) 238-9533

Notes on the trail: Start the ride in the parking lot of the ski area at Hidden Valley Resort. Exit the parking lot and make a left up Parke Drive. At Valley View Drive (just above the upper parking lot) you can either continue up Parke Drive (which is easier), or turn right onto Valley View Drive; Valley View Trail (which is very steep) is 40' up the road on the left.

For the easier (and longer) climb continue up Parke Drive, make a left onto Gardner Road at the stop sign, and then take the next right, the Lookout Trail (there's a sign). Follow the trail 100 yards and make the next right; continue following Lookout Trail, which parallels Gardner Road. Either way the loop starts on the Lookout Trail, at the intersection of Valley View and Gardner Roads.

NORTH WOODS RAMBLE

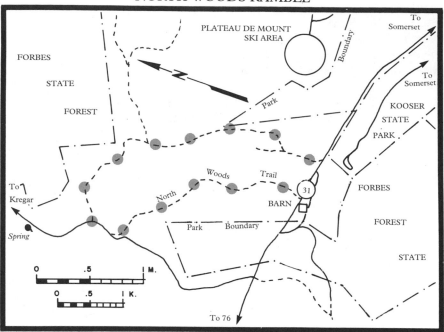

RIDE 22 *NORTH WOODS RAMBLE*

This 3-mile loop ride features some excellent views of the mountains of western Pennsylvania. Little technical skill is required, though there is one short section of loose rock. The first quarter mile is hard-packed; the next mile is a gradual climb on a grass trail. There are no steep hills. The top of the climb is a two-wheel-drive road, and the return trail is all grass. "Ramble" is a good name for this easy ride.

Somerset County is visible from the top of the trail, and there's a good view of Laurel Ridge looking north into the forest regeneration area. This region is typical of Pennsylvania forests and meadows. In addition to the views and excellent pedaling, you can visit a stone springhouse on the return.

General location: Forbes State Forest in the Laurel Highlands of western Pennsylvania. The ride begins at The Barn, the cross-country ski shop at Hidden Valley Resort.

Elevation change: There's a 300′ climb in the first 1.5 miles.

Season: Late spring through fall are the best times to ride this loop. Spring

Photo by author

is usually very muddy. Expect snow from November through March. Avoid riding during deer hunting season, which typically begins on the first Monday after Thanksgiving.

Services: All services are available at Hidden Valley Resort. Camp at Kooser State Park, 2 miles east of Hidden Valley on PA 31.

Hazards: Watch for rocks while riding through the forest regeneration area on North Woods Trail. And look out for groundhog holes (which can devour front wheels, causing the dreaded face-plant) in the fields at the end of the ride.

Rescue index: Help is quickly reached at The Barn on PA 31.

Land status: Private land and state forest land.

Maps: Pick up the Hidden Valley Resort trail maps and Department of Forestry Snowmobile Trail Maps from Hidden Valley Resort.

Finding the trail: Hidden Valley Resort is located on PA 31 between Somerset and Donegal, Pennsylvania. From points north and west take the Pennsylvania Turnpike to Exit 9/Donegal. Continue 8 miles east on PA 31 to Hidden Valley. From Washington, DC, and points south and east, take the Pennsylvania Turnpike to Exit 10/Somerset. Continue 12 miles west on PA 31 to Hidden

Valley. Stop at The Barn (Hidden Valley's cross-country ski shop) on PA 31, 300 yards east of the Hidden Valley Resort entrance. Park behind the building.

Sources of additional information:

Mountain Bike Shop
Hidden Valley Resort
One Craighead Drive
Somerset, Pennsylvania 15501
(800) 458-0175, ext. 473

District Forester
Forbes State Forest
P.O. Box 519
Laughlintown, Pennsylvania 15655
(412) 238-9533

Notes on the trail: Start this easy trail at The Barn by pedaling out of the parking lot on the lower road and riding toward the stone house. Cross PA 31 (watch for traffic) just past the house, and keep left once you enter the driveway. Then follow the North Woods signs.

On the return you can either follow the dirt road back to PA 31, or follow the trail through the field on the left (an apple tree marks the beginning of the trail). This trail passes through a short section of woods followed by a view of orchards. And a note to allergy sufferers—in late summer the fields can become overgrown with goldenrod.

RIDE 23 *KUHNTOWN LOOP*

Riding the trails and roads on this 15-mile loop is a good introduction to the history of the Laurel Highlands. North Woods and Schaffer Trails were once railroad lines used to haul logs out from logging operations. The dirt roads provided access for early settlers who have long since moved on. The smooth sections of road near the Pennsylvania Turnpike are used by modern-day logging operations. Toward the end of the ride there's a stone spring house along the dirt road.

This ride, designed for experienced and well-conditioned cyclists, takes you to the heart of the Laurel Ridge area. The trails and roads are typical of many others found in the region. The top of the ridge provides several views of the surrounding mountains. Most of the ride is in woods, and with the rise and fall of elevation is representative of the region's topography. The first 2.5 miles are on grassy ski trails. After the warming hut at the bottom of

KUHNTOWN LOOP

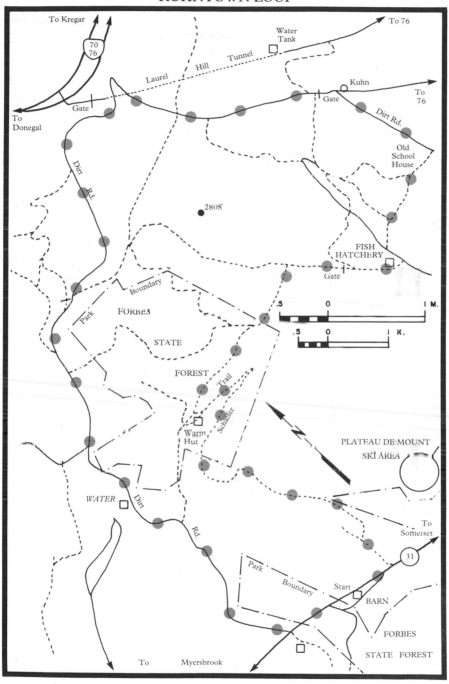

Schaffer Trail the surface is mostly dirt and gravel. Some sections are rutted and washed-out dirt road. There is a long, steep climb over loose rock after the fish hatchery. The climb out of the valley near the Pennsylvania Turnpike is mostly packed dirt. Once you reach the road at the top it's dirt road for the remainder of the ride.

General location: Forbes State Forest, 12 miles west of Somerset, Pennsylvania. The ride begins and ends at The Barn, the cross-country ski shop at Hidden Valley Resort.

Elevation change: The first 1.5 miles begin with a 300' climb followed by a 300' descent over the next 2 miles. A steep, half-mile climb after the fish hatchery is difficult due to the loose surface. Once at the top there is a slight elevation gain back to the very top of the ridge for the next 1.5 miles. A fast 250' descent to the Turnpike (with a sharp left turn) is followed by a 400' ascent (with 2 steep climbs) over the next 2 miles of the dirt trail. The road back is level with a fast descent near the end. The total elevation gain is about 800'.

Season: Late spring through fall are the best seasons to ride this loop. Spring can be very muddy from snowmelt. Expect snow between November and March. Avoid riding in deer hunting season, which begins in late November.

Services: All services are available at Hidden Valley Resort. Camp at Kooser State Park, 2 miles east of Hidden Valley on PA 31.

Hazards: Watch for rocky sections and four-wheel-drive traffic on some of the roads. There is a sharp left turn with loose gravel on the descent into the Turnpike area.

Rescue index: There are a number of residences near the fish hatchery and along the dirt road after the steep climb. After climbing the dirt trail past the Pennsylvania Turnpike, help is best reached at Hidden Valley Resort.

Land status: State forest, public roads, and private property.

Maps: Department of Forestry Snowmobile Trail Maps; Bakersville and Seven Springs USGS series quads.

Finding the trail: Hidden Valley Resort is located off PA 31 between Somerset and Donegal, Pennsylvania. From points north and west take the Pennsylvania Turnpike to Exit 9/Donegal. Continue 8 miles east on PA 31 to Hidden Valley. From Washington, DC, and points south and east, take the Pennsylvania Turnpike to Exit 10/Somerset. Continue 12 miles west on PA 31 to Hidden Valley. Stop at The Barn (Hidden Valley's cross-country ski shop) on PA 31, 300 yards east of the Hidden Valley Resort entrance. Park behind the building.

Sources of additional information:

> Mountain Bike Shop
> Hidden Valley Resort
> One Craighead Drive

Photo by author

Somerset, Pennsylvania 15501
(800) 458-0175, ext. 473

District Forester
Forbes State Forest
P.O. Box 519
Laughlintown, Pennsylvania 15655
(412) 238-9533

Notes on the trail: See North Woods Ramble for details on the start of this ride.

Allegheny National Forest and Clarion

A glance at a road map reveals that a sizeable portion of central and western Pennsylvania is, well, empty—no roads, no towns, no superhighways. Cynics would say there's nothing there. Mountain bikers, on the other hand, know better. Empty space on a road map just might mean great off-road riding.

In this case they're right. Most of this empty territory is the Allegheny National Forest, 740,000 acres of wilderness in the northern Allegheny Mountains. The forest boasts 170 miles of hiking trails (including the 95-mile North County Trail, a National Scenic Trail), hundreds of camping sites, the Allegheny Reservoir Scenic Drive (part of the coast-to-coast Bike Centennial Route), and the 27-mile-long Allegheny Reservoir.

In addition, the Forest Service is busy expanding a system of off-road-vehicle trails, such as the Marienville, Willow Creek, and Rocky Gap O.R.V. Trails. These trails are maintained, well marked, and perfect for mountain biking. Furthermore, while the trails allow mountain bikes year-round, they're only open to motorized vehicles from Memorial Day through late September, leaving the trails free for mountain bikers the rest of the year.

So where do you start exploring this huge forest? Clarion, south of Allegheny National Forest on Interstate 80, is a perfect place. Clarion University of Pennsylvania doubles the population of the town to 14,000 when classes are in session. And where there are college students, you can usually find a good bike shop. In Clarion it's High Gear, located at 5th and Wood streets in downtown Clarion.

The shop serves as the focal point for Clarion's cycling community. On a typical sunny Friday afternoon the shop bustles with activity: A group of five riders returning from a ride in the national forest; owner Steve Shaffer and former employee Anthony DeBaldo assembling a unicycle and then test riding it around the repair stand; a group poring over topo maps before a ride on the state game lands around Clarion. The phone rings every two minutes. R.E.M. is on the CD player. A visiting writer declines a test ride on the unicycle; he's too busy taking notes. It's that kind of place.

High Gear also sponsors races (weekly time trials, and several road and mountain bike races) and teaches bike maintenance at the college. Twenty-six-year-old Steve Shaffer started the business while a sophomore at Clarion University and moved to his present quarters in 1990.

Everybody associated with the shop is into cycling, including Steve's college co-op student, Michelle, nominally a non-cyclist. Steve insists that she ride an exercise bike for 20 minutes before leaving the shop. "She's got to ride *something* if she's going to work here," says Steve. It's that kind of place.

RIDE 24 *MARIENVILLE ALL-TERRAIN-VEHICLE TRAIL*

This all-terrain-vehicle trail is just one of countless recreational trails throughout Allegheny National Forest, but it's especially popular with local mountain bikers. The many rustic wooden bridges over fast mountain streams are great places to stop, relax, and soak up the wilderness experience in this half-million acre forest. The ride is almost entirely through woods, so there are few signs of civilization. Check out the excellent views of the surrounding ridges at the gas line swath. Part of the trail winds along Spring Creek, a small trout stream. Wildlife, including white-tailed deer and wild turkeys, are often seen while riding this loop. Old oil and gas well relics are also visible along the trail.

Most of this 12-mile loop is along wide, smooth trails. There are a couple of short stretches along gas pipelines that are narrow, steep, rocky, and rutted. There are several steep climbs, including one toward the end of the ride that only strong climbers will ascend without dismounting. Most of the trail is hard-packed dirt and fast when dry. Occasionally there are short stretches of logging, fire road, and gas line right-of-ways that have rough, rutted sections. Watch for shallow diversion ditches (dug to prevent washouts) on the descents.

General location: In Allegheny National Forest, about 35 miles north of Clarion, Pennsylvania.

Elevation change: The ride starts at 1,900′ of elevation. At the gas line the trail drops 100′ over a half mile. At mile 2.5 a 320′ descent begins and is followed by a 340′ climb over 1 mile. After rolling over two 100′ climbs and descents there is a gradual 300′ drop over 1.5 miles. At the creek the trail turns around before a steep 360′ climb over a half mile. The last climb is on the gas line and rises about 100′ after a 135′ drop. The total elevation gain on the ride is about 1,100′.

Season: The best months for riding this trail are from April through the fall. The trail is open to motorized off-road vehicles from Memorial Day through September 24, and for a brief time in the winter. Mountain bikes are permitted year-round, but be cautious when motorized vehicles are present. Fall is pleasant with the changing foliage and cooler temperatures. Avoid riding in deer hunting season, which starts in the late fall.

Services: All services are available in Clarion.

Hazards: Keep alert for motorized off-road vehicles. On descents look out

MARIENVILLE ALL-TERRAIN-VEHICLE TRAIL

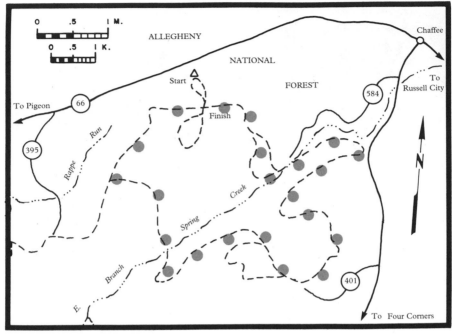

for diversion ditches dug across the trails to prevent erosion, which can drop daydreaming cyclists instantaneously.

Rescue index: The trail is well traveled in the summer months, and most of it is accessible from various maintenance and logging roads. Marienville Ranger Station is located 6 miles south on PA 66. The nearest phone is in Russell City, 3 miles north on PA 66.

Land status: National forest.

Maps: Trail maps are available at the trailhead and at the ranger station in Marienville. There are also 9 checkpoints with maps located along the trail. The USGS 7.5 minute topo is Lynch.

Finding the trail: The trail starts on PA 66 about 9 miles north of Marienville and 10 miles south of Kane, Pennsylvania. Park at the ORV Trailhead/Parking Area.

Sources of additional information:

District Ranger
Marienville Ranger District
Marienville, Pennsylvania 16239
(814) 927-6628

High Gear
34 S. 5th Street
Clarion, Pennsylvania 16214
(814) 226-4763

RIDE 25 *MILLCREEK TRAIL*

This 11.5-mile (one-way), out-and-back ride starts along the Clarion River and winds through State Game Lands #74 along Mill Creek. As you pedal these easy, pleasant state game land maintenance roads and trails the creek is usually in sight. Birds and wildlife are everywhere; keep an eye open for signs of beaver activity. The stream is usually stocked with trout, so packing a fly rod is a popular option. There are a number of springs along the trail. The greatest attraction of this ride is the beauty of the forest and the stream. Pack a lunch and make a leisurely day of it.

This ride requires almost no technical skill, except for stream crossings, which can be portages. The terrain varies from hard-packed dirt road to grassy meadows to single-track in the woods. There are many small stream crossings.

General location: Five miles northeast of Clarion, Pennsylvania.

Elevation change: The ride starts at 1,100' of elevation and gains 120' over the first half mile. The rest of the ride is a gradual uphill grade along the creek to an elevation of 1,400'.

Season: This ride is best from mid-summer through late fall. Sections of the trail are marshy in the spring and early summer. There are also a number of small streams that may be difficult to cross after heavy rains.

Services: All services are available in Clarion.

Hazards: Water crossings can be high after wet weather or in the spring and early summer.

Rescue index: Most of the trail is accessible by four-wheel-drive vehicles from various back roads that connect to it. These roads can be used to reach help.

Land status: State game land.

Maps: The USGS 7.5 minute quads are Strattanville and Corsica.

Finding the trail: From Clarion, drive east on US 322 to Strattanville. Turn left onto Millcreek Road. Look for the Penelec Recreation Area sign after about one-quarter mile. Stay on the dirt road for approximately 3 miles to the park. Park at the picnic area.

Sources of additional information:

High Gear
34 S. 5th Street

MILLCREEK TRAIL

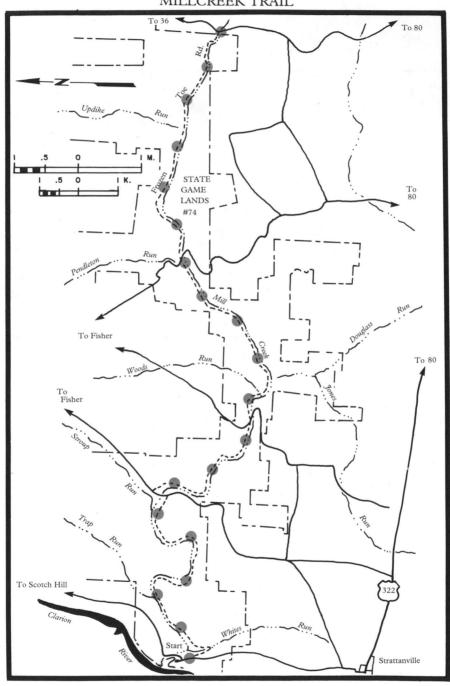

Clarion, Pennsylvania 16214
(814) 226-4763

Notes on the trail: This is a great leisure ride. On warm spring days the trail is lined with blooming trees and flowers. For riders wanting to make a loop out of the ride, obtain a local road map. Connect Frozen Toe Road (great name) back to Fisher Road and then back to the parking area.

RIDE 26 *BUZZARD SWAMP*

This is an easy 11-mile loop ride on cross-country ski trails. It demands only two easy climbs on paved and dirt roads leading to and from the plateau where the swamp is located. The ride starts and ends on paved and dirt roads, while the rest of the route is through meadows and forests on easy, grassy jeep trails used for cross-country skiing in the winter. However, the trails in Buzzard Swamp can be wet and soggy, especially in the spring or after a hard rain.

Buzzard Swamp is along a flyway for migrating Canada geese that stop here in early spring and late fall, so consider packing binoculars and a bird book. It's a unique area with 14 ponds, streams, bogs, meadows, and mixed hardwood and pine forests unique to Allegheny National Forest.

General location: Allegheny National Forest, about 25 miles north of Clarion, Pennsylvania.

Elevation change: Buzzard Swamp sits on a plateau. There are two 150' descents and climbs on the roads leading to and from the area.

Season: The loop is rideable spring through fall. While spring can be wet and muddy, summer and fall riding is great. Avoid riding in the deer hunting season, in the late fall. Expect snow between November and March.

Services: All services are available in Clarion. The Bucktail Motel in Marienville has an excellent restaurant.

Hazards: The trails can flood in the spring. Avoid riding in deer hunting season, in the late fall.

Rescue index: There are some residences along the dirt roads leading in and out of the area.

Land status: National forest.

Maps: Maps are available at the ranger station 1 mile north of Marienville. The USGS 7.5 minute topo is Marienville East.

Finding the trail: The ride starts in the center of Marienville, about 25 miles north of Clarion on PA 66. Park near the Bucktail Hotel.

BUZZARD SWAMP

Sources of additional information:

District Ranger
Marienville Ranger District
Marienville, Pennsylvania 16239
(814) 927-6628

High Gear
34 S. 5th Street
Clarion, Pennsylvania 16214
(814) 226-4763

Notes on the trail: From the center of town ride down Loleta Road, between the Bucktail Hotel and the Kelly Motel. Turn left on Forest Service Road 157. Follow the Buzzard Swamp Trail signs. After passing through the area, turn left at the gate onto Lomonaville Road and continue back to town.

RIMERSBURG RIDE-O-RAMA

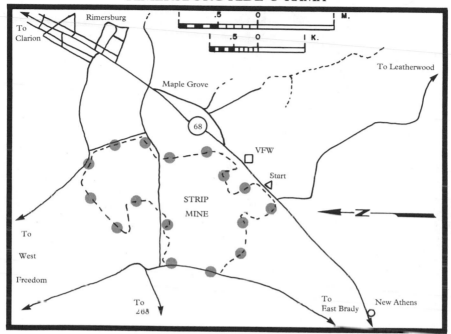

RIDE 27 *RIMERSBURG RIDE-O-RAMA*

This 350-acre unreclaimed strip mine is the favorite playground of Clarion-area hammerheads. There are hundreds of hills and jumps on which you can hone your mountain biking skills, burn off excess calories, and generally goof off. One hill located in the southeast end (near the entrance road) is reminiscent of the first drop on a huge roller coaster. Non-experts and the sane can choose from a wide variety of less death-defying drops.

With hundreds of hills and jumps the area can be ridden tamely or aggressively, slow or fast. Good bike handlers (or those who aspire to improve) will get an excellent workout. The area is almost always hard-packed and fast to ride. The surface is mostly packed shale.

General location: Fifteen miles south of Clarion, Pennsylvania.

Elevation change: The elevation doesn't change more than 25' or 30' over the entire area.

Season: All year. The trails are well ridden by dirt bikes and four-wheelers, so the surface is always packed and in good condition.

Services: All services are available in Clarion, about 15 miles northeast of Rimersburg.

Hazards: This is a great place to fine-tune your bike handling skills, but you must know your limits. Be careful of loose shale in some spots and occasional interruptions by motorized dirt bikes.

Rescue index: There is a phone at the VFW across the road from the entrance.

Land status: Private. Call High Gear in Clarion to confirm that the area is open to the public.

Maps: USGS 7.5 minute quad is Rimersburg.

Finding the trail: Rimersburg is located on PA 68 about 15 miles south of Clarion and 20 miles northeast of Butler, Pennsylvania. Drive 1 mile south of Rimersburg; the entrance is on the right across from the VFW. Turn right and park along the entrance road.

Sources of additional information:

High Gear
34 S. 5th Street
Clarion, Pennsylvania 16214
(814) 226-4763

State College

State College, Pennsylvania, located near the center of the state, is aptly named: the 30,000-student campus of Pennsylvania State University dominates the town. To a mountain biker's eye, however, the town's major attractions are the mountains and neat-as-a-pin farmland that surround it. Riding a mountain bike right out of town is not only feasible, but the preferred way to reach the nearby hills.

So it's no surprise that State College is a mountain bike haven. With recent growth causing downtown congestion, mountain bikes are now the preferred way to get around. These days it seems like every Penn State student rides a mountain bike to class.

To support this kind of mountain bike activity, State College boasts several bike shops. And the biggest, The Bicycle Shop on West College Avenue, is impressive. Its large showroom is dominated by high quality, big ticket bikes, including both road and mountain tandems. The secret to the shop's large selection is sales volume.

"Bikes are the favorite form of transportation in State College," says sales manager Mike Hermann. "Every year we get a big rush of kids who spend between $300 and $500 for a bike. And it's a bargain for them, when you consider the cost of parking and car insurance." And every four years there's a complete turnover of students, guaranteeing continued sales.

The Bicycle Shop actively supports mountain biking by sponsoring several races throughout the year. On Sundays there's usually an informal ride led from the shop. The large staff is knowledgeable and willing to help visitors with maps and directions to trailheads. And if you're in the market for a tandem, call Mike Hermann.

RIDE 28 *TUSSEY MOUNTAIN TO WHIPPLE DAM*

This easy, 5-mile, out-and-back ride features classic Appalachian scenery. The woods, rocks, and mountain streams are reminiscent of New England. The verdant green foliage in spring and blazing colors in fall are spectacular. Most of the ride is through thick woods on well-maintained woods roads that pass several springs. The lookout tower provides spectacular views of the surrounding ridges and valleys. While this ride is non-technical, the climb to the fire tower and the climb on the return from Whipple Dam require good stamina.

TUSSEY MOUNTAIN TO WHIPPLE DAM

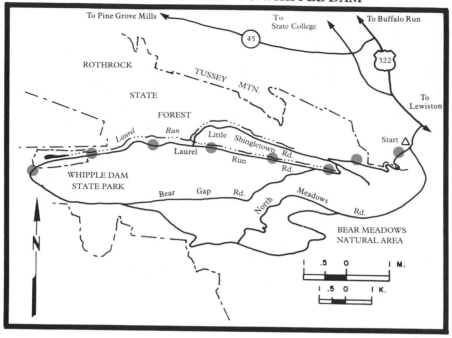

But the rewards are worth it. In summer you can swim at Whipple Dam. Look for a large field of blueberries surrounding the lookout tower—another reason for doing this ride in late summer. In addition to the views from the lookout tower, keep an eye open for the abundant wildlife in the area. You might even see a black bear.

General location: Rothrock State Forest, outside State College, Pennsylvania.

Elevation change: From the start at the ski area to the fire tower is a steep climb of approximately 800′ over 2 miles. On the return from Whipple Dam the elevation gain is about the same, but is spread over 5 miles.

Season: Spring and fall are the best times of year for mountain biking in central Pennsylvania. Summer is hot, humid, and buggy, and snow is possible between November and March. However, since the final destination of this ride is a public swimming area, this is a popular ride in the summer. Avoid riding in deer hunting season, after Thanksgiving.

Services: All services are available in State College. Whipple Dam has water and rest rooms available year-round. A snack bar is open between Memorial Day and Labor Day.

Hazards: Keep an eye peeled for snakes during warm weather, especially along the ridge. Watch for traffic on Laurel Run Road.

Photo by author

Rescue index: This is a well-traveled road, so you should have no problem flagging down a vehicle.

Land status: Pennsylvania state forest land and park.

Maps: The USGS 7.5 minute topo maps are State College and McAlevys Fort.

Finding the trail: From State College, take Business US 322 south to Tussey Mountain Ski Area. Park at the ski area parking lot.

Sources of additional information:

The Bicycle Shop
441 West College Avenue
State College, Pennsylvania 16801
(814) 238-9422

Notes on the trail: After parking, get on your bike and turn right at the first intersection. You will be turning onto a dirt road. From here climb up to the lookout tower. The turnoff to the lookout tower is not marked, but it's simple to find—it's the only left-hand turn within 100 yards of the top of the climb. Look for a gate.

After visiting the tower, retrace the route back down to the main road and continue downhill. From the ski area to the fire tower is all uphill, and from the fire tower to Whipple Dam is all downhill. Stay on the main road to reach Whipple Dam. To return, retrace the route back to the parking lot at Tussey Mountain.

RIDE 29 STATE COLLEGE TO TUSSEY MOUNTAIN VIA LOOKOUT TOWER AND SHINGLETOWN GAP

This is one of the prettiest sections in central Pennsylvania, featuring more than six stream crossings, huge ferns, rhododendron, and pine and mature forests that create a lush, deep-forest feel on the ride. Most of this 15-mile loop ride demands no technical skill. It starts out on paved road in State College, then climbs on dirt road at the Tussey Mountain Ski Area. A single-track descent at the end of the ride is rocky and has many stream crossings. Don't miss the fire tower on Tussey Mountain for great views of the surrounding mountains. Look for the gate on the left about 100 yards from the top of the mountain.

STATE COLLEGE TO TUSSEY MOUNTAIN

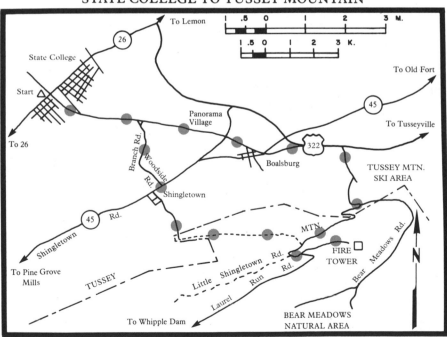

Photo by author

General location: State College, Pennsylvania.
Elevation change: There is about an 800′ elevation gain on the climb up Tussey Mountain. The elevation is lost on the single-track descent to Shingletown.
Season: While rideable April through October, this loop is especially popular in the hot summer months. The thick vegetation guarantees a cool, shady ride on the descent to Shingletown. Avoid riding in deer hunting season, after Thanksgiving.
Services: All services are available in State College.
Hazards: Watch for snakes on the ridges in warm weather and for traffic on the roads.
Rescue index: Other than the descent to Shingletown, all the roads are well traveled. There are residences at the end of the single-track trail to Shingletown.
Land status: State forest land and county roads.
Maps: The USGS 7.5 minute topo maps are State College and McAlevys Fort.
Finding the trail: A convenient place to start this ride is The Bicycle Shop, near downtown State College. Or park anywhere along Business US 322 southbound out of town.

Sources of additional information:

The Bicycle Shop
441 West College Avenue
State College, Pennsylvania 16801
(814) 238-9422

Notes on the trail: From State College pedal out Business US 322 south to the turnoff for Tussey Mountain Ski Area (at Bear Mountain Road, on the right). Ride through the parking area, then turn right at the first intersection onto a dirt road. After leaving the fire tower retrace your route to the first left-hand option. (This is easy to miss—look for a small semi-circle parking area with a closed gate.) Behind the gate are two grassy jeep trails. Ride either one; they eventually meet again. This leads to the single-track (which is technical) and ends at a parking area near a small reservoir.

Follow the paved road down to the stop sign at PA 45. Turn right and go a short distance to Woodside Road, turn left, and then turn right at the "T" intersection onto Branch Road. This takes you back to US 322; turn left to get back into town.

RIDE 30 *PENN ROOSEVELT TO ALAN SEEGER*

This rigorous, 15-mile loop ride offers a special treat—a stop at a virgin forest at the Alan Seeger Natural Area. Hike down the trail (no bikes allowed) to view the huge pine trees. Rumor has it these might be the largest pine trees in North America. The area is thick with rhododendron and a large mountain stream flows through it. Also, the lookout tower is on one of the highest points around and provides great views of the surrounding ridges and valleys.

This ride features steep climbing and challenging terrain as it goes over ridges and through valleys covered with second-growth hardwood forests. There are many views of the surrounding mountains. Expect to shoulder your bike for about 300 yards on the climb out of the Penn Roosevelt picnic area. This is followed by twisting single-track that leads over terrain that changes on almost every turn, demanding total concentration. Next is a hard-packed dirt road that climbs very steeply to the lookout tower.

All the roads on the loop are either hard-packed dirt or paved. The single-track eventually turns into a jeep trail. The tough climbing starts at the intersection of Seeger Road and Stone Creek Road.

General location: Rothrock State Forest, between State College and Lewistown, Pennsylvania.

Elevation change: The ride has 2 major climbs of about 1,000' each. The

PENN ROOSEVELT TO ALAN SEEGER

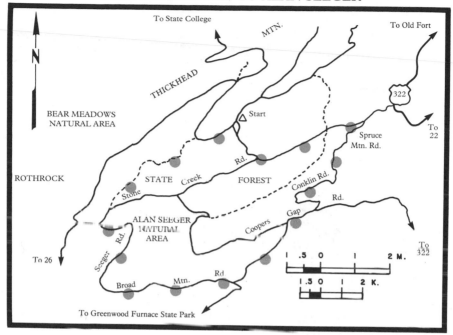

To State College
To Old Fort
MTN.
THICKHEAD
N
322
BEAR MEADOWS
NATURAL AREA
Start
Spruce
Mtn. Rd.
To
22
ROTHROCK
STATE   Creek
FOREST
Conklin Rd.
Stone
Rd.
ALAN SEEGER
NATURAL
AREA
Coopers
Gap
To 26
Seeger   Rd.
To
322
Broad   Mtn.   Rd
.5 0   1   2 M.
1.5 0   1   2 K.
To Greenwood Furnace State Park

first is out of Penn Roosevelt Picnic Area. After the descent into Alan Seeger Natural Area, the second major climb leads 4.5 miles to the lookout tower. There are a couple of smaller climbs followed by a descent back to Penn Roosevelt Picnic Area.

Season: The roads on this loop are rideable from April through October. Spring can be muddy and snow is possible from November through March. Avoid riding in deer hunting season, after Thanksgiving.

Services: All services are available in State College. Water, bathroom facilities, and camping are available at the Penn Roosevelt picnic area.

Hazards: The descent on the single-track section out of the Penn Roosevelt picnic area is very fast and the terrain changes around every corner. Watch for snakes on the ridges in warm weather.

Rescue index: Except for the single-track and jeep trail sections, the whole ride is on public roads. However, this is a remote area that doesn't carry a lot of traffic, especially in late fall and early spring.

Land status: State forest.

Maps: The USGS 7.5 minute topo maps are State College and McAlevys Fort.

Finding the trail: From State College, drive out US 322 south toward Lewistown. Turn right near the bottom of the Seven Mountains descent (at the reservoir) and follow the paved road through Rothrock State Forest to the Penn Roosevelt State Forest picnic area. Park at the campground.

Sources of additional information:

The Bicycle Shop
441 West College Avenue
State College, Pennsylvania 16801
(814) 238-9422

Notes on the trail: The turnoff to the lookout is the only left-hand option available, so you can't miss it. And as the map indicates, there are several options for returning to the Penn Roosevelt picnic area from the lookout tower. They're all fun!

RIDE 31 *STATE COLLEGE TO WHIPPLE DAM AND BEAR MEADOWS*

Bear Meadows is a pristine area that's well worth the long ride. Observation platforms built over the marsh let visitors view birds and fish from ten feet in the air. This is even a nice place to visit on a rainy day, since it's so rich in flora and wildlife. The wet, swamp-like topography draws many birds. And they don't call it Bear Meadows for nothing—keep an eye peeled for both deer and bear. More fun things to do on this ride include climbing the lookout tower at Tussey Mountain and, in summer, swimming at Whipple Dam State Park.

Most of this 25-mile loop ride is on hard-packed dirt roads. The descent on Little Shingletown Road is on a rocky jeep trail. The trail around Bear Meadows Natural Area is rocky, and crossed by fallen logs and many streams. Be warned: This ride requires technical skills and good stamina, since it has two long climbs of around 800' to 1,000' of elevation gain each.

General location: Rothrock State Forest, near State College, Pennsylvania.

Elevation change: There's a steep 800' climb to the lookout tower at Tussey Mountain. The loop then descends and climbs about 800' to Bear Meadows Natural Area.

Season: Rideable between April and November, although mid-summer can be hot and humid. Spring can be muddy, and expect snow from November through March. Avoid riding in deer hunting season, after Thanksgiving.

Services: All services are available in State College. Whipple Dam has water and rest rooms; between Memorial Day and Labor Day a snack bar is open.

Hazards: Watch for snakes on the ridges in warm weather. Be alert for traffic on the dirt roads.

Rescue index: Whipple Dam and Bear Meadows are both popular areas.

STATE COLLEGE TO WHIPPLE DAM AND BEAR MEADOWS

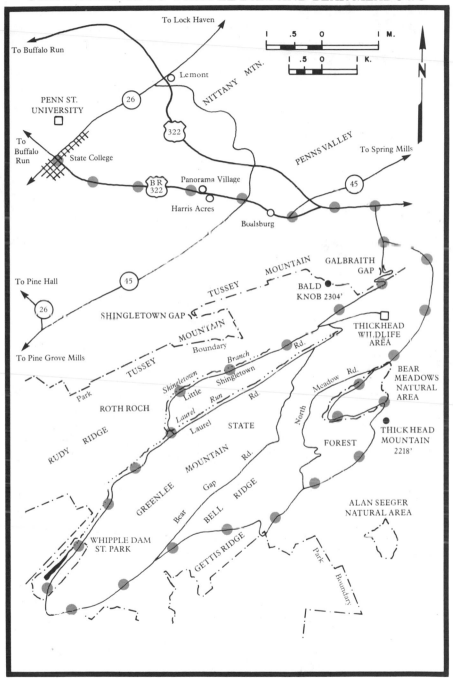

Little Shingletown Road, however, is remote, with no residences or farms along it.

Land status: Pennsylvania state forest and parks.

Maps: The USGS 7.5 minute topo maps are State College and McAlevys Fort.

Finding the trail: From State College, pedal out Business US 322 south to the turnoff for Tussey Mountain Ski Area (at Bear Mountain Road, on the right). After the lookout tower watch for the turn onto Little Shingletown Road (which isn't marked) at the very top of the climb. The turn is at the same elevation as the tower.

Sources of additional information:

The Bicycle Shop
441 West College Avenue
State College, Pennsylvania 16801
(814) 238-9422

Notes on the trail: Bear Meadows Natural Area is a day-use-only area that is in pristine condition, since no fishing or boating is allowed. The large, flat bog, punctuated by a slow-moving stream, changes appearance with the seasons, making it a popular destination throughout the year.

RIDE 32 *STATE COLLEGE TO ALAN SEEGER*

This 45-mile, out-and-back ride, popular with racers training for competition, features three major ascents of 800' to 1,000' of elevation gain each. Overall, this is a ride for experienced, hard-core mountain bikers. Most of this ride is along forest roads that provide frequent views of the surrounding ridges and valleys. Try to allow enough time to explore Bear Meadows and Alan Seeger Natural Areas.

While there are several steep ascents and descents on the dirt roads, watch out for the extremely technical trail that drops from the lookout tower to Alan Seeger Natural Area. It's only for the very experienced. Most riders should backtrack down the dirt road, which is one of the steepest, fastest drops in the region.

Other neat features on this ride include the lookout tower above the Alan Seeger Natural Area, which offers excellent views. And there's a short hiking trail (no bikes allowed) in Alan Seeger that shouldn't be missed. Bear Meadows Natural Area is a bog that features a wide variety of wildlife.

General location: The ride starts in State College, runs through Bear Meadows Natural Area to Alan Seeger Natural Area, and then returns to State College.

STATE COLLEGE TO ALAN SEEGER

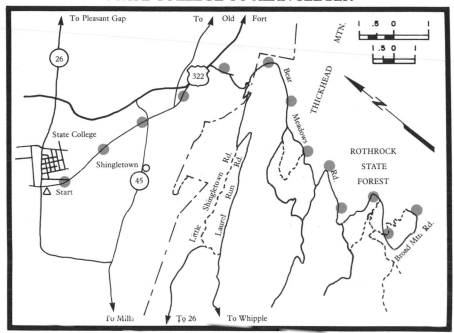

Elevation change: There are 3 major climbs: Tussey Mountain to Bear Meadows Natural Area, Alan Seeger Natural Area to the lookout tower and, on the return, Alan Seeger to Bear Meadows. The ride then drops for the return to State College. Total elevation gain is about 3,000′.

Season: Rideable between April and November. Mid-summer can be hot and humid. Expect snow after November and through March. Spring can be muddy. Avoid riding in deer hunting season, after Thanksgiving.

Services: All services are available in State College.

Hazards: The descent from the lookout tower into Alan Seeger Natural Area is very difficult and should only be attempted by expert riders.

Rescue index: Most of the ride is along traffic-bearing roads. However, traffic gets lighter as the ride moves away from US 322.

Land status: State forests, state and county roads.

Maps: The USGS 7.5 minute topo maps are State College and McAlevys Fort.

Finding the trail: From State College, pedal out Business US 322 south to the turnoff for Tussey Mountain Ski Area (at Bear Mountain Road, on the right). At Tussey Mountain Ski Area turn right onto Meadows Road.

Sources of additional information:

The Bicycle Shop
441 West College Avenue
State College, Pennsylvania 16801
(814) 238-9422

Notes on the trail: Mike Hermann, the sales manager at The Bicycle Shop in State College, has this warning about the optional descent from the lookout tower to Alan Seeger Natural Area: "We originally named this trail 'Herm's Ride from Hell' when we first attempted it, and people do get hurt riding this. To be ridden well, it must be ridden fast. This section of trail is for extreme mountain bikers—only the hard-core need apply!"

Bald Eagle State Forest

Bald Eagle State Forest, located near the geographical center of Pennsylvania, lies midway between State College to the west and the Susquehanna River to the east. Named after a famous Indian chief, the forest comprises 191,858 acres in the ridge and valley region of the state. The dominant features are sandstone ridges that rise as much as 2,300 feet above sea level. The many streams in the area originate in the forested ridges and drain southeasterly toward the Susquehanna River.

With over 340 miles of roads, as many miles of foot trails, and 300 miles of designated snowmobile trails, Bald Eagle State Forest draws mountain bikers from throughout Pennsylvania and the Northeast. Since 1987 the Bald Eagle Mountain Bike Jamboree has been held at R. B. Winter State Park (one of four state parks located in the forest) and offers a wide selection of rides, full technical support, maps, and camping. The Jamboree is held every October and attracts hundreds of mountain bikers for three days of riding during the peak of the fall foliage season.

When pedaling north-central Pennsylvania, stop by The Bicycle Peddler in Lewisburg to pick up maps and get final directions to trailheads. Owner Mike Kryzytski is a rabid mountain biker who will make sure you get the most from your visit to the area. And don't forget to ask Mike for the dates of this year's Bald Eagle Mountain Bike Jamboree.

RIDE 33 COWBELL HOLLOW / TOP MOUNTAIN TRAIL

This 15-mile loop ride is a typical north-central Pennsylvania combination of forest roads and trails. It features Top Mountain Trail, one of the best mountain bike rides in Bald Eagle State Forest. This abandoned jeep trail, which varies from smooth to very rocky, is fast and challenging, with lots of turns, short climbs, and descents. It also has excellent views of the surrounding mountains. Sugar Valley Narrows Road is a hard-packed dirt road, while all the other forest roads on this ride are hard-packed dirt covered with loose stones. Cowbell Hollow Trail is one of the most rideable single-track trails in this area—but watch out for deadfalls.

With steep climbs and rocky, technical single-track, this trail is for experienced riders. Less experienced mountain bikers will find large parts of the loop rideable, but should have good stamina and be ready to push their bikes over the rocky sections of trail. White Deer Creek, which is crossed twice, is

COWBELL HOLLOW/TOP MOUNTAIN TRAIL

one of the larger creeks in the area. It's a rocky, fast-flowing trout stream that has some excellent camping spots along it. Mook's Spring on Running Gap Road, 100 yards south of the Top Mountain Trail intersection, is a dependable source of water.

General location: The ride starts in Bald Eagle State Forest, 10 miles northwest of Lewisburg, Pennsylvania (60 miles north of Harrisburg).

Elevation change: The ride begins at 1,000' of elevation and climbs to over 1,750' on Cowbell Hollow Trail. After descending to about 1,100' at White Deer Creek, the trail climbs to 1,800' on Top Mountain Trail. Descend to 1,300' on White Deer Creek Road and follow the creek back to 1,000' at the start. Total elevation gain is around 1,500'.

Season: The best time to ride this loop is between April and October. Spring can be very muddy. The best views are in the fall after the leaves are off the trees. (But don't ride in deer hunting season, usually after Thanksgiving.) The winter months are risky. Expect snow after November, and the forest roads are often ice-covered, even after long spells of warm weather.

Services: All services are available in Lewisburg, Pennsylvania. Camp at R. B. Winter State Park, about 12 miles southwest of this loop.

Hazards: Sections of Top Mountain Trail are extremely rocky. In winter and early spring expect parts of the trails to be covered with ice.

Photo by author

Rescue index: There's light traffic along White Deer Creek Road. Interstate 80 parallels most of this ride.

Land status: Pennsylvania state forest.

Maps: Pick up a Bald Eagle State Forest public use map at The Bicycle Peddler in Lewisburg. USGS 7.5 minute quads are Carroll and Williamsport S.E.

Finding the trail: Take Exit 29 from I-80 (10 miles west of PA 15). From the exit ramp, go down the hill a few hundred yards to the dirt road and park near the intersection with Sugar Valley Narrows Road.

Sources of additional information:

Department of Environmental Resources
Bureau of Forestry
P.O. Box 147
Laurelton, Pennsylvania 17835-0147

The Bicycle Peddler
PA 45 West
Lewisburg, Pennsylvania 17837
(717) 524-4554

Notes on the trail: This ride starts from an interstate exit that inexplicably leads directly onto a desolate state forest road. From your car, ride west on Sugar Valley Narrows Road, then bear left onto Garden Hollow Road, which is followed by an almost immediate left onto Cooper Mill Road. There's a steep climb to the top; on the downhill, turn left onto Cowbell Hollow Trail at the first 180-degree hairpin turn (look for a sign). This up-and-down jeep trail turns into a brushy single-track. It descends to White Deer Creek. Cross the creek at the small bridge and turn right onto White Deer Creek Road.

Make a sharp left almost immediately onto Running Gap Road and climb to the top. Turn right on Top Mountain Trail. Following this single-track is self-evident; but if in doubt, follow the blue blazes and bear left. Turn right at the first forest road, Cooper Mill Road. Follow it downhill (you may have a short climb first, depending on which branch of Top Mountain Trail you finished on) to White Deer Creek Road. Turn right and ride to the end. Turn right again and ride back to your car.

RIDE 34   *THE BEAR GAP RIDE*

This 12-mile figure-8 ride is a challenging route designed for experienced mountain bikers. However, intermediate riders with good stamina and the willingness to walk some sections will be able to complete the double loop.

Most of the trail is through second-growth hardwood forests, with many vistas of the surrounding ridges and valleys. Stop at Sand Mountain Tower and climb to the top for breathtaking views, which are especially spectacular on a clear day at dusk or during a full moon. You can also swim at the state park.

These forest roads are mostly hard-packed dirt covered with loose stones. Spring Mountain Trail is relatively flat and rideable by novice mountain bikers. Parts of Bear Gap are expert only, but are short enough to walk. The Old Tram Trail is moderately rocky.

General location: R. B. Winter State Park, 15 miles west of Lewisburg, Pennsylvania.

Elevation change: Start at 1,600' of elevation and climb the Cracker Bridge Trail to 1,700'. Climb to 1,767' at the intersection of Cooper Mill and Sand Mountain Roads. Drop down Bear Gap Trail to around 1,000' and climb back up again to 1,767' at Sand Mountain Road. On the return to the park you will reach 2,047' at the fire tower. Total elevation gain is about 1,400'.

Season: Generally rideable between April and November. Spring can be very muddy. Autumn, after the leaves are off the trees, offers the best views. The trails and roads can be icy in winter, even after prolonged warm spells. Expect snow from November through March.

THE BEAR GAP RIDE

Services: All services are available in Lewisburg, Pennsylvania, 18 miles east of R. B. Winter State Park.

Hazards: Bear Gap Trail is very rocky and in wet weather can be filled with flowing water. Avoid riding in deer hunting season, after Thanksgiving.

Rescue index: R. B. Winter State Park is usually staffed. Traffic can be flagged down on PA 192.

Land status: Pennsylvania state forest.

Maps: The USGS 7.5 minute topos are Carroll, Williamsport S.E., and Hartleton. Also, pick up a copy of the Bald Eagle State Forest public use map at The Bicycle Peddler in Lewisburg.

Finding the trail: R. B. Winter State Park is 18 miles west of Lewisburg, Pennsylvania, on PA 192. Follow the signs to the camping area. Park in the lot between the lake and the camping area.

Sources of additional information:

Department of Environmental Resources
Bureau of Forestry
P.O. Box 147
Laurelton, Pennsylvania 17835-0147

The Bicycle Peddler
PA 45 West
Lewisburg, Pennsylvania 17837
(717) 524-4554

Notes on the trail: From the parking lot, ride north on the paved park road a half mile uphill to the first intersection with a dirt forest road; turn right onto Sand Mountain Road. Go to the first intersection (Boyer Gap Road is to the right) and take Cracker Bridge Trail to the left. At the bottom of the hill, turn right and follow the Old Tram Trail east to Cooper Mill Road and turn right. Turn left at the top, after the long climb. Very soon you'll reach a fork; bear left (which is almost straight) and continue to Bear Gap Trail (no trail sign).

Here's how to verify you're on Bear Gap: The trail goes slightly downhill at first, with a grassy meadow on the left, followed by a steep downhill through trees and across a small stream. Follow the trail downhill to Spruce Run Road. Turn left. At the next intersection, go left onto Cooper Mill Road.

Repeat the climb on Cooper Mill Road. At the top turn right onto Sand Mountain Road. After the short climb to the top you'll see the fire tower. Continue downhill on Sand Mountain Road. At Boyer Gap Road turn left, then turn right onto Bake Oven Trail and back to the park.

RIDE 35 *CHERRY RUN / PENN'S CREEK RAILROAD BED*

While this is a long ride with several rocky single-tracks and three long climbs on forest roads, beginning mountain bikers with good stamina will enjoy it. Most of the route is along hard-packed forest roads covered with loose sand and gravel. The single-track trails on the ride are rocky and technical. The section of Old Mingle Road from the grave (see below) to the railroad bed is along a narrow, steep bank that requires good bike handling skills. The Mid-State Trail is steep and rocky.

This 20-mile ride has lots to offer besides a great workout. Along Penn's Creek there is great swimming in the summer, an abandoned railroad tunnel to ride through, and the century-old grave of a drowning victim erected by his heart-broken lover. The Joyce Kilmer Natural Area, on the left along Bear Run at the beginning of the ride, is a 77-acre tract of virgin white pine and hemlock. Hike down the trail at the sign on Bear Run (bikes aren't allowed) to explore the forest.

There are many vistas of the surrounding forest-covered ridges. The abandoned rail bed along Penn's Creek is one of the most beautiful spots in the state. The creek is huge and flows through a big valley covered with a mature

CHERRY RUN/
PENN'S CREEK RAILROAD BED

forest free of underbrush. With no road along the creek, the area has a real wilderness feeling to it.

General location: Bald Eagle State Forest, 25 miles west of Mifflinburg, Pennsylvania.

Elevation change: The ride starts at about 1,100' of elevation and slowly climbs to 1,900' on Bear Run Road. Rupp Hollow is a ridge with an elevation of about 1,700' along its length; you then drop to 1,200' at Old Mingle Road. The road drops to just below 1,000' of elevation at Penn's Creek. At the former trestle, start a slow climb to 1,200' at Cherry Run Road. Climb to 1,717' at Rupp Hollow Road. Along Paddy Mountain Road the elevation climbs to 2,100', then drops to below 900' at PA 45. Total elevation gain is around 1,900'.

Season: Rideable from April through November. Spring can be muddy; the best views are in late fall after the leaves are off the trees. Avoid riding in deer hunting season, after Thanksgiving. Expect snow from November through March.

Services: All services are available in Lewisburg, 25 miles east of the ride.

Hazards: The mud on Old Mingle Road in wet weather is the worst in north-

Photo by author

central Pennsylvania. The single-track is rocky and technical. The downhill on Paddy Mountain Road is fast and technical.

Rescue index: This ride is in the heart of Bald Eagle State Forest and mountain bikers are, for the most part, on their own. The village of Weikert, on Penn's Creek past Cherry Run, has year-round residents. Traffic can be flagged down on PA 45.

Land status: State forest.

Maps: Bald Eagle State Forest public use map, available at The Bicycle Peddler in Lewisburg.

Finding the trail: Take PA 45 west from Mifflinburg through Hartleton and past Laurelton Center. After entering the state forest, look for a left turn onto Bear Run Road. The parking lot is 100 yards down the road on the left.

Sources of additional information:

Department of Environmental Resources
Bureau of Forestry
P.O. Box 147
Laurelton, Pennsylvania 17835-0147

The Bicycle Peddler
PA 45 West
Lewisburg, Pennsylvania 17837
(717) 524-4554

Notes on the trail: After parking, pedal uphill on Bear Run Road to the end. Turn left on Woodward Gap Road and then turn right on Rupp Hollow Road. Turn left onto the Mid-State Trail, a rocky, downhill single-track. Turn right onto Old Mingle Road and follow it to the dead end at Penn's Creek. To find the unnamed trail to the left, look about 100 yards above the creek bank. Follow the creek downstream along the rocky remnants of the logging trail. Look for the tombstone of a drowning victim. Turn toward the creek at the tombstone and continue downstream a short distance to a cabin; turn left at the cinder path and ride through an abandoned railroad tunnel.

Continue along this old railroad grade to the former site of a trestle. Leave the grade and go left (uphill), which leads to Cherry Run Road, followed by a long climb to Rupp Hollow Road. Turn right and continue straight. (The road's name changes to Paddy Mountain Road.) At the end of the downhill turn left and continue to PA 45; turn left again and return to the parking lot.

Jim Thorpe

In the western Pocono Mountains of Pennsylvania, the Lehigh River cuts a spectacular 1,000-foot-deep gorge through table-top mountains and thousands of acres of state park and game lands. Taking advantage of 30 miles of abandoned railroad grade along the river, Pennsylvania created Lehigh Gorge State Park, 6,000 acres of spectacular park land that stretches south from an Army Corps of Engineers dam near Wilkes Barre to a town with the unlikely name of Jim Thorpe, Pennsylvania. This combination of scenic river gorge, state game lands, and a restored Victorian-era village results in one of the best mountain biking destinations in the East.

The rich history of the area is also an attraction, especially to mountain bikers. This is coal country, and many of the old rail lines used to haul coal from mines to river ports are now converted trails that make for easy pedaling. In the mid-nineteenth century industry was booming and, as the transportation hub of the region, so were the towns of Mauch Chunk and East Mauch Chunk (today's Jim Thorpe). Canal, railroad, and river traffic converged in the towns. Millionaires built mansions, hotels, an opera house, and churches in fine Victorian style on the hillsides overlooking the Lehigh River. When the boom ended later in the century the towns and the mountainous region around them became a popular summer resort known as "The Switzerland of America."

The Great Depression of the 1930s clinched the area's decline and the towns fell into disrepair. Unemployment took its toll and young people fled the region. In the early 1950s the local newspaper started an economic development fund and urged citizens to contribute a nickel per week. In 1954 the communities were rewarded for their spunk when the widow of Jim Thorpe, the hero of the 1912 Stockholm Olympic Games (who died a pauper in a Philadelphia hospital in 1953), agreed to let the two towns merge under the great athlete's name and build a monument and mausoleum for him.

The 1980s marked the beginning of an era of prosperity and restoration for this handsome town on the Lehigh. Tourism is now big business. Shops, restaurants, bed-and-breakfasts, and lots of cars now line the streets of Jim Thorpe. You'll also see plenty of mountain bikes.

And no wonder. With Lehigh Gorge State Park at its doorstep and miles of hiking trails winding through the town to the overlooks nearby, Jim Thorpe was made for fat-tired bikes. The trails, converted from old railroad right-of-ways, are on two-percent grades, making for effortless riding. Close by are thousands of acres of state game lands, which extends the variety of mountain biking from the town.

116

Since 1986 Jim Thorpe has hosted the Mountain Bike Weekend, held every June in nearby Mauch Chunk Lake Park. Bill Drumbore and Galen Van Dine, local riders who help organize the event, discovered mountain biking when it was virtually unheard of in the East. (Bill built his first mountain bike in a garage using old 10-speed and BMX parts. It's stored in the basement of the Hotel Switzerland in Jim Thorpe and displayed in the bar during the Mountain Bike Weekend.) Every year Bill and Galen help organize and plan mountain bike rides for the hundreds of mountain bikers who converge on the town for a weekend of camaraderie and great cycling. They also assisted in the trail descriptions that follow.

Here's how to get there. Jim Thorpe is located between Allentown and Scranton, off the Northeast Extension of the Pennsylvania Turnpike (about 90 minutes from Philadelphia). From New York City take Interstate 80 west to PA 209 south, about a three-hour drive.

RIDE 36 *THE WEEKEND WARRIOR*

The mountains in the western Poconos were sheared by glaciers, making the tops smooth and rolling—and perfect for mountain biking. This entire 14-mile ride, which can be ridden as a loop or a figure-8, follows double-track roads on top of Broad Mountain. The road passes through mixed-hardwood forests (mostly oak with some maple and gray birch) interspersed with open fields. The mountain borders the Lehigh River Gorge, providing different views of the river and mountains, and glimpses of hawks soaring at eye level.

The optional ride to the first overlook is down a rocky power line cut; the view up the river gorge (almost 1,000 feet deep) makes it worth the return climb. The second overlook is even better. The village of Jim Thorpe, with Flagstaff Park towering over it (see Galen's Surprise), straddles both sides of the river flowing deep inside the gorge.

General location: Five miles north of Jim Thorpe, Pennsylvania, off PA 93.

Elevation change: The optional, out-and-back drop down the power line to the first overlook is about 350'. The elevation at the start is about 1,700' and gradually drops to about 1,300' at the second overlook. There is about 600' of climbing spread over the entire ride.

Season: Summer and fall are the best seasons to ride this loop. The mountaintop is relatively cool in the summer and the fall colors are spectacular (early and mid-October). Spring can be very muddy and snow is possible from November through March. These are state game lands, so avoid riding during fall hunting season.

THE WEEKEND WARRIOR

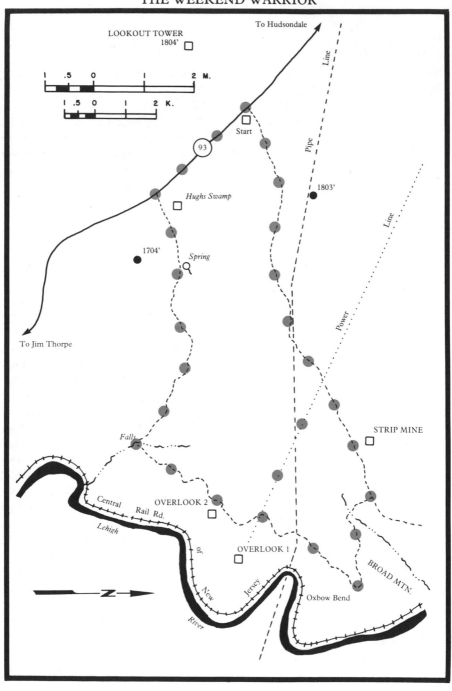

Services: All services are available in Jim Thorpe. Mountain bikes can be rented at Blue Mountain Sports.

Hazards: The descent to the first (optional) overlook is steep and rocky. Watch for heavy truck and car traffic on PA 93 for the last mile of the ride.

Rescue index: PA 93 is the only traffic-bearing road on the loop. There are no residences on the ride. The farthest point from PA 93 is about 5 miles.

Land status: State game lands.

Maps: Copies of the Mountain Bike Weekend Maps are available at Blue Mountain Sports in Jim Thorpe. The USGS topo maps are Christmans and Weatherly quadrangles.

Finding the trail: From Jim Thorpe, Pennsylvania, go north on PA 209 for 2 miles to the first traffic light (PA 93) and turn right. Go approximately 3 miles and park in the second lot on the right near the gate.

Sources of additional information:

Carbon County Tourist Promotion Agency
P.O. Box 90
Railroad Station
Jim Thorpe, Pennsylvania 18229
(717) 325-3673

Blue Mountain Sports
34 Susquehanna Street
Jim Thorpe, Pennsylvania 18229
(717) 325-4421

Notes on the trail: The recommended way to ride this loop is a figure-8. From the second pulloff on PA 93, ride out the fire road beyond the gate. After 2.5 miles, turn right and follow the power lines. At the intersection a mile later, go straight for the descent to the first overlook. Return to this intersection from the overlook and turn right. (It would be a left if you were coming down the power lines.) Follow this loop for 2.5 miles back to the first intersection. Turn left and retrace the ride along the power lines; at the intersection where you went straight to the overlook, now turn right.

After a half mile there is a "T" intersection; turn left to reach the second overlook. Double back to the "T" and go straight. Follow the road for 3 miles (through 2 stream crossings and a steep climb) to the next intersection; continue straight. At the gate in the parking lot on PA 93, turn right and ride 1 mile along the road back to your car.

RIDE 37   *GALEN'S SURPRISE*

This 14-mile loop ride is a great example of the tremendous diversity of off-road riding that Jim Thorpe offers. For example, the view from Flagstaff Park of the Lehigh River Gorge and the town of Jim Thorpe spans a whopping 65 miles. The park, containing a restaurant, a nightclub, and a view to die for, was known as "The Ballroom of the Clouds" during the Swing Era of the 1930s and 1940s and was home base for the Dorsey Brothers Band. Sound too civilized for a mountain bike ride? Relax—the next section of the ride features bone-jarring single-track, followed by fast double-track along a ridge and a steep descent to a huge lake.

The ride starts with an easy cruise on the Switchback Trail, but then climbs for 1.5 miles to the top of Mauch Chunk Ridge and Flagstaff Park. Next is two miles of rough single-track on a narrow, rocky trail. You will follow the ridge on an old dirt road, and make a right for a steep descent along a power line cut to the Shoreline Trail. Most of the ride on the ridge is through second-growth hardwood forest. After the descent, follow the wooded shoreline of Mauch Chunk Lake. This trail twists through evergreen forests and has views of the lake and Mauch Chunk Ridge. Look for the bird sanctuary and observer's shack built on the marshy lake shore. There's an excellent view of the entire lake and the wetlands teem with birds. The shack is also a good shelter in a storm. Keep an eye peeled for wildlife (including black bear) while riding.

General location: The ride begins in Mauch Chunk Lake Park, located 3 miles west of Jim Thorpe, Pennsylvania, on PA 209 (the Lentz Trail Highway).

Elevation change: This ride does all of its climbing on the paved road to Flagstaff Park—about 450′ of elevation gain. After that it's all ridge riding, followed by a steep descent to the lake.

Season: Summer is excellent—consider a swim at the lake following the ride. In fall the spectacular foliage is mirrored on the lake. Spring can get very muddy, especially along the lake. Expect snow between November and March. Avoid riding in hunting season (late fall).

Services: All services are available in Jim Thorpe. Mountain bikes can be rented at Blue Mountain Sports.

Hazards: Watch for cars on the paved road up to Mauch Chunk Ridge. The drop off the ridge at the power lines is very steep.

Rescue index: No point on the trail is more than a couple of miles from paved roads. Also, Mauch Chunk Lake Park is staffed from April through October.

Land status: The trail along Mauch Chunk Ridge is on private property. Obtain permission to ride at Flagstaff Park (just past the turnoff for the

GALEN'S SURPRISE

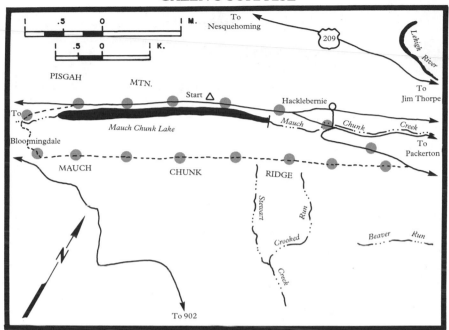

single-track trail). Mauch Chunk Lake Park is owned by the Carbon County (Pennsylvania) Parks and Recreation Commission.

Maps: Maps showing this ride are available at Blue Mountain Sports in Jim Thorpe. The USGS topo is the Nesquehoning quadrangle.

Finding the trail: Mauch Chunk Lake Park is located 3 miles from Jim Thorpe, Pennsylvania, on PA 209 (the Lentz Trail Highway). The Switchback Trail is located at the park entrance. Park at the office or at any of the other parking lots.

Sources of additional information:

Mauch Chunk Lake Park
P.O. Box 7
Jim Thorpe, Pennsylvania 18229
(717) 325-3669

Blue Mountain Sports
34 Susquehanna Street
Jim Thorpe, Pennsylvania 18229
(717) 325-4421

Notes on the trail: The ride starts on the Switchback Trail, which crosses PA 209 at the entrance of Mauch Chunk Lake Park. Follow it past the dam, where it bears left. At the intersection with the paved road turn right and climb 1.5 miles to the top of the ridge; the trailhead is on the right. Continue a short distance on the road to Flagstaff Park, catch the view, and get permission to ride the ridge trail.

Double back to the single-track (now on the left). After about 2 miles the trail turns into a grassy road for another 3 miles. At the "T" intersection turn right and descend at the power lines. Look for the single-track to the left that goes into the woods (about two-thirds of the way down). In the woods, follow the path over 2 wooden bridges and emerge in a field. Turn right and keep the woods to your right as you bear around to the lake. Once you arrive at the lake the Shoreline Trail is easy to find.

RIDE 38 *LEHIGH GORGE STATE PARK*

The Lehigh River cuts a spectacular gorge through the Poconos, and this pleasant ride through Lehigh Gorge State Park provides great views from the bottom up. The fast-moving river, steep walls of rock, waterfalls, and thick vegetation characterize the trail along its 30 miles. The Lehigh River is almost always in sight, frequently coursing over rocks and rapids. On this easy ride the emphasis is on the scenery, not bike handling. The grade along this wide, cinder-covered trail is virtually unnoticeable riding north (upriver), and riding downriver is even easier. On long rides take head winds into consideration: It's usually best to ride out with the wind in your face and return with a tail wind. And while this is usually ridden as an out-and-back ride, it's easy to set up a shuttle for a one-way ride—say, Jim Thorpe to Rockport.

Highlights: At the first river crossing north of Jim Thorpe, explore an abandoned railroad tunnel adjacent to the bridge. At various points along the trail, look for ruins of the old canal that parallels the river. Look up and you'll see many waterfalls emptying into the river through siltstone and sandstone rock formations.

General location: Jim Thorpe, Pennsylvania.

Elevation change: Negligible.

Season: Summer and fall are the best seasons. The fall foliage viewed from the bottom of the gorge is dramatic. Spring can be wet and muddy. Expect snow from November through March. Hunting is permitted in the park, so avoid riding in the late fall.

Services: All services are available in Jim Thorpe. Mountain bikes can be rented at Blue Mountain Sports.

LEHIGH GORGE STATE PARK

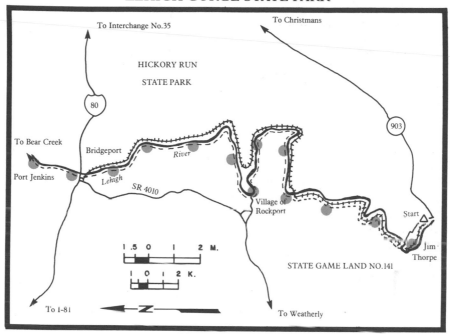

Hazards: The trail is along, and occasionally crosses, railroad tracks still in use.

Rescue index: The trail is closed to motor vehicles and is in a deep gorge surrounded by state game lands, so help is only available at park entrances.

Land status: State park.

Maps: Pick up maps at Blue Mountain Sports and the tourist bureau in Jim Thorpe.

Finding the trail: From Jim Thorpe, either drive or pedal your bike across the Lehigh River on PA 903 and turn left onto Coalport Road. The entrance to the Coalport Access Area is on the left.

Sources of additional information:

Department of Environmental Resources
Lehigh Gorge State Park
RD 2 Box 56
Weatherly, Pennsylvania 18255
(717) 427-8161

Blue Mountain Sports
34 Susquehanna Street
Jim Thorpe, Pennsylvania 18229
(717) 325-4421

RIDE 39   *THE SWITCHBACK TRAIL*

Here's an easy 10-mile loop that includes forest trails, great views of the Lehigh River Gorge, a ramble through old Jim Thorpe, and a spin along a babbling mountain stream. And if that sounds too good to be true, consider this: there aren't any steep climbs, either.

The trail is in two sections—the Back Track and the Down Track, references to the days when the trail was a gravity railroad. Loaded coal cars traveled the Down Track to waiting barges and returned to the coal mines empty on the Back Track. Today the Back Track follows a wooded ridge (watch for deadfall) into Jim Thorpe; the Down Track returns to Mauch Chunk Lake Park along the stream. A wide cinder path winds through some woods in the heights above the town. The grade never exceeds two percent.

Watch out for: a steep, rocky descent into town on the Back Track; a side trail to "The Point," a rock outcropping with an unobstructed view north of the Lehigh River Gorge where hawks soar at eye level; a young black bear spotted around dusk on the Down Track.

General location: Jim Thorpe, Pennsylvania.

Elevation change: The ride starts at Mauch Chunk Lake Park and descends about 600′ in elevation to Jim Thorpe. Recovering the lost altitude on the 2 percent grade back up to the park is very easy.

Season: Summer and fall are the best seasons for riding. Spring can be very muddy, especially on the Back Track. Stay out of the woods during deer hunting season (late fall). Expect snow between November and March.

Services: All services are available in Jim Thorpe. Mountain bikes can be rented at Blue Mountain Sports.

Hazards: There is a steep, rocky descent from the Back Track into Jim Thorpe that novice riders may want to walk.

Rescue index: The Back Track section is along a mountain ridge away from paved roads. The rest of the trail is either in town or parallels PA 209.

Land status: County park lands.

Maps: Blue Mountain Sports and the tourist bureau in Jim Thorpe carry maps.

Finding the trail: From Mauch Chunk Lake Park, ride out the main entrance, turn left onto PA 209 and ride a half mile to where the Back Track intersects

THE SWITCHBACK TRAIL

on the right. (Here's a shortcut, if you don't mind pushing your bike 100 yards up a very steep bank: Turn right from the park entrance and look for a dirt road on the left. Follow it straight up the side of the mountain to the Back Track section and turn right.)

Sources of additional information:

Carbon County Tourist Promotion Agency
P.O. Box 90
Railroad Station
Jim Thorpe, Pennsylvania 18229
(717) 325-3673

Blue Mountain Sports
34 Susquehanna Street
Jim Thorpe, Pennsylvania 18229
(717) 325-4421

Notes on the trail: The Switchback Trail is built on the right-of-way of one of America's first railroads, the gravity railroad between old Mauch Chunk and the coal mines in Summit Hill. Cars full of coal rolled to waiting barges in Jim Thorpe; mules pulled the empty cars up a steep incline where they rolled back to the mines. (Steam power later replaced the mules.) The gravity railroad began operating in 1828 and ran until 1933. After the Civil War and the decline of the canal system that the railroad fed, it was converted into a passenger ride, foreshadowing the development of the roller coaster.

One last note: While the ride can be started in Jim Thorpe, be sure to ride out of town on the Down Track section, to avoid a steep climb on the Back Track.

RIDE 40 *SUMMER'S LOOP*

This 15-mile loop on Pennsylvania state game land is characterized by deep forests, making this a nice ride on hot days. An added attraction is the great view of the Lehigh River Gorge, especially in fall when the foliage is turning. The mountain laurel is in full bloom in mid-June. Keep on the lookout for wildlife, including deer, black bear, and birds.

While this ride is entirely on forest roads, there are sections of steep descents and climbs on rutted surfaces that make it challenging, especially if ridden fast. After starting on pavement the trail changes to dirt, with some stretches of coarse gravel. On the return leg there's a creek crossing followed by a packed-dirt uphill. Midway through the ride the trail passes over the Rockport Tunnel, a live railroad tunnel that runs through the mountain. The view of the Lehigh River Gorge is one of the best and one that few visitors to the area ever see. A series of steep, short climbs ends the ride.

General location: Summer's Loop is 10 miles from Jim Thorpe, Pennsylvania, in the western Pocono Mountains.

Elevation change: The elevation changes are minor, with the lowest point of the ride at 1,100' of elevation and the highest only 1,680'. This difference accumulates over many short climbs.

Season: Summer and fall are the best seasons. The mountain is usually covered by snow in winter and deep mud from melting snow in early spring. Avoid riding during hunting season (late fall).

Services: All services are available in Jim Thorpe. Mountain bikes can be rented at Blue Mountain Sports.

Hazards: The biggest danger on this ride, with its easy grades and wide roads, is running out of water. Watch out for snakes in warm weather and avoid riding in deer hunting season (late fall). Be careful on the long descents.

Rescue index: There's the small private community of Christmansville near the start of the ride. If you've begun the descent toward Drake's Creek and need help, keep going in that direction to your car.

SUMMER'S LOOP

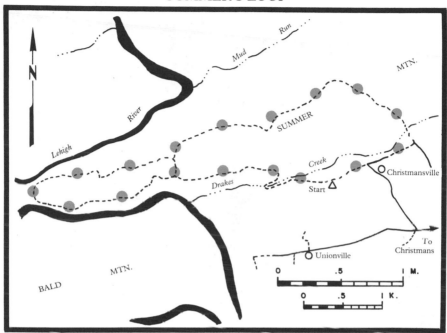

Land status: State game lands.

Maps: The topo map for this ride is the Christmans USGS quadrangle.

Finding the trail: To reach Summer's Loop, drive north from Jim Thorpe on PA 903 for 10.5 miles. At the sign for Penn Forest Garage (directly across from Smith's Hardware Store), turn left onto Unionville Road. Follow this road (don't turn off on side roads) for 2.5 miles to a power line and turn right onto Schoolhouse Road. Drive to the "Y" intersection and take the dirt road to the left. About a half mile down the road look for a small open area by the power line; park there. To start the ride, head back out the dirt road to the "Y" intersection and go straight. Follow the road to another "Y" intersection. Look for a house on the corner and a gate across the road to the left. Take the left past the gate and ride uphill. Go straight until the road turns to dirt at a "Y" intersection. Turn right to begin the loop.

Sources of additional information:

Blue Mountain Sports
34 Susquehanna Street
Jim Thorpe, Pennsylvania 18229
(717) 325-4421

Notes on the trail: Pennsylvania state game lands provide a lifetime of mountain biking opportunities, but offer nothing in the way of road signs, trail signs, blazes, or anything to help riders find their way around. Carry a topo map and compass, and give yourself enough time to explore. And don't forget your spirit of adventure.

NEW YORK

Shawangunk Mountains / Catskill State Park

In a two-hour drive north of the cold concrete canyons of New York City, intrepid mountain bikers are transported to the scenic Hudson Valley. Overlooking the valley to the west is Catskill Park, featuring 650,000 acres of mountains and forests—and some of the best mountain biking and alpine scenery in the East. South of the park, the Shawangunk (SHON-gum) Mountains have become a favorite destination for off-road riders.

The Hudson Valley's rich history is also a boon to mountain bikers. The region was settled in the early seventeenth century, and the many carefully carved carriage trails crisscrossing the nearby Shawangunks reflect nearly three centuries of use. For off-road cyclists, this translates into many miles of moderate-grade climbing through spectacular mountains. Dramatic rock outcroppings and vistas of mountain ridges and lakes mark almost every turn along many of these trails.

If riding carriage trails sounds a little too tame, the Shawangunks also feature excellent single-track trails. For hammerheads seeking anaerobic bliss, all-day rides leading to distant peaks are easy to plan.

With New York City only a few hours away the Shawangunks get a lot of use by hikers and increasingly over the last five or so years by mountain bikers as well. When I visited on a mid-week morning the trails in Minnewaska State Park were filling up with hikers, and at least a dozen mountain bikes were being unloaded in the parking lot. The word is out: the Shawangunks are a hot place to bike.

With the growing popularity of the Shawangunks as a mountain bike destination, it hasn't taken long for an entrepreneurial spirit to see a need and fill it. Bob Henninger is an expert-class mountain bike racer who operates two bike shops in the Catskills—his original shop in Kingston, and a second shop in New Paltz (where Bob rents mountain bikes and organizes tours).

He calls the Shawangunk Mountains "the East Coast Boulder, Colorado," and anticipates the continued growth of mountain biking's popularity throughout the nineties. With a decade of riding experience in the area, Bob is a regional expert on where to ride off-road. Whenever you're looking for a mountain bike adventure in the Shawangunks, Catskill Park, or the Hudson Valley, stop in at one of his shops to talk about mountain bikes, good trails to ride, and to get directions to the trailhead. The rides that follow are some of Bob's favorites.

MINNEWASKA STATE PARK

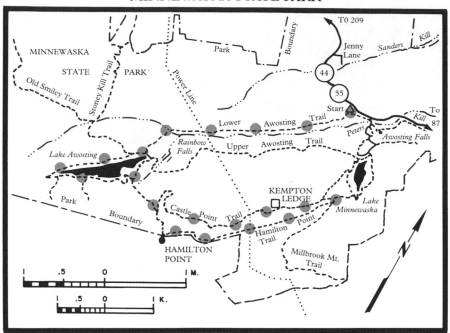

RIDE 41   *MINNEWASKA STATE PARK*

For spectacular mountain scenery, this 17-mile loop ride may qualify as one of the best on the East Coast. The carriage roads carved out of the mountains gently switchback up the mountain face, revealing higher and grander views of the surrounding mountains and lakes at each turn. From Castle Point the nearly 360-degree view is breathtaking, as high ridges recede in the distance in all directions. The scenery never lets up.

And for more good news, you don't need to be a LeMond or Tomac to enjoy this ride. Although there are some long climbs, most of the riding is on six-foot-wide converted carriage roads. The gentle grades require endurance, not technical riding ability. The trails are well maintained and heavily used.

General location: Minnewaska State Park lies 25 miles southwest of Kingston, New York, off NY 44/55 in the Shawangunk Mountains.

Elevation change: The loop begins at around 1,400' of elevation and gently climbs to about 2,100' at Castle Point. Total elevation gain is around 1,000'.

Season: These well-groomed trails make for fine riding year-round. Fall, with

Photo by author

its spectacular foliage, is a favorite season with most visitors, with spring and summer right behind. Expect snow between November and March.

Services: All services, including bike shops and rentals, are available in New Paltz and Kingston.

Hazards: The park is popular with hikers, so maintain a reasonable speed when descending on the carriage trails. Watch for wheel-eating crevasses when riding on the large rock formations that lead to the overlooks.

Rescue index: The park is heavily used by both hikers and mountain bikers, even on weekdays.

Land status: State park.

Maps: The USGS 7.5 minute topos are Gardiner and Napanoch. A trail map is available at the park entrance.

Finding the trail: From New York State Thruway (Interstate 87) Exit 18, turn left onto NY 299 west. Go through the village of New Paltz and cross the iron bridge. Continue on NY 299 until it ends 6 miles later. Turn right onto NY 44/55. The park entrance comes in about 4 miles, on the left.

Sources of additional information:

Minnewaska State Park
New Paltz, New York 12561
(914) 255-0752

Catskill Mountain Bicycle Shop
RD 6 Box 386
Kingston, New York 12401
(914) 336-2737

Catskill Mountain Bicycle Shop
5 ½ N. Front Street
New Paltz, New York 12561
(914) 255-3859

RIDE 42 *WALLKILL VALLEY RAIL TRAIL*

This beautiful, 12-mile hiking/biking trail passes through two quaint seventeenth-century villages, skirts farms, goes through woods, and crosses over rivers and streams. The elevated rail bed provides a view of the surrounding area including woodland ponds, the Wallkill River, and the Shawangunk Mountains in the distance. Wildlife frequently sighted along the trail includes wood turtles, woodcocks, songbirds, broadwing hawks, great horned owls, fox, white-tailed deer, and raccoons.

The well-maintained cinder trail is essentially flat. It can be ridden as an out-and-back, or as a loop by returning to the start via one of 21 paved roads that cross the trail. The trail passes through the New Paltz Historical District, which features seventeenth-century stone houses and the old railroad station that served the trains on this former Conrail route. There's also a Mexican restaurant, a bistro, a bakery, and several pizza parlors to round out a leisurely ride.

General location: The ride begins in the town of New Paltz, 15 miles south of Kingston and 1.5 miles from the New York State Thruway (I-87).

Elevation change: Negligible.

Season: The best riding is from late spring to mid-fall.

Services: All services, including two bike shops and rentals, are available in New Paltz. Gardiner has several bed-and-breakfast inns.

Hazards: Parts of the southern section of the trail are frequently covered with water after heavy rain. The bridge over the Wallkill River has been slated for repair; if the work isn't completed before your visit take special care.

WALLKILL VALLEY RAIL TRAIL

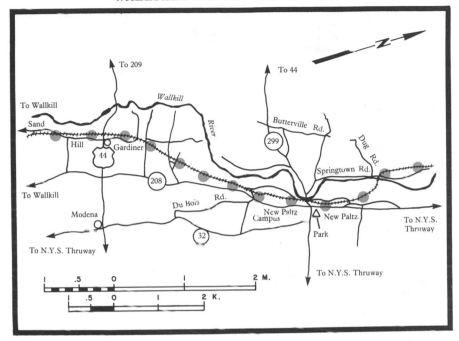

Rescue index: Help can be flagged down on the paved roads which cross the trail or from nearby residences.

Land status: The linear park is jointly owned by the village of New Paltz and the Land Trust of Wallkill Valley.

Maps: The USGS quadrangles are Gardiner and Rosendale. Brochures of the trail include a map and are available at the Town Hall on North Chestnut Street in New Paltz—phone (914) 255-0100.

Finding the trail: From I-87 take Exit 18 (NY 299) west for 1.5 miles to New Paltz, where the Wallkill Valley Rail Trail crosses the road. Park on a side street in the village or in the lot near the Historic District.

Sources of additional information:

Wallkill Valley Rail Trail Association
P.O. Box 1048
New Paltz, New York 12561

New Paltz Chamber of Commerce
257 ½ Main Street
New Paltz, New York 12561
(914) 255-0243

Catskill Mountain Bicycle Shop
5 ½ N. Front Street
New Paltz, New York 12561
(914) 255-3859

RIDE 43 *VERNOOY KILL FALLS TRAIL*

On this scenic ride in the mountains of Catskill Park watch for wildlife such as bear, deer, porcupine, turkey, and a wide variety of bird life. Other attractions include a beautiful waterfall and swimming hole surrounded by pines and shrubs about 2 miles into the ride. The trail passes through dense forests of pines, maples, and oaks, and along streams, waterfalls, and swamps. And don't forget to pack a fly rod. Vernooy Kill is an excellent trout stream.

This 10-mile loop, however, is for the technically adept mountain biker. It features rough, washed-out fire roads and technical single-track trails. There are steep climbs and long, technical descents that will challenge expert riders. Additional challenges include slippery wet rocks, black muck, and swamps. This is a ride for strong cyclists.

General location: Upper Cherrytown Road near Kerhonkson, New York, in the southern Catskill Mountains.

Elevation change: The ride starts with a long climb on technical single-track that gains about 1,000′ over 1.5 miles. This is followed by some gradual climbing and then rolling hills on a fire road. About 6 miles into the loop the trail begins to descend the mountain. The total elevation gain is around 1,200′.

Season: Local riders say that summer is the best time of year for this ride, for it's warm enough to swim and the trails are usually dry. In fall the foliage is considered "better than Vermont." Expect snow from November through March.

Services: All services are available in Kingston, New York.

Hazards: Watch for wet, slippery rocks. Watch out for other trail users on steep descents.

Rescue index: The trails are all within 5 miles of roads with residences and traffic.

Land status: State park.

Maps: The USGS 7.5 minute quadrangles are Peekamoose Mountain, Roundout Reservoir, and Kerhonkson.

Finding the trail: Take Exit 19 (Kingston) from the New York State Thruway (I-87) to NY 209 south, toward Ellenville. Go about 16 miles, through Accord. Turn right at Kerhonkson onto Pataukunk Road. At the intersection with Cherrytown Road continue straight onto Sampsonville Road. Bear left onto

VERNOOY KILL FALLS TRAIL

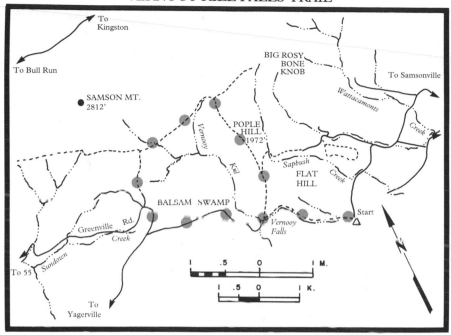

Lower Cherrytown Road. The name changes to Upper Cherrytown Road in Cherrytown. Continue to the parking area on the left at the state trail marker. Park here.

Sources of additional information:

Catskill Mountain Bicycle Shop
RD 6 Box 386
Kingston, New York 12401
(914) 336-2737

Catskill Mountain Bicycle Shop
5 ½ N. Front Street
New Paltz, New York 12561
(914) 255-3859

Notes on the trail: When first reaching the falls at the beginning of the ride take the trail to the right. When returning to this point on the loop you will return from the left, crossing over a wooden hiking bridge.

Syracuse

Syracuse, near the geographical center of New York, sits on the edge of the great northeastern sweep of the Appalachian Mountains. Its proximity to Lake Ontario, Adirondack Park, the Finger Lakes, and numerous hills and swamps affords a wide variety of riding to mountain bike enthusiasts.

A good example is Old Erie Canal Park, which starts in Syracuse and includes 35 miles of partially restored canal. The towpath gives mountain bikers not only glimpses of the region's history and early commerce, but a look at the considerable natural diversity of the area. The canal, begun in 1817, took advantage of a comparatively level route between the Hudson River and Lake Erie through the only break in the Appalachian chain. Finished in 1825, the canal was the work of self-made engineers, and was the greatest engineering feat of its time.

Another popular off-road destination near Syracuse is Highland Forest, a county-owned and -operated park on a tall hill overlooking lush farmland. Popular as a cross-country skiing area in the winter, the park welcomes mountain bikers to its trails in the warmer months. While foot trails are closed to cyclists, over 20 miles of ski trails and all roads and fire lanes are open to mountain bikes.

Syracuse is close to Adirondack Park, which at six million acres is the largest park east of the Rockies. While the park is an immense area containing 2,000 miles of hiking trails, mountain biking is relatively limited. For one thing, the old systems of logging roads that make up most of the trails rarely link up, making loop rides scarce. And in the spectacular—and highly popular—High Peaks region near Lake Placid, off-road cycling is discouraged because of the large numbers of hikers who visit the area and resistance from the powerful Adirondack Mountain Club.

But all is not lost in the Adirondacks. Moose River Recreation Area, on the western edge of the park, is one destination open to mountain bikers. What it lacks in stunning vistas and loop rides, it makes up for with the many miles of trails to explore in a rugged wilderness setting.

Another good mountain biking area in Adirondack Park is Streeter Lake. The trails lead to a beautiful, moss-covered meadow near two lakes. An overnight shelter overlooking the lake has been described as one of the most beautiful spots in the Adirondacks.

Steve Johnson is a Syracuse-based cyclist who lent his knowledge and expertise of the area in putting together several of these rides. Steve works out of his home teaching bicycle maintenance and repairing bikes. He's also active with the Onandoga Cycling Club, which promotes both road and mountain biking. If you're in Syracuse and have any questions about cycling in the area, give him a call at Meltzer's Bicycle Store, (315) 446-6816.

RIDE 44 *ERIE CANAL STATE PARK BICYCLE PATH*

This historic trail along the Erie Canal slowly curves eastward from Syracuse through farmland, wetlands, woods, and meadows which are home to white-tailed deer, woodchucks, and painted turtles. On this ride don't forget to bring binoculars and a bird book, for many types of woodpeckers, hawks, osprey, and a large number of great blue heron (with a wingspan over 5 feet) feed along the canal. Red maple, elm, and black willow trees predominate along the trail. The fall foliage peaks in early to mid-October.

The 38.5-mile (one-way) trail follows the old towpath used when mules pulled barges on the Erie Canal. Most of the towpath is flat, hard-packed dirt and stone that is 5- to 8-feet wide and maintained for bicycling and hiking. No technical riding skills are required. Road bikes with touring tires should have no problems on the first 15 miles. The towpath stops and roads parallel to the canal must be ridden after Durhamville for about 2 miles (NY 46), and from Lock Road to the New York State Barge Canal (NY 46).

In the first 2 miles the trail traverses huge stone aqueducts built to carry the canal over rivers and streams. Cedar Bay Picnic Area (.8 miles from the start) has picnic and playground facilities, bathrooms and water, as well as a Canal Center with historic information and displays (open on summer weekends). The large footbridge at Cedar Bay is a replica of the bridges that carried foot traffic and horses across the canal in the nineteenth century. Further along the trail are Green Lakes State Park, Poolsbrook Picnic Area (with the ruins of an 1800s brick factory), dry docks (used to maintain and repair canal boats) under restoration, the Canastota Canal Museum and, at the end of the trail, the Erie Canal Village, where you can catch a ride on a canal boat pulled by a mule!

General location: The trail begins at Butternut Drive in Dewitt, about 1 mile from the Dewitt exit of Interstate 481, and continues along the old Erie Canal to the Erie Canal Village near Rome, New York.

Elevation change: Negligible.

Season: The trail is rideable from spring to mid-fall. Bugs are a nuisance in June and in the evenings from July through September. Wear goggles or glasses, especially near dusk. Bugs in the daytime are usually no problem after June.

Services: Water, food, and beverages are available during the summer months

ERIE CANAL STATE PARK BICYCLE PATH

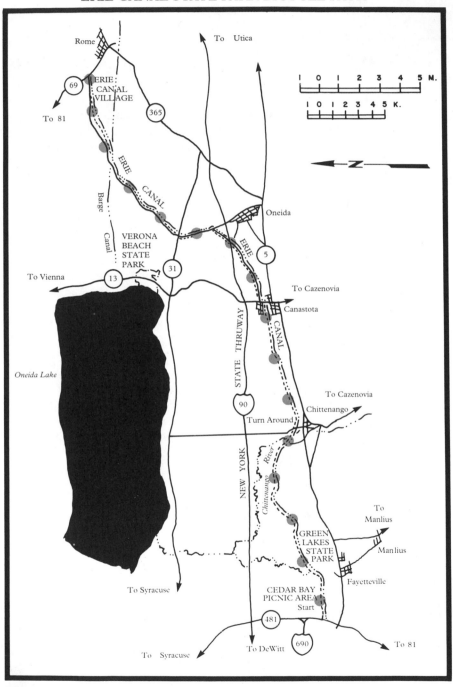

Rome
ERIE CANAL VILLAGE
69
To 81
To Utica
365
ERIE CANAL
Barge Canal
VERONA BEACH STATE PARK
To Vienna
13
31
Oneida
5
ERIE
To Cazenovia
Canastota
CANAL
STATE THRUWAY
Oneida Lake
90
Turn Around
NEW YORK
To Cazenovia
Chittenango
Chittenango River
To Manlius
GREEN LAKES STATE PARK
Manlius
Fayetteville
To Syracuse
CEDAR BAY PICNIC AREA
Start
481
To Syracuse
To DeWitt
690
To 81

1 0 1 2 3 4 5 M.
1 0 1 2 3 4 5 K.

N

at Green Lakes State Park and the towns of Dewitt, Chittenango, Canastota, and Durhamville. Water is also available at Cedar Bay picnic area and Pools Brook Picnic Area. Overnight camping and swimming are available at Green Lakes State Park and nearby Verona Beach State Park. Bicycle service is available at Nipponose Adventure Outfitters in Dewitt.

Hazards: Watch for high-speed motor traffic when crossing the many roads that intersect with the trail.

Rescue index: The canal is popular and well-traveled; also, traffic can be waved down at intersections.

Land status: State park.

Maps: Maps of the Erie Canal Bicycling Path are sometimes available on the post at the bridge in Cedar Bay Park. Maps of Green Lakes State Park are available at the park office. The USGS quad maps are Syracuse East, Manlius, Canastota, Oneida, Sylvan Beach, and Verona.

Finding the trail: The trail begins at Butternut Drive in Dewitt, New York. From NY 5 (Erie Boulevard) in Dewitt, take Kinne Road east. Continue past a cemetery on the left and over I-481. Turn left immediately after the bridge onto Butternut Drive. The parking area is at the bottom of the hill on the right. The ride can also start at the parking area at Cedar Bay Park (.8 miles from Dewitt). Take Kinne Road east from NY 5 in Dewitt and continue to the end. Turn left at the "T" intersection and follow the road around a sharp, uphill curve to the right. Cedar Bay Picnic Area is on the left at the top of the hill.

Sources of additional information:

New York State Parks
Recreation and Historic Preservation
Empire State Plaza, Agency Building 1
Albany, New York 12238
(518) 474-1456

Onondaga Cycling Club
P.O. Box 6307
Teall Station
Syracuse, New York 13217

Meltzer's Bicycle Store
2714 Erie Blvd. East
Syracuse, New York 13224
(315) 446-6816

RIDE 45 *HIGHLAND FOREST*

About 30 miles south of Syracuse is a wonderful destination for mountain bikers: Highland Forest, a 2,759-acre county park and reforestation area atop a small, wooded mountain. This 10-mile loop ride, a good introduction to the park, passes through mixed-hardwood forest and conifers (at the southern end of the park) on wide, grassy cross-country ski trails. The hardwood forests are predominantly maple, ash, and beech, while conifers are mostly Norway spruce and red and white pines. In the summer and fall the trails are shaded by the trees, providing cool cycling in hot weather.

While on the loop, stop and see an operating sawmill that makes picnic tables and other park equipment. On Road 16, about 8 miles into the ride, is Highland Tree—largest in the park. But the best part of Highland Park is the quiet, and the sense of isolation imparted by the forest on top of the small mountain.

The well-maintained fire roads and ski trails on this loop make for fairly easy riding. While some of the climbs are long, few are steep; bike handling skill requirements are minimal. Since the clay soil holds water long after rain, expect to get at least a little wet. And keep an eye peeled for deadfalls on Road 30, midway through the ride.

General location: Highland Forest is 30 miles south of Syracuse, New York.

Elevation change: The ride begins at the park office at about 1,700' of elevation and climbs to around 1,800' on the paved road at the sawmill. In the woods the trail drops about 200', passes a shelter on the left, and is followed by a short, steep climb. Over the next couple of miles the elevation slowly drops to about 1,500' at the end of Road 32. Along Road 30 the elevation is slowly regained. On Road 20 the elevation drops, then regains about 200'. The rest of the ride is fairly level, with a few long descents and easy climbs back up. The total elevation gain is about 1,000'.

Season: The trails are open to mountain bikes from May 1 through November 1. This area gets a lot of snow and Highland Forest is a popular cross-country skiing spot. Because of the high clay content of the soil, the trails tend to stay soggy long after it rains.

Services: All services are available in Syracuse. Water and rest rooms are located near the park office.

Hazards: Carry a forest map, available at the park office. Not all the trails and roads in the forest are marked, and a wrong turn could lead you out of the park.

Rescue index: The main park road, which carries traffic, runs north and south through the park.

HIGHLAND FOREST

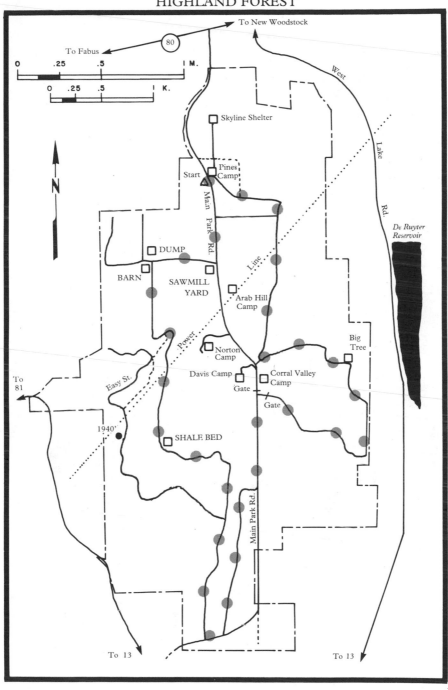

Wide, cross-country ski trails in Highland Forest offer mountain bikers non-technical —and well-shaded—routes. *Photo by author*

Land status: Onondaga County park.

Maps: A trail map is available at park headquarters. The USGS 7.5 minute topo is De Ruyter.

Finding the trail: From Syracuse drive south 18 miles on I-81 to the Tully exit. Drive east on NY 80 for 12 miles. The park is on the right. Park in the lot near the main office.

Sources of additional information:

Highland Forest
Box 31
Fabius, New York 13063
(315) 683-5550

Onondaga Cycling Club
P.O. Box 6307
Teall Station
Syracuse, New York 13217

Meltzer's Bicycle Store
2714 Erie Blvd. East
Syracuse, New York 13224
(315) 446-6816

RIDE 46 *MOOSE RIVER RECREATION AREA*

The greatest attraction to Moose River is the intense wilderness feel that comes from riding inside a 50,000-acre recreation area deep inside Adirondack Park. And the second greatest attraction? It's the network of trails that leads to the many ponds and streams deep in the forest. Adding to the sense of deep-woods isolation are tens of thousands of acres of other public lands surrounding Moose River. Many foot trails lead into the ridges and mountains in the West Canada Lakes Wilderness Area (no mountain bikes permitted).

Camping and mountain biking go together very well here. Moose River is scattered with campsites (all primitive, most with privies); many are perched on scenic spots over streams. There is also a swimming beach at the Limekiln Lake campground, near the west entrance to the area.

The Moose River Plains, which are the heart of the region, are surrounded by mixed-hardwood and pine forests interspersed with many lakes and ponds. While dramatic views aren't the rule, the area where the main road crosses the Moose River has a wide open look with low ridges visible in the distance. A ride to one of the ponds results in a dramatic change in scenery when a

MOOSE RIVER RECREATION AREA

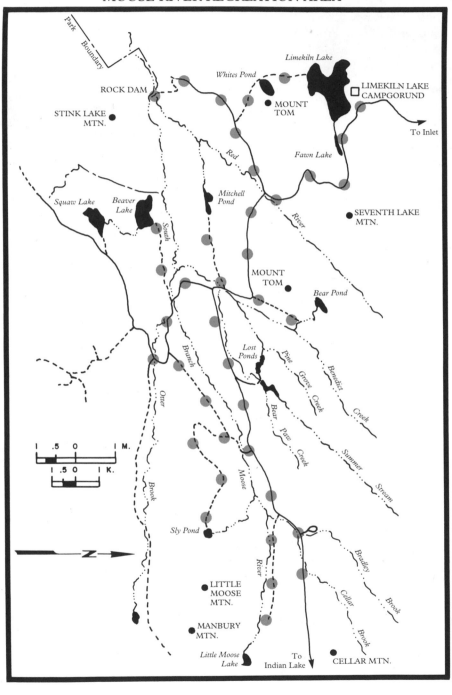

Photo by author

large pond comes into view. These trails follow a maze of abandoned logging roads through the recreation area. More than 27 miles of easy-to-ride access trails lead to ponds and streams scattered throughout the rolling terrain, providing a wide variety of out-and-back rides. These trails connect to a 41.3-mile main road system. The double-track trails (closed to motor vehicles) are usually grassy and flat, are often wet, and are frequently narrow, overgrown, and crossed by deadfalls. The main road system is hard-packed dirt, passable in two-wheel-drive vehicles, and well maintained.

General location: About 5 miles from Inlet, Hamilton County, New York, in western Adirondack Park.

Elevation change: The elevation of the area is around 2,000′. Frequently, the only descent on a trail occurs on the approach to a pond or stream. On most of the trails the maximum elevation gain or loss is only a few hundred feet. The area is surrounded by higher ridges and mountains that are in wilderness areas (off-limits to mountain bikes).

Season: Moose River Recreation Area is open from Memorial Day through the end of deer hunting season in the late fall. Avoid the area in blackfly season, which starts around Memorial Day and lasts through the Fourth of July.

Services: The closest town is Inlet, which has groceries and lodging. There is a spring on the main road 1.3 miles from where it crosses the Moose River.

Hazards: Avoid riding in deer hunting season, in the late fall. When camping, keep food and garbage secure against black bears.

Rescue index: The primary roads carry light traffic. There is a ranger residence at the Limekiln Lake entrance.

Land status: State park.

Maps: A trail map is available at the park office at the Limekiln Lake entrance. The USGS 7.5 minute topo maps are Old Forge and West Canada Lakes.

Finding the trail: From Inlet, New York, on NY 28, turn onto Limekiln Road and drive about 3 miles to the entrance of the recreation area. There is another entrance at the east end on Cedar River Road, which intersects NY 28/30 near Indian Lake. This entrance may be closed during or after inclement weather. Register at either gate. From either the Limekiln Lake or Cedar River entrance, drive about 5 miles into the area and park at a campsite.

Sources of additional information:

Forest Ranger
Limekiln Lake
Inlet, New York
(315) 357-4403

Meltzer's Bicycle Store
2714 Erie Blvd. East
Syracuse, New York 13224
(315) 446-6816

Notes on the trail: The Moose River Recreation Area is open for public use from Memorial Day through the end of deer hunting season. To get the most out of this scenic area, plan a leisurely camping trip and explore by mountain bike the many trails in the area.

RIDE 47   *STAR LAKE/STREETER LAKE TRAIL*

Two beautiful lakes, a tenth of a mile apart, are the destination of this Adirondack Park ride. The lakes are quite different. Streeter Lake is darkly colored, which is typical of Adirondack lakes. But Crystal Lake, one-fifth the size of its neighbor, is clear with a white sandy bottom. A large, moss-covered field near the lakes was once used to grow potatoes for potato chips—an incongruous yet beautiful sight. The Streeter Lake Lean-to is a great place to camp and is widely considered one of the most scenic spots in the Adirondacks.

This 13-mile loop ride passes through rolling terrain with low hills, ex-

STAR LAKE/STREETER LAKE TRAIL

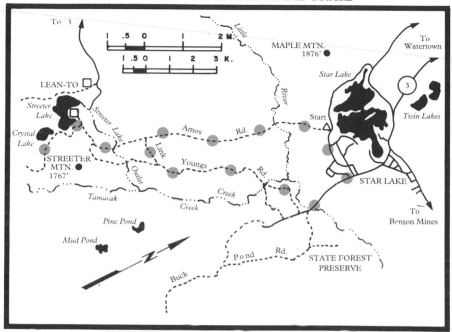

posed outcrops of crystalline rocks, bogs, swamps, and streams. The forests consist of second-growth hardwoods that include sugar maple, black cherry, and beech. The area supports a large deer population, black bear, moose, Eastern coyote, fisher, beaver, porcupine, raccoon, and rabbits. The trail is a mixture of single-track and fire roads which roll through deep forests.

While there isn't much climbing on this ride, marshy and wet conditions require some strength and good bike handling ability. The trail and road conditions vary from marshy to sandy, with some hardpack on dirt roads and grassy areas in meadows. Except for minor stream crossings this is a non-technical ride in a beautiful setting.

General location: The ride is in western Adirondack Park and starts in Star Lake, located on NY 3 between Watertown and Tupper Lake, New York.

Elevation change: Star Lake, at the start of the loop, is at an elevation of about 1,450'. Streeter Lake has an elevation of 1,487'.

Season: The trail is usually rideable from late spring through early fall. Avoid the area from Memorial Day through the Fourth of July, when blackflies take over the Adirondacks. The mountains can get cold at night in the summer, so be prepared if an overnight trip is planned. Avoid riding in deer hunting season, which usually starts in October.

Services: There is a grocery store and gas station in Star Lake and a motel in Fine, New York (6 miles west on NY 3). A restaurant, the Cranberry Lake Inn, is 10 miles east on NY 3.

Hazards: The biggest hazard is the remoteness of the area. Carry a map and compass.

Rescue index: Traffic can be waved down on Youngs Road and Lake Road.

Land status: State park.

Maps: The Adirondack Mountain Club Northern Region Map is an excellent trail map of the area. The USGS 7.5 minute topo maps are Oswegatchie and Oswegatchie S.E.

Finding the trail: From NY 3 in Star Lake turn south onto Griffin Road to Lake Road. Turn right and park at the trailhead on the left.

Sources of additional information:

> Adirondack Mountain Club
> 174 Glen Street
> Glens Falls, New York 12801
> (518) 793-7737

> Meltzer's Bicycle Store
> 2714 Erie Blvd. East
> Syracuse, New York 13224
> (315) 446-6816

Notes on the trail: The trail starts as a single-track that is maintained for summer use and cross-country skiing in the winter. Follow the yellow markers as the trail winds south and crosses a couple of streams by footbridge.

The lakes can be used as a base for exploring more trails that lead out of the area. To complete the loop return on the trail from Star Lake, then bear right on the Youngs Road section of the trail. After 5 miles the trail ends at Youngs Road. Turn left and then take the second left, which leads to Lake Road and the start of the loop.

Ithaca

The town of Ithaca, located at the southern tip of 40-mile-long Cayuga Lake in the Finger Lakes region of central New York, is best known as home to Cornell University and Ithaca College. And true to form for a college town, Ithaca has a large cycling community. During warm weather, road riders and racers are a common sight as they train in the long glacial valleys that surround the town.

Many of these dedicated Ithaca cyclists switch to mountain bikes in the fall, when the racing season is over and the black fly population in the woods is KO'd by frost. They're on to a good thing. Ithaca is surrounded by state forests featuring spectacular gorges, numerous waterfalls, and many miles of trails and dirt roads. Moreover, the fall foliage in the Finger Lakes is legendary. The combination of nearby state forests, fall weather, and great trails makes for excellent mountain biking.

But a word of caution. These state forests are honeycombed with technical single-track trails and dirt roads, and appeal to strong riders with good bike handling skills. Less-experienced riders may wish to avoid the single-track and stick to the dirt roads.

Another caveat. Virtually no trail signs are posted to help visitors find their way around these state forests. Plan accordingly by bringing a topo map and compass, and allowing plenty of time. Since the forests are small and laced with unsigned roads and single-track trails that defy step-by-step directions, the trail descriptions that follow depict the area as a whole, without specific routes.

Ithaca-area riders Ed Zieba and Henry Schomacker recommended Hammond Hill, Yellow Barn, and Shindagin Hollow State Forests as the best mountain biking areas close to town. They ought to know. Ed races both road and mountain bikes and lives at the edge of Hammond Hill State Forest. (With a backyard like that, no wonder he wins races.) Henry, who died in 1990, was a devoted cyclist and the reigning champion technical single-track descender among the Ithaca elite. His spirit rages on in the woods and hollows around Ithaca.

RIDE 48 · *HAMMOND HILL STATE FOREST*

Spectacular descents on the main seasonal roads and serpentine single-track trails make Hammond Hill the most popular mountain bike destination around Ithaca. An example: "Hammond Roubaix" is a stretch of single-track that's notorious with local hammerheads and named after the infamous Paris-Roubaix bicycling classic. For experts only, the trail weaves its way through a rough, stony, muddy creek bed that is best ridden from north to south. Other trails wind through thick pine stands planted in uniform rows. Some descents are several miles long (notably the trail down to Six Mile Creek and Six Hundred Road). Loop rides of 5, 10, 15 or more miles are possible here.

Hammond Hill, although rated difficult by local mountain bikers, is still within the capabilities of strong recreational bikers. The forest contains many short climbs (usually less than 1 mile) that are often steep for short stretches. From the top of Hammond Hill, the elevation gain and loss moderates. Good bike handling skills are necessary to negotiate narrow trails with sharp drop-offs on the shoulders. The constantly changing terrain—leaf-covered hard-pack, boggy sections with deep ruts, dry creek beds with pizza-sized shale chips and baseball-sized rocks—makes riding in this area a real challenge.

Hammond Hill Road is an unpaved seasonal road, hardpack at the start but with changing conditions on the climb that vary with the seasons. The trails off the main seasonal roads generally are narrow double-track used by snowmobiles or single-track hiking trails used by all-terrain vehicles. All the trails tend to be wet except after dry spells. Most of the roads and trails in this area cut through verdant forest, a mixture of deciduous and coniferous species. A variety of pine, much of it planted in the 1930s by the Civilian Conservation Corps, stands interspersed with birch, beech, cherry, oak, maple, and many other hardwood species.

Fall is the prettiest time of year in the forest, but spring can also be delightful, if a bit wet. Peak time for fall riding is mid- to late October, when the foliage is spectacular. The area is bisected with gorges and creeks containing small waterfalls and swimming holes. Some open spots along ridge tops offer great views of the surrounding hills, which are dotted with farms and fields. Hammond Hill is also home to a wide variety of wildlife. Look for white-tailed deer, hawks, red-winged blackbirds, chickadees, grosbeaks, cardinals, woodpeckers, sparrows, and finches. Occasionally, great blue herons and barn and horned owls are spotted. Also common are gray and red squirrels, and the ubiquitous chipmunk.

General location: The forest is located between the towns of Caroline and Dryden, 8 miles east of Ithaca, New York.

HAMMOND HILL STATE FOREST

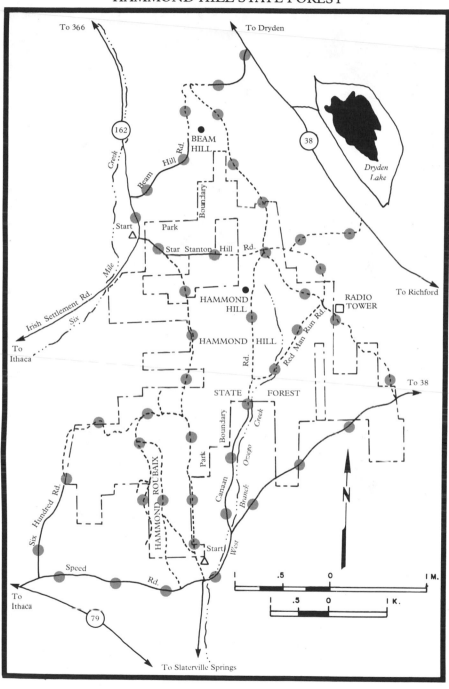

Elevation change: The north end of Hammond Hill Road begins with an elevation of 1,500' and climbs to Hammond Hill, elevation 2,014', the highest point in the forest. The starting point at the south end of the forest is at an elevation of 1,300'. The average gain in vertical feet from the valley to the ridges is between 500' and 800'. Many trails are roller coasters with negligible elevation gain.

Season: The best riding is in the fall, when conditions are driest and most of the bugs are gone. Deerfly and blackfly season lasts from July into September; insect repellent is a must. Spring is the wettest season. Winter is great for "Idita-biking" because the snow-covered trails are packed down by snowmobiles. Avoid riding in deer hunting season, which starts in mid-November.

Services: All services are available in Ithaca. A grocery store is located on the corner of Midline Road and NY 79. A natural spring is located in front of the courthouse next to the store.

Hazards: Watch for four-wheel-drive and logging vehicles on the seasonal roads. The area is popular with moto-cross motorcycles. The forest is littered with deadfall, hanging branches, and fallen limbs. Don't forget bug repellent during blackfly season, from July into September.

Rescue index: Most trails are within walking distance of paved roads where passing motorists can be flagged down. There are also a few isolated residences in the forest.

Land status: State forest.

Maps: The USGS 7.5 minute topo is Ithaca East.

Finding the trail: There are 2 places to start rides in Hammond Hill State Forest. The northern beginning point is reached by driving east from Ithaca on NY 79 to Slaterville Springs; turn left onto Midline Road, which changes name to Irish Settlement Road. Hammond Hill Road is on the right, 4.4 miles from NY 79. Pull off and park near the intersection.

To reach the southern starting point continue through Slaterville Springs on NY 79 for .5 miles to Harford Road and turn left. Go straight for 2 miles to the intersection of Hammond Hill Road and Flatiron Road, and turn left onto Hammond Hill Road. Park at the foot of the hill.

Sources of additional information:

The Bike Rack Bicycle Shop
Collegetown
Ithaca, New York 14850
(607) 272-1010

Ed Zieba
522 Harford Road
Brooktondale, New York 14817
(607) 539-7672

Notes on the trail: As with other state forest lands around Ithaca, trails and roads are not marked in Hammond Hills State Forest. The best approach to riding the area is to bring the Ithaca East topo map, a compass, and a spirit of adventure. Since even local mountain bikers who know the area occasionally get disoriented (lost, they say, is too strong a word), you can avoid frustration by allowing plenty of time and carrying extra food, water, and tools.

RIDE 49   *YELLOW BARN STATE FOREST*

Local hammerheads all agree: Come to Yellow Barn for the screaming descents. But that's not all. Views of the surrounding hills from clearings are spectacular on the many loop rides ranging from 5 to 10 miles in length that you can do here. (For longer rides it's easy to link up with nearby Hammond Hill State Forest via a short ride on paved road.) Yellow Barn's mix of forest includes deciduous and coniferous trees typical to the Finger Lakes area. Many small creeks flow through the forest into small gorges and then to the major creeks that feed the Finger Lakes. These gorges often have waterfalls and small circular swimming holes.

Short, steep climbs are the trademark of mountain biking in Yellow Barn State Forest. The area is often wet and muddy, increasing the power output needed on climbs. The short, rapid descents off the top of the ridge require good bike handling skills. Yellow Barn Road is an unpaved seasonal road that's rocky in sections. Many of the trails in the forest are rutted from logging activity. Furthermore, Yellow Barn is infamous for its lake-sized puddles and oozy mud. Like all other forests in the Ithaca area, the terrain changes constantly. Trails along the pipeline and power line are single-tracks used by moto-cross motorcycles and are usually hardpack.

General location: About 8 miles east of Ithaca, New York.

Elevation change: The southern end of Yellow Barn Road is at an elevation of 1,460′. The highest point in the forest is 1,888′. The northern end (at NY 13) is 1,140′. The average elevation gain is between 400′ and 700′ on any particular climb.

Season: The best riding starts in the early fall and continues through mid-November. Spring tends to be wet, and summer riding can be plagued by heat, humidity, and bugs. The fall foliage is excellent. Lake-effect snow flurries from the north occur frequently, so carry extra clothes when riding in the fall.

Services: All services are available in Ithaca, 8 miles from the forest. A small grocery store is located at Midline Road and NY 79; the courthouse next to it has a spring.

YELLOW BARN STATE FOREST

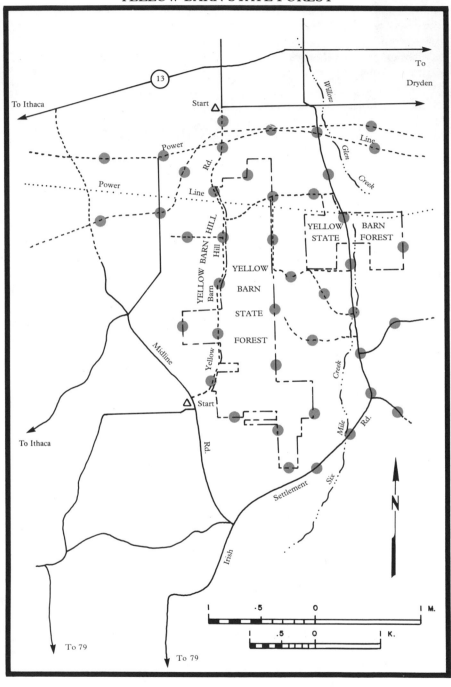

Hazards: Avoid the towers when riding on the power lines. Also, ruts made by logging trucks are dangerous on the descents. Bring bug repellent during blackfly season, from July into September.

Rescue index: The area is within walking distance of paved roads where cars can be waved down. There are many private residences along the paved roads at the southern end of the forest.

Land status: State forest.

Maps: The USGS 7.5 minute topo is Ithaca East.

Finding the trail: There are 2 starting points for rides in Yellow Barn. To reach the southern starting point take NY 79 east from Ithaca to Slaterville Springs and turn left onto Midline Road. Go straight 2 miles to the intersection with Irish Settlement Road (at a dip in the valley). Turn left, following Midline Road for another 2 miles to Yellow Barn Road, at the sign for the Dusenberry Sportsmen's Club. Turn right and park anywhere along the shoulder at the foot of the hill.

To reach the northern starting point take NY 13 east from Ithaca toward Dryden. Turn right on Yellow Barn Road, drive to the unpaved section, and park at the plow turnaround.

Sources of additional information:

The Bike Rack Bicycle Shop
Collegetown
Ithaca, New York 14850
(607) 272-1010

Ed Zieba
522 Harford Road
Brooktondale, New York 14817
(607) 539-7672

Notes on the trail: This area shares a trait with other New York state forests—no trail signs are posted. Explore the area by riding loops that radiate from the central unpaved road. The forest is also crisscrossed by cleared power lines and pipelines that are rideable. Carry a topo map and allow plenty of time for the ride.

RIDE 50 *SHINDAGIN HOLLOW STATE FOREST*

Ithaca mountain bikers consider Shindagin Hollow a double-whammy: the riding is both technical *and* steep. This beautiful forest is known for its twisting descents punctuated by roots lying across the trails. The single-track trails

SHINDAGIN HOLLOW STATE FOREST

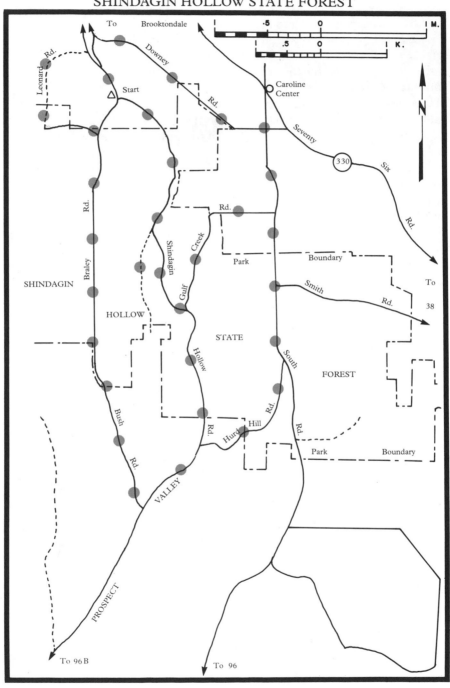

are fast and narrow, and they pass close to trees. Ruts created by moto-cross motorcycle activity add to the difficulty of the trails. In general the climbs are gradual and short, but there are lung-searing exceptions.

The forest is covered with mixed deciduous and coniferous trees, and small gorges and glens bisect the hillsides. Many creeks and waterfalls add to the beauty, while Prospect Valley offers bucolic views of small dairy farms nestled in a gorge. Shindagin Hollow Road and Braley Hill Road are unpaved, hard-packed dirt roads suitable for two-wheel-drive vehicles. But most of the riding in Shindagin is on narrow single-track, which can be wet and covered with standing water. The trails are fast when dry. All roads above the valleys tend to be unpaved.

Since the forest is a maze of single-track trails connected by seasonal roads, it accommodates all riding styles. Loop rides of 5, 10, and 15 miles or longer are possible. Huge pine stands in the forest are great places to take a break and feature a pristine, cathedral-like ambience.

General location: About 10 miles southeast of Ithaca, near the town of Caroline in Tompkins County, New York.

Elevation change: Shindagin Hollow Road and Braley Hill Road start at an elevation around 1,400'. Bald Hill, the tallest peak in the area, is around 1,850'. The average elevation at the tops of the trails is about 1,600'. Shindagin Hollow bottoms out near 1,100'.

Season: The best time to ride this area is from mid- to late October through mid-November. The fall foliage is spectacular in the Shindagin Hollow Valley. Spring can be wet. Heat, humidity, and bugs are strong arguments against summer riding. After the first frost conditions improve dramatically. Avoid riding in deer hunting season, in late November.

Services: All services are available in Ithaca, a 20-minute drive. There is a small grocery store in Brooktondale on Central Chapel/Brooktondale Road. There are no sources of potable water in the forest.

Hazards: Deep ruts made by moto-cross motorcycles can grab front wheels, resulting in a face-plant. Watch for four-wheel-drive trucks and logging vehicles. Some hills have washouts cut into trails to drain runoff, which can pitch unwary riders over the handlebars. Blackfly season runs from July into September, so bring repellent.

Rescue index: Most trails are within walking distance of paved roads, where cars can be waved down. The main roads in the forest carry light traffic.

Land status: State forest.

Maps: The USGS 7.5 minute topo is Ithaca East.

Finding the trail: From Ithaca, drive east on NY 79 for 4 miles to the Brooktondale exit. Turn right and go straight for about 5 miles, where Brooktondale Road becomes Central Chapel Road. Continue straight and bear right onto Braley Hill Road at the fork (Shindagin Hollow Road is to the left). Park at the foot of the hill.

Sources of additional information:

The Bike Rack Bicycle Shop
Collegetown
Ithaca, New York 14850
(607) 272-1010

Ed Zieba
522 Harford Road
Brooktondale, New York 14817
(607) 539-7672

Notes on the trail: Shindagin Hollow State Forest shares many characteristics of the other forests in the Ithaca area—great single-track, beautiful views, tough climbs, and no trail signs.

The key to riding the single-track is to find the trails that branch off the main roads. A topo map, a compass, and a philosophical attitude about getting lost are indispensable. Just allow plenty of time.

Corning

Corning, a small town famous for its glassworks, is located in southeastern Steuben County, just above the Pennsylvania border in central New York state. Geographically, this part of the state rests on a section of the Appalachian Plateau that is sharply eroded by river valleys. The result is that the landscape is dominated by large hills that rise as much as 1,200 feet above the narrow valley floors.

Here's a brief outline of the topography: The principal river valleys in the region are formed by four rivers—the Tioga, the Canisteo, and the Cohocton, all of which join to create the fourth river—the Chemung, near Corning. The Chemung then flows eastward through the center of Corning to meet the Susquehanna River, which continues through Pennsylvania and Maryland to spill into Chesapeake Bay. The best mountain bike trails in the Corning area are on the hills over these river valleys.

In addition to being famous for its glass industry, Corning serves as the Southern Gateway of the popular Finger Lakes vacation area; tourism is second only to industry in the region's economy. The town has some 15 hotels and motels, and several campgrounds to accommodate visitors, making it a good base of operations for exploring the region.

The mountain biking around Corning is mostly on wide dirt roads that lead up to the tall hills between the river valleys. Vistas of forests and orderly farmlands stretch into the distance from the summits. In fall the foliage of the wide variety of trees is brilliant.

Jeff Loik is the founder of the Crystal City Mountain Bike Club in Corning. He has been an avid mountain biker for over four years, and has pioneered many rides in the Corning area. The following rides are some of his favorites.

RIDE 51 HIGMAN HILL / BLENCOWE ROAD TRAIL

The Southern Tier of New York state, with its Finger Lakes region and large state forests, is a naturalist's paradise. This 9-mile out-and-back ride is a good example. Thanks to the reforestation efforts of the Civil Conservation Corps in the 1930s, this area contains a myriad of tree species. From the overlook at the top of the first climb is a view north down the NY 414 valley toward Beaver Dams, New York. The railroad through this valley in the 1800s and early 1900s was the primary route into northern New York state. Looking left and right are views of General Sullivan's Trail, which was carved during

HIGMAN HILL/BLENCOWE ROAD TRAIL

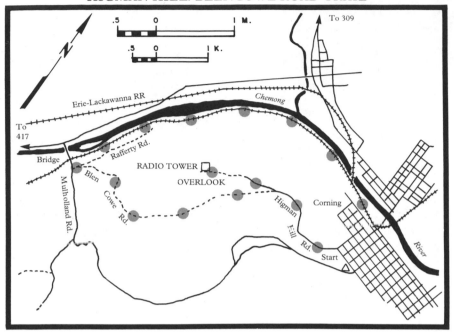

the Indian wars of the 1700s and 1800s. (General Sullivan was given charge of clearing hostile Indians from the area.) Stop at the radio tower for the best view of the Chemung River Valley to the east and the Post Creek Valley to the north. Also, at the top of the climb, look for an informal "playground" for off-road vehicles and mountain bikes on the right.

This is an easy ride, requiring no technical skills. Most of it is on four-wheel-drive roads and dirt roads maintained by New York State Electric and Gas. Good aerobic fitness is required for the climb. All the roads on this ride are wide, hard-packed dirt. Following the linkup with the Erie-Lackawanna railroad track (at the bottom of Blencowe Road), large stones used to maintain the tracks make for a bumpy ride. Keep an eye open for wildlife on this ride, particularly the many types of hare and white-tailed deer.

More historical notes: The early settlers made great use of the fertile Chemung Valley for the growing of grains, corn, and tobacco. The periodic flooding of the Chemung River provided rich, workable soil and an ample supply of water for irrigation. The level top of Higman Hill was mostly logged clear of trees and was planted with grain for livestock and human consumption. For the most part the hill has now been abandoned due to its inaccessibility. The last reference to any settlement is seen in the remains of the burned-out farmhouse at the start of the Blencowe Road descent.

General location: Higman Hill, outside Corning, New York.

Elevation change: The first mile of the ride climbs about 650', followed by about 4 miles of level riding. The last mile or so is a steep descent. The elevation is about 1,100' at the start and rises to 1,736' for a total elevation gain of 636'.

Season: This ride is good year-round, except for early spring (which is usually muddy) and late fall (during hunting season). Mid-summer may be hot and humid, so remember to carry plenty of water. In late September and early October the famous western New York fall foliage sets the rolling hills ablaze with a multitude of colors.

Services: All services are available in Corning.

Hazards: Keep alert for four-wheel-drive traffic when riding. Watch out for off-camber turns on the Blencowe Road descent, which are further complicated by 3 half-covered culverts. At high speeds these can throw your bike off-line.

Rescue index: There is a house with a phone on the left at the bottom of Blencowe Road.

Land status: Seasonal-use roads maintained by New York State Electric and Gas Company.

Maps: The USGS 7.5 minute topo is Corning.

Finding the trail: The dirt road starts at the corner of Sixth Street and Washington Street in Corning. Park on either side of the road.

Sources of additional information:

Corning Bike Works
96 E. Market Street
Corning, New York 14830
(607) 962-7831

RIDE 52 *SUGAR HILL TRAIL*

Great views of forests, hills, valleys, lakes, and fertile farmland are the highlight of this long but scenic ride. Reforestation efforts provided the Sugar Hill area with a variety of trees, including the apple trees harvested for raw fruit and cider making. (The sugar from the apples is what gives the area its name.) The 360-degree view from the top of Sugar Hill includes Lamoka Lake and Wanet Lake, which are joined by a canal. No technical bike handling ability is required on this 20-mile loop, since it follows seasonal-use and abandoned dirt roads. However, a wide variety of road surfaces and large elevation gains make this ride challenging. The first 2.5 miles are fairly steep and rough. Look for a large stand of pine trees on the left during the return leg of the loop.

SUGAR HILL TRAIL

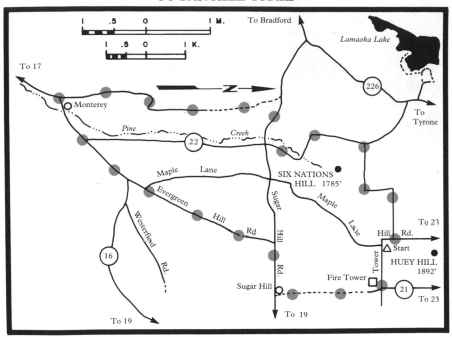

They were hand-planted to study methods of halting soil erosion in the area.

The first mile or so is on a hard-packed dirt road followed by 2.5 miles of steep climbing on an unmaintained dirt road that can be rough and rutted, especially after wet weather. This is followed by 3 miles of fairly straight and level single-track. The return trip is partially on a paved road, and includes a climb on the unpaved Evergreen Hill Road.

General location: Twelve miles north of Corning, New York.

Elevation change: The ride begins at the summit of Sugar Hill, elevation 2,080′, and descends to around 1,212′ halfway through the ride. The elevation is slowly recovered at the finish for a total gain of 878′.

Season: The best time to ride this loop is from mid-summer through late fall. Spring can be muddy and fall has spectacular foliage. For the hearty rider, mid-winter offers hard fast trails and views of the frosted and snow-covered hillsides.

Services: All services are available in Corning. Overnight camping is permitted in the fire tower area, and there are 4 lean-tos available.

Hazards: Watch for traffic on County Road 16.

Rescue index: The fire tower is usually manned in the summer. Also, traffic can be waved down on CR 16. The closest town is Monterey.

Land status: New York State Recreation Area.

Maps: Maps of Schuyler County are available at the Schuyler County Highway Department in Watkins Glen.

Finding the trail: Sugar Hill is located west of Watkins Glen and north of Corning. From Corning take NY 414 north; turn left onto CR 19 at North Beaver Dams. From Watkins Glen take CR 16 past the speedway to CR 21, which leads to Sugar Hill Road. Park near the tower.

Sources of additional information:

Corning Bike Works
96 E. Market Street
Corning, New York 14839
(607) 962-7831

RIDE 53 POST CREEK TRAIL

This is a flat, easy trail that is perfect for a quick ride in the morning or on a late summer afternoon. The railroad switching yard, the Ferenbaugh Campground, and the turnaround point at the end of the trail are interesting sights. And for anglers there is excellent fishing in Post Creek.

The approach to this 5-mile (one-way), out-and-back trail passes through Penn Central Railroad switching yard, which is used to transport large supplies of salt from underground mines near Seneca Lake. Paralleling the trail is Post Creek, a popular stocked brown trout stream (that produced a record 4-pound, 21.5-inch trout caught by Jeff Loik in 1989). The trail is lined by a wide variety of trees and passes through farmland. The ride is along a dirt road used by utility trucks. The road is frequently muddy and there are a few creek runoff crossings.

General location: Corning, New York.

Elevation change: Negligible.

Season: Summer is the best time of year to ride this trail. Other seasons tend to be wet and muddy.

Services: All services are available in Corning. Camp at the Ferenbaugh Campground, which is along the route.

Hazards: Watch for a few runoff crossings (used to prevent erosion) on the trail. Keep alert for trains.

Rescue index: Help is available at Ferenbaugh Campground or in Corning.

Land status: Private—New York State Gas and Electric Company and Penn Central Railroad.

Maps: The USGS 7.5 minute topo is Corning; the Steuben County Highway map also shows this route.

POST CREEK TRAIL

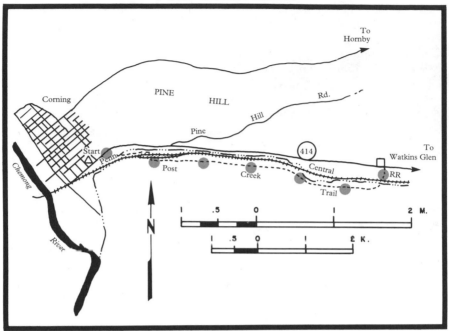

Finding the trail: The ride starts near the north side of Corning. Park in the Hotel Central parking lot, near Spruce Street (past the railroad bridge on Baker Street).

Sources of additional information:

> Corning Bike Works
> 96 E. Market Street
> Corning, New York 14839
> (607) 962-7831

Notes on the trail: Ride out Baker Street in Corning, through the railroad overpass to the Hotel Central Bar and Grill (which, by the way, serves very good food). Turn right into the lot and continue past the baseball field behind the bar. Follow the road to the left that passes over a wood plank bridge. Parallel the railroad tracks for about .5 miles to the first railroad track crossing; turn left. Go about 30 yards to a small turnoff on the right (past a small railroad pump building). Ride up a short hill to the main trail on the left.

Follow the Post Creek Trail about 3 miles, where it reconnects with the railroad tracks. Follow the tracks to the campground. Here, either turn around or link up with NY 414 south for a loop ride on a paved road that leads back to Corning.

Western New York State

The huge Allegany National Forest in northwestern Pennsylvania continues north into New York as the 65,000-acre Allegany State Park, the largest in the New York state park system. Even more enticing to mountain bikers are the 80 miles of hiking trails, 25 miles of cross-country ski trails, and more than 50 miles of snowmobile trails found in the park.

The topography of Allegany State Park is marked by steep, wooded hillsides, huge rock outcroppings, fast mountain streams, deep valleys dotted with grassy meadows, and wooded wetlands. The park is forested with Allegheny Plateau hardwoods that yield legendary fall foliage. Wildlife is abundant. Look for white-tailed deer, black bear, fox, raccoon, porcupine, hawks, owls, woodpeckers, wild turkey, and numerous breeding and migratory songbirds.

North of the Allegheny River, the topography evokes Vermont. The mountain biking up here is different than in the forest—two of the rides that follow wind their way through small towns and state-owned forest lands along a combination of dirt and paved roads.

In Olean, New York, Hojo's House of Wheels serves as mountain bike headquarters for the area. Owner Tim Houseknecht sponsors both road and mountain bike races and carries maps of nearby Allegany State Park and other prime mountain biking locations. And should misfortune strike and require a fast bike repair, trust Hojo's to do a timely and correct job. After all, with 65,000 acres of state park to explore, who wants to waste time?

RIDE 54 *ART ROSCOE SKI CENTER RIDE*

The foothills of the Allegany Mountains remind a lot of visitors of Vermont, with low ridges blanketed with forests of maple, pine, and oak. Stone Tower, at the top of the first climb on this scenic, 19-mile loop, provides excellent views of these surrounding mountains, forests, and Red House Lake. For the best scenery try to catch the fall foliage in early October.

The 10-foot-wide ski trails winding through the forests are delightful to pedal. Be sure to stop and enjoy the views from the Stone Tower and the overlook on Christian Hollow Ski Trail. On the climb, keep your eyes peeled for a beaver dam. In summer you can end the ride with a swim at Red House Lake.

No technical skills are required to ride these roads and ski trails— just be in fairly good physical shape. The route is fairly long with only a few steep (but

ART ROSCOE SKI CENTER RIDE

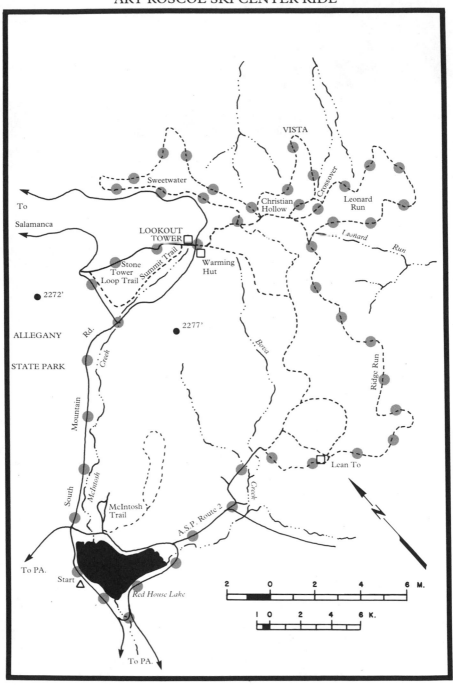

VISTA

Sweetwater

To
Salamanca

LOOKOUT
TOWER

Crossover

Christian
Hollow

Leonard
Run

Leonard
Run

Stone
Tower
Loop Trail

Summit Trail

Warming
Hut

● 2272'

● 2277'

Creek

Bova

Ridge Run

Rd.

ALLEGANY

STATE PARK

Mountain

Lean To

McIntosh

South

McIntosh
Trail

Creek

A.S.P. Route 2

To PA.

Start △

Red House Lake

2   0   2   4   6 M.

1 0   2   4   6 K.

To PA.

short) climbs on the ski trails. The ride starts out with a steady 3-mile climb on paved road followed by a mile on a packed-stone surface. The majority of the riding is on grassy, well-packed cross-country ski trails.

General location: Allegany State Park, Salamanca, New York, in the Red House Lake Area.

Elevation change: The ride starts at Red House Lake at an elevation of 1,456', then climbs to the Stone Tower at 2,202'. At the entrance to the cross-country ski trails the elevation is 2,300'. On the 3 trails (Sweetwater, Christian Hollow, and Leonard Run) the elevation gain is about 400'. Ridge Run descends gradually to the old Bova Ski Run, where the trail drops dramatically. The total elevation change is around 1,150'.

Season: The best season to ride this area is fall, for the trails are dry and the foliage is spectacular. In summer a long hot ride can be rewarded with a swim in Red House Lake. Spring riding tends to be soggy, due to snow thaw. Expect snow between November and March.

Services: All services available in Olean.

Hazards: Watch out for steep descents on the ski trails. Avoid riding during deer hunting season in the late fall.

Rescue index: There are cabins at the entrance to the ski trails where help may be found in an emergency. Otherwise, go to the administration building at Red House Lake.

Land status: New York state park.

Maps: The USGS 7.5 minute topo is Red House. Trail and topo maps are available at the administration building near Red House Lake.

Finding the trail: Take NY 17 (the Southern Tier Expressway) 5 miles west of Salamanca, New York, to the Red House exit. Follow the signs to the park entrance. (There is a $3 admission fee between Memorial Day and Labor Day.) Drive 1.6 miles to the intersection and bear right. Red House Lake is on the left. Park in one of the lots halfway around the lake.

Sources of additional information:

Allegany State Park
Administration Building
Salamanca, New York 14779
(716) 354-2545

Allegany State Park
Art Roscoe Ski Touring Area
Administration Building
Salamanca, New York 14779
(716) 354-2535

Hojo's House of Wheels
213 North Union Street

Olean, New York 14760
(716) 373-BIKE

Hojo's House of Wheels
9059 Main Street
Clarence, New York 14031
(716) 632-2631

Notes on the trail: To reach the trail from the parking lot, ride back past the state park administration building (clockwise around the lake) to the first stop sign. Go straight and up the hill to begin the ride.

To expand your mountain biking options even further, ask at the administration building for a copy of the snowmobile trail map. This adds about 30 miles of cycling in the area.

RIDE 55 *JOHN BUSACK CATTARAUGUS TRAIL*

Excellent views of the surrounding forests and mountains are the major attraction on this popular 37-mile loop. This part of New York state is often overlooked; the hills aren't as big, but the topography is similar to Vermont. The route passes through beautiful forests, predominantly red oak, white oak, and maple that create a riot of brilliant colors in the fall. The best time to catch the foliage is in early to mid-October.

This non-technical ride requires only minimal mountain biking skills. But its length and many climbs require good endurance. The route follows a mix of paved and unpaved roads. The unpaved roads are all hard-packed dirt, but some stretches only get seasonal maintenance. Watch for rough sections, especially in the spring.

General location: The loop starts and ends in Allegany, New York, and winds through forests to the surrounding towns to the north in Cattaraugus County.

Elevation change: The ride starts at 1,413' of elevation in the town of Allegany and reaches its highest point in Hinsdale (2,210'). There is about 2,700' of climbing, with individual climbs ranging from 500' to 800'.

Season: Fall is the best season for this ride. The daytime temperatures are very comfortable, averaging in the mid-60s. Summer can be muggy and the dirt roads in spring can get muddy. Expect snow between November and March. Avoid riding in deer hunting season, which starts in the late fall.

Services: All services available in Olean.

Hazards: Most of this ride is through farm country, so be on the lookout for traffic and dogs.

Rescue index: There are residences and farms all along the ride.

JOHN BUSACK CATTARAUGUS TRAIL

Land status: County roads and state-owned land.

Maps: County road maps are available at the Chamber of Commerce in Olean.

Finding the trail: Take NY 17 (Southern Tier Expressway) to Exit 24, which is 5 miles west of Olean, New York. Drive west on NY 417 for 1 mile to the first stop light and turn left. Drive about 1 block to the Fireman's Park on the left and park. The park is on Five Mile Road, which begins the ride.

Sources of additional information:

Chamber of Commerce
Exchange National Bank Building
North Union Street
Olean, New York 14760
(716) 372-4433

Hojo's House of Wheels
213 North Union Street
Olean, New York 14760
(716) 373-BIKE

Hojo's House of Wheels
9059 Main Street
Clarence, New York 14031
(716) 632-2631

RIDE 56 *HOLIDAY VALLEY*

This challenging ride goes through some of the most scenic areas of western New York. Even though the wilderness is long gone from this part of the state, the combination of forests, farms, and small towns makes for delightful cycling. There are excellent views of the surrounding mountains from the ridges and Little Rock City, and from the ski runs in Holiday Valley Resort. The maple, oak, and pine forests make for spectacular foliage in the fall. The area's scenery is often compared to Vermont.

The technical skills required are minimal, although there are plenty of optional ski and service trails at Holiday Valley which require more bike handling technique. Since there are many steep climbs, good endurance is a must for this out-and-back ride, which covers a variety of paved and unpaved roads over its 28-mile round-trip length. Half the unpaved roads only get seasonal maintenance, so they can be in rough shape, especially in the spring.

If getting dirty and muddy turns you on, stop at Holiday Valley Resort for a map and permission to ride their ski trails and service roads. These are actually logging roads, which are steep, rocky, and covered with deadfall.

General location: The ride starts and ends in the town of Ellicottville, New York, and winds through state lands and the town of Great Valley.

Elevation change: The lowest elevation on the ride is at Great Valley (1,477') and the highest is Little Valley (2,250'). There are 2 major climbs near Great Valley of about 800' each.

Season: The best time of year for this ride is autumn, because of the area's cool temperatures (the average high is in the mid-60s) and the spectacular fall foliage. Summer can be muggy and the dirt roads in spring are usually muddy because of snowmelt. Expect snow between November and March.

Services: All services available in Olean.

Hazards: Watch for traffic and the occasional loose dog.

Rescue index: There are residences and farms all along the ride.

Land status: County roads and state-owned land.

Maps: The USGS 7.5 minute topo maps are Salamanca and Ellicottville.

Finding the trail: From NY 17 (the Southern Tier Expressway) take Exit 23, US 219 North toward Ellicottville. From the Buffalo area take US 219 south

HOLIDAY VALLEY

toward Salamanca to Ellicottville. Park at the main lodge at Holiday Valley Ski Resort on US 219.

Sources of additional information:

Holiday Valley Ski Resort
Ellicottville, New York 14731
(716) 699-2345

Hojo's House of Wheels
213 North Union Street
Olean, New York 14760
(716) 373-BIKE

Hojo's House of Wheels
9059 Main Street
Clarence, New York 14031
(716) 632-2631

Notes on the trail: From the main lodge at Holiday Valley, pedal down Holiday Valley Road and cross over US 219 to the railroad tracks. Follow the tracks south to the town of Great Valley and turn right onto Mutton Hollow Road. Follow it to McCarthy Hollow Road. Turn right onto Hungry Hollow Road, then turn left onto Rock City Road. Continue on to Little Rock City, then turn around and return to Hungry Hollow Road and turn left. Turn right onto Whig Street. Continue to Mutton Hollow Road and turn right. Then retrace the route back to Holiday Valley.

Holiday Valley welcomes mountain bikers and holds a mountain bike race in the fall. Stop in for a map of the ski trails and service roads, and permission to mountain bike on their property.

Glossary

This short list of terms does not contain all the words used by mountain bike enthusiasts when discussing their sport. But it should be sufficient as an introduction to the lingua franca you'll hear on the trails.

ATB all-terrain bike; this, like "fat-tire bike," is another name for a mountain bike

ATV all-terrain vehicle; this usually refers to the loud, fume-spewing three- or four-wheeled motorized vehicles you will not enjoy meeting on the trail—except of course if you crash and have to hitch a ride out on one

bladed refers to a dirt road which has been smoothed out by the use of a wide blade on earth-moving equipment; "blading" gets rid of the teeth-chattering, much-cursed washboards found on so many dirt roads after heavy vehicle use

blaze a mark on a tree made by chipping away a piece of the bark, usually done to designate a trail; such trails are sometimes described as "blazed"

BLM Bureau of Land Management, an agency of the federal government

buffed used to describe a very smooth trail

clean while this can be used to describe what you and your bike *won't* be after following most trails, the term is most often used as a verb to denote the action of pedaling a tough section of trail successfully

deadfall a tangled mass of fallen trees or branches

diversion ditch a usually narrow, shallow ditch dug across or around a trail; funneling the water in this manner keeps it from destroying the trail

double-track the dual tracks made by a jeep or other vehicle, with grass or weeds or rocks between; the mountain biker can therefore ride in either of the tracks, but will find that whichever is chosen, no matter how many times he or

175

	she changes back and forth, the other track will appear to offer smoother travel
dugway	a steep, unpaved, switchbacked descent
feathering	using a light touch on the brake lever, hitting it lightly many times rather than very hard or locking the brake
four-wheel-drive	this refers to any vehicle with drive-wheel capability on all four wheels (a jeep, for instance, as compared with a two-wheel-drive passenger car), or to a rough road or trail which requires four-wheel-drive capability (or a *one*-wheel-drive mountain bike!) to traverse it
game trail	the usually narrow trail made by deer, elk, or other game
gated	everyone knows what a gate is, and how many variations exist upon this theme; well, if a trail is described as "gated" it simply has a gate across it; don't forget that the rule is if you find a gate closed, close it behind you; if you find one open, leave it that way
Giardia	shorthand for *Giardia lamblia,* and known as the "backpacker's bane" until we mountain bikers expropriated it; this is a waterborne parasite that begins its life cycle when swallowed, and one to four weeks later has its host (you) bloated, vomiting, shivering with chills and living in the bathroom; the disease can be avoided by "treating" (purifying) the water you acquire along the trail [see "Hitting the Trail"]
gnarly	a term thankfully used less and less these days, it refers to tough trails
hammer	to ride very hard
hardpack	used to describe a trail in which the dirt surface is packed down hard; such trails make for good and fast riding, and very painful landings; bikers most often use "hardpack" as both a noun and adjective, and "hardpacked" as an adjective only (the grammar lesson will help you when diagramming sentences in camp)
jeep road, *jeep trail*	a rough road or trail which requires four-wheel-drive capability (or a horse or mountain bike) to traverse it
kamikaze	while this once referred primarily to those Japanese fliers who quaffed a glass of sake, then flew off as human

bombs in suicide missions against U.S. naval vessels, it more recently has been applied to the idiot mountain bikers who far less honorably scream down hiking trails, endangering the physical and mental safety of the walking, biking, and equestrian traffic they meet; deck guns were necessary to stop the Japanese kamikaze pilots, but a bike pump or walking staff in the spokes is sufficient for the current-day kamikazes who threaten to get us all kicked off the trails

multi-purpose   a BLM designation of land which is open to multipurpose use; mountain biking is allowed

out-and-back   a ride in which you will return on the same trail you pedaled out; while this might sound far more boring than a loop route, many trails look very different when pedaled in the opposite direction

portage   to carry your bike on your person

quads   bikers use this term to refer both to the extensor muscle in the front of the thigh (which is separated into four parts), and to USGS maps; the expression "Nice quads!" refers always to the former, however, except in those instances when the speaker is an engineer

runoff   rainwater or snowmelt

signed   a signed trail is denoted by signs in place of blazes

single-track   a single track through grass or brush or over rocky terrain, often created by deer, elk, or backpackers; single-track riding is some of the best fun around

slickrock   the rock-hard, compacted sandstone which is *great* to ride and even prettier to look at; you'll appreciate it more if you think of it as a petrified sand dune or seabed, and if the rider before you hasn't left tire marks (through unnecessary skidding) or granola bar wrappers behind

snowmelt   runoff produced by the melting of snow

snowpack   unmelted snow accumulated over weeks or months of winter, or over years in high-mountain terrain

spur   a road or trail which intersects the main trail you're following

technical   terrain that is difficult to ride due not to its grade (steepness) but because of obstacles—rocks, logs, ledges, loose soil . . .

topo   short for topographical map, the kind that shows both linear distance *and* elevation gain and loss; "topo" is pronounced with both vowels long

trashed   a trail which has been destroyed (same term used no matter what has destroyed it . . . cattle, horses, or even mountain bikers riding when the ground was too wet)

two-wheel-drive   this refers to any vehicle with drive-wheel capability on only two wheels (a passenger car, for instance, compared with a jeep), or to an easy road or trail which a two-wheel-drive vehicle could traverse

water bar   earth, rock, or wooden structure which funnels water off trails

washboarded   a road with many ridges spaced closely together, like the ripples on a washboard; these make for very rough riding, and even worse driving in a car or jeep

wilderness area   land that is officially set aside by the Federal Government to remain *natural*—pure, pristine, and untrammeled by any vehicle, including mountain bikes; though mountain bikes had not been born in 1964 (when the U.S. Congress passed the Wilderness Act, establishing the National Wilderness Preservation system) they are considered a "form of mechanical transport" and are thereby excluded; in short, stay out

wind chill   a reference to the wind's cooling effect upon exposed flesh; for example, if the temperature is 10 degrees Fahrenheit and the wind is blowing at 20 miles per hour, the wind-chill effect (that is, the actual temperature to which your skin reacts) is *minus* 32 degrees; if you are riding in wet conditions things are even worse, for the wind-chill effect would then be *minus 74 degrees*!

windfall   anything (trees, limbs, brush, fellow bikers) blown down by the wind

Photo by Dave Hammond

When not hard at work on his next mountain bike trail guide or writing articles for *VeloNews, Dirt Rag,* or the *Baltimore Sun,* JOE SURKIEWICZ revels in conquering technical single-track trails, riding his road bike, and savoring the early films of Barbara Stanwyck. He lives in Baltimore, Maryland, with his wife Ann Lembo and their cat Wally.

The Mountain Bike Way to Knowledge
is through William Nealy

No other great Zen master approaches William Nealy in style or originality. His handwritten text, signature cartoons, and off-beat sense of humor have made him a household name among bikers. His expertise, acquired through years of meditation (and some crash and burn), enables him to translate hard-learned reflexes and instinctive responses into his unique, easy-to-understand drawings. Anyone who wants to learn from the master (and even those who don't) will get a good laugh.

Mountain Bike!
A Manual of Beginning to Advanced Technique

The ultimate mountain bike book for the totally honed! Master the techniques of mountain biking and have a good laugh while logging miles with Nealy.

Soft cover, 172 pages, 7" by 10"
Cartoon illustrations
$12.95

The Mountain Bike Way of Knowledge

This is the first compendium of mountain bike "insider" knowledge ever published. Between the covers of this book are the secrets of wheelie turns, log jumps, bar hops, dog evasion techniques, and much more! Nealy shares his wisdom with beginner and expert alike in this self-help manual.

Soft cover, 128 pages, 8" by 5 1/2"
Cartoon illustrations
$6.95

From Menasha Ridge Press
1-800-247-9437

Out here–there's no one to ask directions

. . . except your **FALCON**GUIDE.

FALCONGUIDES is a series of recreation guidebooks designed to help you safely enjoy the great outdoors. Each title features up-to-date maps, photos, and detailed information on access, hazards, side trips, special attractions, and more. The 6 x 9" softcover format makes every book an ideal travel companion as you discover the scenic wonders around you.

FALCONGUIDES... leading the way!

FALCONGUIDES   *Perfect for every outdoor adventure!*

FISHING
Angler's Guide to Alaska
Angler's Guide to Minnesota
Angler's Guide to Montana
Beartooth Fishing Guide

FLOATING
Floater's Guide to Colorado
Floater's Guide to Missouri
Floater's Guide to Montana

HIKING
Hiker's Guide to Alaska
Hiker's Guide to Alberta
Hiker's Guide to Arizona
Hiker's Guide to California
Hiker's Guide to Colorado
Hiker's Guide to Hot Springs
   in the Pacific Northwest
Hiker's Guide to Idaho
Hiker's Guide to Missouri
Hiker's Guide to Montana
Hiker's Guide to Montana's
   Continental Divide Trail
Hiker's Guide to Nevada
Hiker's Guide to New Mexico
Hiker's Guide to Oregon
Hiker's Guide to Texas
Hiker's Guide to Utah
Hiker's Guide to Virginia
Hiker's Guide to Washington
Hiker's Guide to Wyoming
Hiking Softly, Hiking Safely
Trail Guide to Glacier National Park

MOUNTAIN BIKING
Mountain Biker's Guide to Arizona
Mountain Biker's Guide to
   Central Appalachia

Mountain Biker's Guide to
   Northern New England
Mountain Biker's Guide to
   Southern California

ROCKHOUNDING
Rockhound's Guide to Arizona
Rockhound's Guide to Montana

SCENIC DRIVING
Arizona Scenic Drives
Back Country Byways
California Scenic Drives
Oregon Scenic Drives
Scenic Byways
Scenic Byways II
Trail of the Great Bear
Traveler's Guide to the Oregon Trail

WILDLIFE VIEWING GUIDES
Arizona Wildlife Viewing Guide
California Wildlife Viewing Guide
Colorado Wildlife Viewing Guide
Idaho Wildlife Viewing Guide
Indiana Wildlife Viewing Guide
Montana Wildlife Viewing Guide
North Carolina Wildlife Viewing Guide
North Dakota Wildlife Viewing Guide
Oregon Wildlife Viewing Guide
Texas Wildlife Viewing Guide
Utah Wildlife Viewing Guide
Washington Wildlife Viewing Guide

PLUS—
Birder's Guide to Montana
Hunter's Guide to Montana
Recreation Guide to
   California National Forests
Recreation Guide to
   Washington National Forests

Falcon Press Publishing Co.   •   *Call toll-free 1-800-582-2665*

14396840R00079

and the Office of Population of the U.S. Agency for International Development for their generous financial support of the study.

Finally I should like to thank Mr. Don Yoder and all the staff members at the East-West Population Institute, in particular Ms. Sonia C. Albores and Ms. Sandra Ward, for their comments and editorial suggestions, and especially Dr. James T. Fawcett, who introduced me to the research and was coordinator, supervisor, and adviser throughout this innovative study.

In addition, this study is part of a collaborative cross-national investigation undertaken in five other countries—the Republic of Korea, the Philippines, the Republic of China (Taiwan), Thailand, and the United States (Hawaii). The reader who wishes to compare the present findings with those of the other countries should consult the other volumes in this publication series. Volume 1 (Arnold et al., 1975) presents comparative results; the remaining volumes provide more detailed findings from the individual countries.

In carrying out this research, I have been indebted to many people. First, I should like to thank Mr. Shoji Suzuki, who was involved in this study from the beginning, helping to plan and carry out the research, and who was responsible for the final phase of the data analysis. Professor Kiyoshi Shima of Musashino Women's College kindly offered the use of his office as the administrative center for the study and gave us much valuable advice beginning in the pilot study phase.

Next, I should like to thank all the interviewers and coders for their painstaking efforts at the time of the interviews and during the period of data analysis. Without their help, the investigation would never have been possible. I would also like to thank all the personnel who gave us advice on sampling and arranged the urban and rural interviewing. Much credit goes to the statisticians at the office of the prime minister, to personnel at the Institute of Population Studies, to the public health officials of Saitama, Niigata, and Ibaraki Prefectures, and to other local health personnel of the interviewed areas.

I should like to thank those who served as occasional consultants for this project, especially the late Dr. Minoru Tachi, former director of the Institute of Population Problems at the Ministry of Health and Welfare, and Dr. Toshio Kuroda, its subsequent director. Thanks are also due to Mr. Shinichi Mihara, former executive director of the Population Research Council of Mainichi Newspapers, Inc., who helped me to organize a special research group for this project and who introduced a sponsoring organization, the Family Planning Federation of Japan, for the foreign grant. I should like to thank Mr. Chojiro Kunii, executive secretary of the Family Planning Federation, who wholeheartedly offered the Federation as the sponsoring organ for the project grant.

I should also like to thank all the Asian and American coinvestigators of this project, to whom I owe a great intellectual debt—Drs. Fred Arnold, Rodolfo A. Bulatao, Chalio Buripakdi, Sung Jin Lee, and Tsong-Shien Wu. Special thanks must also go to the Ford Foundation

preface

The rapid industrialization and urbanization that have taken place in Japan especially since the Second World War have drastically transformed the structure of the socioeconomic system of the country, which in turn has affected the pattern of fertility. This fertility transition has attracted the attention of demographers and other population scientists. To investigate the process, some cross-sectional methodological approaches have been used to trace the relationship between macrodemographic trends and the individual patterns of behavior that have influenced them.

Nationwide knowledge, attitude, and practice (KAP) surveys, initiated by the Mainichi Newspapers, Inc., in 1950, have partially fulfilled this purpose. But these studies of childbearing and contraceptive behavior do not fully explain how each individual considers fertility in his or her socioeconomic context, or in the temporal and dynamic context of social change.

To fill the gap, a study has been needed that explores cognitive and behavioral aspects of how young couples view children, how such views reflect certain trends when they are grouped into socioeconomic strata, and how these views about children may be related to fertility change in the country as a whole. The study described in this monograph provides considerable information about such issues. Although the research was undertaken during the period of 1972–73, the findings are considered still valid, describing in some detail the attitudes of young couples toward children and shedding light on the fertility decline in the present socioeconomic context.

The
Fallen Angel
Model

Deeper into the Mysteries

Joe P. Provenzano, Ron D. Morgan,
Dan R. Provenzano

En Route Books and Media, LLC
St. Louis, MO

Make the time

En Route Books and Media, LLC

5705 Rhodes Avenue

St. Louis, MO 63109

Cover credit: Dr. Sebastian Mahfood, OP.
Cover Art: St. Michael defeats the Devil by Eugène Delacroix
(1861). Mural on the ceiling of the Chapel of the Holy Angels
in the Roman Catholic Church of Saint-Sulpice, Paris
https://smarthistory.org/delacroix-sulpice/
https://commons.wikimedia.org/wiki/Category:Saint_Michael_
and_the_Dragon_(Delacroix)

ISBN-13: 978-1-952464-86-7
Library of Congress Control Number: 2021940485

Acknowledgments

We have been discussing the ideas in this book with many people over a long period of time and could never mention all of them. However, the following individuals encouraged our effort and helped us organize and present our ideas more clearly: Jay Braun, Bob Chamberlain, Tom Fraschetti, Kevin Hinzman, Dr. Robert Hochberg, Sandy Morgan, Linda Provenzano, Gary Provenzano, and Ron Renckly.

Dr. Tom Sheahen, former Director of the Institute for Theological Encounter with Science and Technology (2008-2021) provided detailed reviews and suggestions for clearer presentations in many areas in the book.

Meet the Authors

The Philosopher — Joe P. Provenzano has an M.S. in Physics and is the author of *Conscious Energy* (previously published as *The Philosophy of Conscious Energy)* and *How to Believe in God and Science — In Three Easy Steps.*

The Deacon — Ron D. Morgan is a deacon in the Catholic Church and is a lifelong follower and student of physics.

The Scientist — Dan R. Provenzano has a Ph.D. in Applied Physics from the California Institute of Technology. Dan works with lasers and fiber optic sensors.

Joe and Ron are retired and live near Dallas, Texas. They have been brothers-in-law for over fifty years and have been developing the ideas and insights in this book for almost that long.

Dan is the son of Joe and his wife, Linda. He is currently an Optical Scientist working in Blacksburg, Virginia. Dan is married with three children and has been involved with these ideas all his life. He wrote the *ProWave Interpretation of Quantum Mechanics* when he was in graduate school in the late 1990's (see Appendix B).

A Note from the Authors

This book is intended for anyone who is seeking to reconcile their belief in God with the findings of modern science. Two of the biggest obstacles to belief in God are materialism and the problem of evil. The ideas in this book help overcome these obstacles.

In fact, that is exactly what happened with Joe and Dan. We have always been scientifically oriented and working through the logic of what we've done, and writing this book has helped our faith. We've become more comfortable with the reality of the spiritual, non-physical realm and have developed a logical solution for the problem of evil. Ron, who began this project with a strong faith, has seen it become even stronger by finding several connections between modern physics and theology. It is our hope that the ideas in this book will help others.

Table of Contents

Appendix A
Physics and the Not-So-Physical

Appendix B

Chapter 1

Mysteries from Science and Scripture

"The day science begins to study non-physical phenomena, it will make more progress in one decade than in all the previous centuries of its existence."

—*Nikola Tesla*

Science has given us amazing technology. Our day-to-day lives depend upon electronics and global communication. However, science for many can be a mystery: How does everything we use actually work? The first part of our book addresses one of the greatest mysteries in science as it relates to the underlying reality of physical substance. The scientific community anticipated that the fundamental particles that compose matter would behave as small, solid entities that obeyed Newton's classical laws of mechanics. It turns out that they did not conform to this expectation. Sometimes, they act like particles, and sometimes they act like waves with mysterious behaviors. Interpreting their underlying nature is not considered a matter of physics, and today most scientists simply use the mathematics of physics to make statistical predictions of the physical outcomes of experiments. Very few are even willing to

discuss "what's really going on," i.e., the nature of the under-lying reality.

Many people wonder about the origin of our planet, our solar system, our galaxy, and the other 100 or more billion galaxies. What did the very beginning of our early physical universe look like? Physicists propose that our universe began in a very small, very hot and unstable state. It then cooled, expanded, and evolved to the physical universe we see around us today. However, science itself cannot address how or why it began because there is no way to experimentally verify what, if anything, happens outside of spacetime.

Actually, many aspects of the early universe itself are mysteries. For example, scientists have discovered that the early universe had near, if not perfect, order. The famous physicist Michio Kaku has compared it to a perfect crystal that was somehow broken and then evolved. At this point, no one has any explanation for why our universe started out this way.

Perhaps the greatest mystery uncovered by modern science is something called the Fine-Tuning Argument. A large number of fundamental constants exist in nature that seem to be finely "tuned" to the values they are, and if any one of them is slightly different, then life and consciousness as we know them could not have evolved.

Scripture and theology provide spiritual wisdom revealing God's will for us in this life and a path to live with Him forever. Nevertheless, there are mysteries in Scripture and in the accepted interpretations of Scripture.

Scripture tells us that everything God created is good. However, it does not tell us exactly how God created the universe. Furthermore, we know that our world is full of suffering, death and evil. We wonder: Why would a good God create a world like this, or more simply, what is the source of evil or where did evil come from?

The most accepted explanation of the evolution of the human body that is consistent with religious belief is that God infuses an immortal soul into each human being. The mystery is how a non-physical entity (the soul) can affect a physical entity (the body)? Physicist and theologian Steven Barr acknowledged this mystery in his book *Modern Physics and Ancient Faith* (p. 226), by saying "... if there is something immaterial about the mind, how does it affect the brain and the body?"

There are also mysteries related to the fall of the angels. What are the general implications of their fall? In particular, how is their fall related to our universe: its creation, its evolution, and our spiritual battles with them?

These scientific and Scriptural/theological mysteries have been around for a very long time. There are no easy answers. There are currently two major paradigms about the underlying nature of reality. One is materialism, which says only the physical is real. The second sees reality as two separate realms: the physical and the spiritual. Both of these paradigms have been unable to provide new insights into these mysteries. In this book, we introduce two original ideas, which together lead

to a new, third paradigm and deeper insights into these mysteries not otherwise possible.

We begin in the next chapter by reporting on what we know from modern physics experiments.

Chapter 2

Introducing the Not-So-Physical

"I am a Quantum Engineer,
but on Sundays I have Principles."
—*John S. Bell*

Not many people argue that the physical world is real. In fact, a lot of people believe that the only real, existing entities are physical entities. For these people, the words "physical" and "real" mean exactly the same thing. The common term for this position is materialism. There is no place for God, angels or non-physical human souls in materialism.

On the other hand, the vast majority of the people who believe in God agree that the physical is real, but they also believe in the existence of a non-physical reality. Most of these people believe that God created both the physical realm and the non-physical, spiritual realm as two separate realms.

Until about a hundred years ago, nobody imagined that particles could exist that were part physical and part non-physical. Then something really strange happened. Physicists discovered that the small, fundamental "particles" of nature exhibited some behaviors and attributes that they could not

explain using physical terms. This was in addition to their other behaviors and attributes that were physical.

Nobody was happy with this. It was obviously unacceptable to the materialists. Even the believers could not make sense of fundamental particles that were part physical and part non-physical. Every possible effort was made to explain how these strange entities really were completely physical. Some of the greatest minds in the world tried and failed.

Then an even stranger thing happened. Just about everyone in the scientific community simply refused to think about or discuss the real existence of the non-physical aspects and non-physical behaviors of these entities. However, in this book we are simply going to accept what the physicists have experimentally discovered actually does occur in nature and follow this line of thought to its logical conclusion. We call it the "not-so-physical" and describe it in the next chapter.

Chapter 3

Describing the Not-So-Physical

"Indeed our sensory experience turns out to be a floating condensation on a swarm of the undefinable."
—*Teilhard de Chardin*

Around the turn of the 20th century physicists believed that classical physics, which describes all physical phenomena in purely physical terms, provided a complete description of the physical universe. Some even claimed that all there was left to do was measure things to the next significant figure.

In the late 1800's and early 1900's, that simple picture of physical reality started to change dramatically. Laboratory experiments began to show that light could behave as a wave in some instances and as a particle in other instances. Soon, it was discovered that all small particles displayed this strange, *not-so-physical,* wave-particle duality.

Even today, a hundred years later, no physical way exists to describe "what's really going on" during elementary particle movement. Appendix A contains several examples of behaviors that cannot be described in purely physical terms. The

situation is even stranger in the very early universe where there was no matter, i.e., no mass, and even the laws of physics as we know them had not yet formed. The early universe is briefly described in Chapter 5 and discussed in more detail in Appendix A9.

However, before proceeding, we need to be more precise about what we mean by the terms: physical, not-so-physical, and non-physical.

By *physical,* we mean something that exists in reality that we can, at least in principle, detect and measure, and that only behaves in ways that can be described by the laws of physics.

The things we experience in everyday life provide simple examples of what we mean by physical entities, things like rocks, the air we breathe, and the moon.

By *non-physical,* we mean something that exists in reality that we cannot detect, we cannot measure, and that behaves in ways that cannot be described by the laws of physics. (For more detail on what we mean by "cannot be described by the laws of physics" see Appendix A5.)

There are a number of non-detectable "beables" that are required in the theories and equations of modern physics. Several examples that satisfy the non-physical criteria are provided in Appendix A3. Of course, angels and other purely spiritual entities are categorized as non-physical by these criteria.

By **not-so-physical** we mean something that exists in reality that has at least one physical aspect and at least one non-physical aspect.

For example, we call an entity not-so-physical if we can detect and measure it but find it has behaviors that cannot be described by the laws of physics. Fundamental particles such as the electron are examples of the not-so-physical. They are detectable and measurable but behave in ways that cannot be described by the laws of physics. For example, physics cannot describe the electron's behavior between the slits in the double-slit experiment and the point of impact on the detector. See Appendix A1 for more details. Another example of the not-so-physical is an entity called the vector potential field. This field is detectable but not measurable. It is not measurable because the actual value of this field at every point has no physical significance. See Appendix A2 for a description of the experiment that proved this unmeasurable field has real existence.

We said earlier that we were going to present two original new ideas in this book. Introducing these distinctions as new categories, or ways of looking at reality, is the first of the two new ideas.

Encountering non-physical aspects of physical reality is not a new phenomenon. In fact, it goes back to the very beginning of physics. Modern physical theories began with Sir Isaac Newton's theory of gravity. The problem of the non-physical has been with us since then. Here's a comment from Newton himself who realized that the force of gravity acts between

material bodies that are separated from each other with nothing in between them. His references to the material and the immaterial mean exactly the same as what we mean by the physical and the non-physical.

> …That gravity should be innate, inherent, and essential to matter, so that one body may act upon another at a distance through a vacuum, without the mediation of anything else, by and through which their action and force may be conveyed from one to another, is to me so great an absurdity that I believe no man who has in philosophical matters a competent faculty of thinking can ever fall into it. Gravity must be caused by an agent acting constantly according to certain laws; but whether this agent be material or immaterial, I have left open to the consideration of my readers" (Stanford Encyclopedia of Philosophy).
> — Isaac Newton, Fourth Letter to Bentley

Of course, the general theory of relativity has replaced Newton's theory and explains gravity is in terms of "spacetime curvature." However, it's still difficult to understand this in purely material terms.

In order to deal with the experimental discovery of these not-so-physical entities, physicists developed a theory known as quantum mechanics. It is not necessary to discuss the experiments in very much detail, or the theory at all, in the

main part of this book. We have, however, provided several descriptions of experiments and a brief description of the theory in Appendix A. The chapters in Appendix A are provided as optional reading for readers who do not know about these areas, but are curious, and would like an introduction. Appendix B includes an original interpretation of quantum mechanics written in 1996 by one of the authors of this book. For a deeper discussion about the discovery, reality and meaning of the not-so-physical and more detail on what we mean by "cannot be described by the laws of physics" see Appendix A5.

The following table provides a summary of this new way of categorizing reality:

	Physical Existence	Real Existence
Physical Entities	*Yes*	*Yes*
Not-so-Physical Entities	*Partial*	*Yes*
Non-Physical Entities	*No*	*Yes*

Table 1. Kind of Entities vs. Types of Existence

There are important implications that come with accepting this way of categorizing reality. In other words, accepting the

fact that the fundamental "particles" and certain fields discovered by physicists really do exist in nature as not-so-physical, and some likely exist as non-physical, has many significant implications. We will discuss four of the most important implications in the remaining pages of this chapter.

The first is that it renders the worldview of pure materialism, where physical equals real, as incomplete and unequipped to explain the blurry nature of reality. Since materialism has always been an obstacle to faith in God, clearly removing this obstacle based on modern physics makes it easier to believe in a spiritual reality.

The second implication is that it could provide an approach to help physicists with one of the toughest issues they are facing today. The issue is that there are new physics theories being developed that make predictions about the existence of entities that cannot be experimentally verified. These theories are not following the scientific method as currently understood because this method demands experimental validation. The problem is that the scientific method as currently understood is based on the assumption that the reality studied by physics is purely physical and, therefore, physically verifiable. However, modern physics experiments, as discussed in this chapter and in Appendix A, have shown that the reality studied by the physicists does not conform to the assumption that it is purely physical. This means that these new theories may be correct even if they make predictions that cannot be experimentally verified. Physicists cannot afford to have important

new theories, that may be correct, discarded because of an outdated paradigm that limits reality to only what we can observe.

There is no easy answer to this issue. However, we think that our distinctions or categories about physical, not-so-physical, and non-physical provide the necessary starting point for addressing the question: What is the "scientific method" today?

The third implication of this view of reality is that it provides insights into the mysteries of complex numbers and why they are so important in modern physics in general and quantum mechanics in particular. The key point is that if we correlate the "real" axis with the physical and the "imaginary" axis with the non-physical, we gain insights into these mysteries. The discussion of this implication is provided in Appendix A10.

The fourth, and most important implication for this book, is that this way of viewing reality is needed to understand the Fallen Angel Model (FAM). This vision of reality, together with FAM, form a new paradigm which provides a deeper understanding of reality.

Before proceeding, we will make two points explicit. We have already presented the first one, but it's included here for completeness.

1. It is beneficial to view reality as composed of three categories: physical, not-so-physical, and non-physical.

2. Entities can be in one category, undergo some kind of change, and then be in another category.

A simple example of the second point is shown in the mysterious double-slit experiment. In this experiment, the "particle," for example an electron, exhibits a not-so-physical behavior. It does this while moving between the slits and the detector, but loses that behavior, at least for an instant, at the moment of detection. The detection is a physical process which occurs at a point. See Appendix A1 for more details. Another example is provided by the evolution of the physical universe itself. We will discuss how the universe began at the Big Bang in a very not-so-physical, or more likely non-physical, state where there was no matter, i.e., no mass. Then part of the universe evolved into not-so-physical particles with mass and some of that combined to produce physical entities. See Chapter 5 and Appendix A9 for more details.

We are now ready to take the next step which involves combining this view of reality with ideas from another discipline.

Chapter 4

Combining Disciplines

"In the history of science, ever since the famous trial of Galileo, it has repeatedly been claimed that scientific truth cannot be reconciled with the religious interpretation of the world. Although I am now convinced that scientific truth is unassailable in its own field, I have never found it possible to dismiss the content of religious thinking as simply part of an outmoded phase in the consciousness of mankind, a part we shall have to give up from now on. Thus, in the course of my life I have repeatedly been compelled to ponder on the relationship of these two regions of thought, for I have never been able to doubt the reality of that to which they point."

— *Werner Heisenberg, 1974*

Insights into the mystery of nature provided by the not-so-physical approach go beyond providing a more complete picture of reality and removing materialism as a roadblock to

faith. They actually provide a way to link the findings of modern science with the basic beliefs of traditional faith in a way never done before. However, in order to do that, we need to combine some ideas from science with some ideas from Scripture. This approach will eventually lead us to a discussion of the Fallen Angel Model (FAM).

Physics and cosmology cannot explain what happened "before" the Big Bang because time as studied by physics began at the Big Bang. To consider the source and nature of the emergence of spacetime, we need to turn to another discipline and think about a different kind of "time." In the latter chapters, we need to use the phrase "before the Big Bang" and when we do so we are referring to a sequence of events in the spiritual realm. We are not referring to time as it is typically used, nor are we implying in any way that God is inside of time. These actions and events cannot be described by physical laws and physical structures. See Appendix A7 for a discussion of "spiritual time."

Before modern science was discovered and developed, theology was considered to be the final authority on matters of the spiritual and the physical. The "credibility pendulum" started completely on the theological side because there was no other side.

Eventually, modern science began to prove theology wrong in some predictions regarding the physical world. As a result, theology lost credibility. Unfortunately, theology's loss of credibility was not limited to the physical realm. Many scien-

tists challenged the existence of God and everything but the purely physical. The credibility pendulum swung too far to the science side.

Then, all of a sudden, physics experimental results revealed that there is more to reality than purely physical objects. Actually, it's a lot worse than that. We discuss in the next chapter and in Appendix A9 how the physical realm, the physical constants, and even the laws of physics evolved from non-physical and not-so-physical fields. As we have pointed out, it is time to embrace this not-so-physical blur and recognize that our physical universe emerged from—and continues to consist of—not-so-physical entities for its very existence.

We live in one universe, but it has several realms or dimensions including the physical, the not-so-physical, and the non-physical realms. In order to include theology, we need to address the spiritual realm. By "spiritual" we are referring to God's Kingdom, which transcends the spacetime, physical realm, and includes angels, human souls, etc., as traditionally understood. The spiritual realm, which involves consciousness, is very different than the non-physical entities discussed in physics theories (See Appendix A3). Nevertheless, the spiritual realm certainly fits our criteria as being non-physical.

It's time to place the credibility pendulum in its correct place, giving proper credit to both science and theology. However, it is necessary to be careful, because past attempts resulted in both disciplines encroaching on each other's domains. We think the discovery of the not-so-physical is the

key to success. Science needs to be focused on, and make predictions in, the physical realm. However, it is deeply involved with the not-so-physical and actually postulates the existence of non-physical fields inside the physical theories. Theology is necessarily focused on the spiritual realm but encounters spacetime as part of God's creation.

If one views the physical and the spiritual realms as two completely different realities, then combining these two disciplines will not be productive. History is full of failed attempts to combine them. However, if one views the physical and the spiritual as two different realms of one underlying reality, then combining science and theology has the potential to be productive. That's because we would have two different perspectives on the same underlying reality.

We have seen one side of this in the previous chapters where physics has led us to view the underlying reality of our universe as fields that are not-so-physical. St. Thomas Aquinas addressed the other side of this in his *Summa Theologica*, Volume I, Question 61, Third Article where he states that "...the angels are part of the universe: they do not constitute a universe of themselves; but both they and the corporeal natures unite in constituting one universe."

We agree with the findings of modern science and with St. Thomas, which see the universe, i.e., God's creation, as one reality. Therefore, combining physics and theology has the potential to give new insights.

Truth cannot change from one discipline to the next. Each discipline sees the same reality from a different perspective. In other words, there are some connections that cannot be made without combining science and theology. It is not enough to say that science and theology can agree. Rather it is much stronger; they must agree.

Theology tells us that God only creates good. The evil we see around us was not created by God and we will explore this mystery further after we introduce FAM.

The Bible was written long before the discovery of modern science and does not tell us exactly how God created everything. However, it does tell us that He did create everything and everything He created was good.

Genesis 1:1 "In the beginning when God created the heavens and the earth …"

Genesis 1:4 "God saw that the light was good. God then separated the light from the darkness."

Genesis 1:31 "God looked at everything he had made and found it very good."

When one thinks about actually trying to combine theology with science in a real way, it becomes clear that the origin of the universe is a good place to start. Science begins at the moment of the Big Bang and studies everything that we can measure after that. On the other hand, spiritual events studied by theology happen outside of spacetime and outside of the realm of science. The origin of the universe is a unique point where these two realms meet. If we want to find some kind of

cause-and-effect relationship between theology and science, then that would be a logical place to start. In the next chapter we will take a closer look at the origin of the universe.

Chapter 5

The Origin of the Universe

"The laws of science, as we know them at present, contain many fundamental numbers, like the size of the electric charge of the electron and the ratio of the masses of the proton and the electron .... The remarkable fact is that the values of these numbers seem to have been finely adjusted to make possible the development of life."

—*Stephen Hawking*

It is a mystery how our universe began or how it could have been created. We have two stories that help us understand creation. One is the story we read in the Bible where God created the universe in six days. The other story is from science where the universe begins in a Big Bang, expanding and evolving into the universe as we know it today over a period of about 14 billion years. Both stories have some problems. Currently, they do not fit together. Our Scriptures tell us that God created everything good, but there is evil in our world. Science tells us that what we observe now came about through evolution. Most

believers are of the opinion that evolution can be reconciled with their doctrines.

As a result, today there are three basic views about how the universe came into being.

First, there is the purely materialist view that relies only on science and random evolution. There is no God in materialism; the universe began and evolved naturally. There are a number of problems with this view. One of the biggest problems is that science has found that the basic constants of nature seem to be "tuned" to be the very specific values they have. If they did not have these values, evolution as we know it could not have happened. In order to avoid some kind of tuning, which implies a designer, materialists postulate an infinite number of universes that have all the possible values of all the constants. Given that, at least one universe would have to have the right values for life and consciousness to evolve. We are obviously in such a universe, and it would seem to us to have been tuned to allow evolution as we know it. The remaining, infinite number of universes are not detectable. This solution is very unsatisfactory to us (the authors) and to a lot of people. See Appendix A8.

Furthermore, many scientists claim that science has determined that some of the advances in evolution are too unlikely to just have happened randomly because the universe is not old enough. So, even if an infinite number of universes does allow for one universe to have the right tuning of constants, many scientists argue that there is not enough time for random

evolution to have made the progress it has made in that universe. For examples that there is evidence of design in our universe, see the work being done by the Discovery Institute. — https://www.discovery.org

Second, there is the purely literal interpretation of the Bible. The problem with this view is that it is inconsistent with what science tells us about the beginning and evolution of the universe.

Third, there is the view that God created the universe as stated in the Bible, but the details of the stories in the Bible cannot be taken literally. They necessarily had to be written in language that made sense to the people at that time. The purpose of the stories was to inform us that God created the universe, but not exactly how He did it. Today, we can discover the details of the process using scientific research. Anyone trying to reconcile science and faith needs to adopt some version of this view. The main problem with God's directly designing the evolving, physical universe is that we know that it is full of evil, suffering, and death. That would imply that God is responsible for all the evil, suffering, and death.

In this book, we will combine ideas from science and theology and propose a new paradigm offering deeper insights into these mysteries. However, before we can bring in ideas from theology, we need to first discuss what science tells us about the early universe. Appendix A9 provides quite a bit of detail on what science has discovered about the early universe. Here's an

overview from that appendix that is sufficient for our purposes here:

> The Big Bang Theory is the most accepted cosmological theory about how our spacetime universe began and evolved. According to the Big Bang Theory, the universe began about 13.8 billion years ago as an expansion of space and time. It started as a collection of fields with no matter in a very small volume. These fields were highly ordered but very unstable and almost immediately started to expand and evolve. The expanding fields of the universe produced matter, stars, and eventually all the elements in the periodic table, and everything else we see in the universe today.

Given this discovery, it should not be surprising that fundamental particles studied by physics today, which are the building blocks of our physical universe, are not-so-physical. We are simply seeing the effects from the non-physical beginning of our universe.

We are now in a position to turn to Scripture and theology.

Chapter 6

Creation of the Angels

"...the angel's immateriality is the cause of why it is incorruptible by its own nature."

—*St. Thomas Aquinas*

The existence and activity of angels is an important aspect of Christian doctrine. They are discussed extensively in Scripture and theology. The angels are pure spiritual creatures, and they were created good. We believe that any discussion of God's creation must include the angels. Many early Church Fathers believed that the angels were created before the physical universe was created.

Saint Augustine said that in Genesis when God said: "Let there be light, and there was light," that this is referring to the creation of the angels. (St. Augustine, *The City of God*, Book XI, Chapter 9). He also said what is meant by: "God divided the light from the darkness; and God called the light Day, and the darkness He called Night." refers to the fall of the angels (Chapter 33).

Fr. Pascal P. Parente has also supported this position.

With many of the Fathers of the Church we believe as very probable that the Angels were created long before the material world. They were certainly created before man, because we find them already distinguished as good Angels and fallen angels on man's first appearance on earth. (from Gen. 3:1ff.; 3:24) …

And in St. Ambrose: "Even though the Angels, the Dominations and the Powers had a beginning, they were already there when this world was made." *Hexaemeron*, I, 5, 19. The same opinion is defended by St. Jerome *(Super Epist. ad Titum, I)*, St. John Damascene *(De Fide Ortho-doxa, III, 3)*, and others. — *Beyond Space*, Rev. Pascal P. Parente, S.T.D., Ph.D., J.C.B., pgs. 10 and 11.

St. Thomas Aquinas addresses this question in his *Summa Theologica*, Volume I, Question 61, Third Article: "Whether the Angels Were Created before the Corporeal World?"

In this Article he states that "…the angels are part of the universe: they do not constitute a universe of themselves; but both they and the corporeal natures unite in constituting one universe." (This is the same quote as presented in Chapter 4).

This line of thinking causes him to think it's more probable that the angels and the physical universe were created at the same time. However, he does not take a firm position on this. He acknowledges that earlier Church Fathers believed the angels were created first, and that this position is "not to be deemed erroneous."

The belief that the angels were created before the physical universe is not contrary to Scripture or to Church doctrine. In fact, it is in agreement with teachings of many of the Church Fathers. Furthermore, as you will see in the next few chapters, our ideas fit very well with St. Thomas Aquinas' position that the angels and the physical universe constitute one universe.

Chapter 7

The Broken Vase

Author's Photo

Suppose you walk into a room and find some strange pieces of glass on the floor. You start to examine them and find that mysteriously many of them fit perfectly together to form nice, smooth, curved surfaces. Why do they do this? It seems like a total coincidence. All these jagged pieces are fitting together, yet they were not touching each other when you entered the

room. You could think of several theories for why the pieces fit together:

1. Random: Maybe it's just luck that the pieces fit together.
2. Many Rooms: Maybe there are lots and lots of rooms with random pieces of glass, and given enough such rooms, there has to be at least one room where they fit together like this.
3. Perception: Maybe the fact that you think they fit together has something to do with how you are observing the pieces.
4. Necessity: Maybe there's something about this kind of glass that it has to be that way.
5. Designed: The pieces fit so perfectly together that clearly, they have to somehow be the result of a design.
6. Holistic Design. Maybe a vase fell and broke!

Let's explore the two cases where some sort of design is needed to explain what's going on: cases #5 and #6. These are two vastly different ways that design could be involved. #5 says that the designer designed each piece so that they would be curved the way they are and fit together the way they do.

Now we get to #6, where the parts were once part of a higher design, i.e., a vase. Of course, a vase designer should get more credit because a vase is much more useful and beautiful than the individual parts. Furthermore, the designer may not be

responsible for the fact that it was broken. So, don't blame the designer and creator of the vase if you cut yourself while examining the pieces. Also, the creator may have created many more useful and beautiful items that did not fall, and they remain out of view.

Options 1-5, as you may realize, are depictions of reality put forth by prominent thinkers in modern times. One of the purposes of this book is to provide option #6 and introduce a new view of the origin of our universe. We do this by accepting the blurry nature of reality from modern physics and making the case that our universe is designed, not at the physical level, but at a much higher level. You will see later in this book how this simple concept can be used to provide insights deeper into the mysteries discussed in Chapter 1.

It's very interesting to note that physicists like Michio Kaku, quoted below, are starting to think about the beginning of the physical universe as a breaking of something with perfect, or near-perfect, order. They see our universe as being in a broken, or dare we say, in a "fallen" state.

> ...think of a beautiful crystal that shatters...but at the beginning of time when the universe was first created, that's when the crystal existed in its perfect form. We call it the Superforce. A single Superforce held this crystal together. But then we had the Big Bang which shattered this crystal giving us the shattered universe of today. When you look around you, and you see the different forces, moun-

tains, clouds, planets — it's broken. We live in a horribly broken world, but at the instant of creation there was perfection… —Michio Kaku

— https://www.youtube.com/watch?v=RUlVFzl_BJs

This quote comes just after the 4-minute mark in the video. Dr. Kaku also provides a similar discussion in his book: *Parallel Worlds: A Journey Through Creation, Higher Dimensions and the Future of the Cosmos* (p. 84).

Chapter 8

The Fallen Angel Model (FAM)

"It was pride that changed angels into devils; it is humility that makes men as angels."

—*St. Augustine*

Our theology and Scripture tell us that some of the angels rebelled and fell from heaven.

Then war broke out in heaven; Michael and his angels battled against the dragon. The dragon and its angels fought back, but they did not prevail and there was no longer any place for them in heaven. (Catholic Bishops, *New American Bible*) — Revelation 12: 7-8

Luke 10:18: "Jesus said, 'I have observed Satan fall like lightning from the sky'." Many critical interpretations of this passage would favor the sentiment that Jesus was telling his disciples they would have power over the evil one. However, this is the exact language He used, as recorded in Scripture. The following quote is from Scott Hahn:

Saint Augustine and Saint Ambrose insisted that the 'heavens' and the 'lights' we read about in Genesis represent the realm of pure spirits. (Physical light does not appear till several verses later, on the fourth day.) God created these angels of light, as He created everything to be 'good'. Yet He also created them to be free, because only free creatures can experience love. Love cannot be coerced, or it ceases to be love. So, God presented the angels with a decision, and some of them chose not to return His love. The book of Revelation seems to allude to this event, though in symbolic language, when it says that 'a third of the stars of heaven' (Revelation 12:4) were darkened (8:12) and cast down. — Scott Hahn, *Joy to the World: How Christ's Coming Changed Everything,* New York: Image, 2014 (pp. 84-85).

The idea that the fallen angels were somehow "darkened" implies that they lost something like power or energy when they fell. This idea has been with us for centuries. This darkening is reflected in many works of art, such as, for example, the image shown on the cover of this book.

St. Thomas Aquinas, who is commonly called the Angelic Doctor, also referred to them as "darkened." In fact, he had much to say about the fallen angels and what they lost when they sinned and were thrown out of heaven. In his great work the *Summa Theologica,* he presented his thoughts in a question-and-answer format. Each general topic or question is

addressed by several articles in which there are a number of specific questions and answers. For example, Vol I, Question 64, "The Punishment of the Demons," the First Article is: Whether the Demons' Intellect is Darkened by Privation of the Knowledge of All Truth? Henceforth, we'll refer to articles by the short-hand notion provided in the *Summa*. In this case, it would be Vol I (Q. 64, A. 1).

The important thing for us to do now is to, as best as we can, consider what the angels lost when they were darkened and thrown out of heaven. In the following few paragraphs, we'll summarize what St. Thomas wrote about this in the *Summa*.

It's important to note that St. Thomas felt strongly that God did not take away anything from the fallen angels that was part of their nature.

> For it follows from the very nature of the angel, who, according to his nature, is an intellect or mind: since on account of the simplicity of his substance, nothing can be withdrawn from his nature, so as to punish him by subtracting from his natural powers, as a man is punished by being deprived of a hand or foot or something else. (Q. 64, A. 1)

He goes on to say in this article that although God did not take away any knowledge that came with their nature, He did take away some of the other knowledge that He had freely

given them. That freely given knowledge was twofold: knowledge about "Divine secrets" and ... knowledge which "produces love of God." The first kind was not totally removed but was reduced. The second kind was completely removed, resulting also in a complete loss of charity.

In Q. 62, A. 3 and Q. 109, A. 1, St. Thomas says that he believes that all the angels were created in sanctifying grace, which is not something that they would have had by their very nature. However, those that fell lost their sanctifying grace.

In Q. 62, A. 6, St. Thomas argues that more gifts of grace and glory were given to the angels who had more natural gifts.

In Q. 63, A. 7, St. Thomas argues that since the sin of the angels was a sin of pride, and not a propensity to sin, that the higher angels were more likely to sin.

In Q. 109, A. 4, St. Thomas argues that the angels are ordered by their nearness to God, and those nearer to God have power over those who are further from Him. Therefore, the good angels have power over the bad angels. The bad angels lost their angelic order and some of their power when they fell.

St. Thomas said that when the fallen angels lost these gifts, that they lost nothing that was theirs by virtue of their nature. In summary, St. Thomas described what they lost: some knowledge that was given to them, their love of God, sanctifying grace, their angelic order—or standing in relationship to God, and the power that came with that order.

From physics, we have learned that the universe began as unstable, non-physical and not-so-physical fields with high

order, i.e., very low entropy, which naturally leads to the question: Why is this the case? Professor Robert M. Wald, University of Chicago, provides the following insight:

> It seems to me to be far more plausible that the answer to the above question as to why the very early universe was in a very low entropy state is that it came into existence in a very special state. Of course, this answer begs the question, since one would then want to know why it came into existence in a very special state, i.e., what principle or law governed its creation. I definitely do not have an answer to this question. But I believe that it will be more fruitful to seek an answer to this question than to attempt to pursue dynamical explanations.
> —https://arxiv.org/pdf/gr-qc/0507094.pdf

As we pointed out earlier, physicist Michio Kaku has compared the very early universe to a perfect crystal that was somehow broken and then evolved. At this point, no one has any explanation for why our universe started out this way.

Linking these events from science and theology, where one caused the other, opens the door to a new idea or model about the creation of the physical universe. We call this idea the **Fallen Angel Model, or simply FAM.** It is the second of the two original ideas we present in this book. Together, they provide a new, third paradigm for understanding reality.

The other two paradigms are (1) materialism and (2) assuming that the spiritual and the physical are separately created realities. This new paradigm offers insights deeper into the mysteries of science and Scripture that are not possible with either of the current two paradigms.

The Big Bang was the beginning of the physical, spacetime universe. It is a realm of impermanent order and rapid change. It's reasonable to consider that it came from the fall of the angels and that God saw it for what it was, an imperfect, evolving universe. He could have ignored it and focused only on the good angels remaining in heaven. However, that is not what He did. God saw the imperfect, evolving universe as good and full of potential, but needing a Redeemer. This kind of love is reflected in the parable where a good shepherd would go searching for one lost sheep. — Matthew 18:12–14 and Luke: 15:3–7

The FAM idea comes from combining events from physics and theology. We are presenting no new physics, but we are presenting a new speculative theological idea. Actually, what we are proposing is a possible cause and effect linkage of an event from science with an event from Scripture. This linkage puts together everything we have been discussing into a top-down model of creation. It is made possible because the not-so-physical forms a bridge between the non-physical and the physical, and entities can change from one category to another.

This model fits together all the pieces of the puzzle from both physics and theology in a comprehensive way that the other models do not.

Before we go any further, we need to make an important distinction between FAM and the idea that the physical universe is evil and came from evil sources. Perhaps the most common expression of this is Gnosticism. *The Catechism of the Catholic Church* (*CCC*) specifically expresses this in section 285:

> ...Still others have affirmed the existence of two eternal principles, Good and Evil, Light and Darkness, locked, in permanent conflict (Dualism, Manichaeism). According to some of these conceptions, the world (at least the physical world) is evil, the product of a fall, and is thus to be rejected or left behind (Gnosticism)...

We realize that at first glance FAM sounds similar to Gnosticism, but it is very different. With Gnosticism, the substance of the universe itself is evil. With FAM, the substance of the universe resulted from what the fallen angels lost. They lost a number of God's gifts, especially order and power. These gifts were directly from God, were all good and in no way evil. None of the fallen angels' nature or evilness was in these gifts. However, there were consequences of their fall.

In order to better understand the idea behind FAM, consider the following analogy. When an electron goes from a

higher to a lower energy state, a photon of definite wavelength and frequency is emitted. In the physical realm, we observe that light is emitted by the electron in changing states. Imagine the immense amount of spiritual energy that would have been released when the angels fell from their perfect order to their lower order, losing most of the gifts and power God had given them.

FAM describes the change of state resulting from the fall as the beginning of space and time in the Big Bang. We certainly cannot explain the exact mechanism of this change of state. This mystery is at the interface between the realms of theology and physics. Collaboration between physicists and theologians, focusing on the not-so-physical aspects of reality, might lead to some insights into this mechanism.

The fall of the angels and the resulting disorder is similar to hitting a drum too hard or picking a guitar string too hard. In both cases, the instruments break and can no longer function as before. The sin of the angels is a sin of pride or of wanting power beyond their nature. They wanted to be more than the creatures they were made to be. In this transformation, or change of state, spacetime began.

The fallen angels are spiritual beings that are connected to space and time.

For our struggle is not with flesh and blood but with the principalities, with the powers, with the world rulers of this

present darkness, with the evil spirits in the heavens. - Ephesians 6:12

Current cosmology supports decreasing entropy looking back towards the Big Bang and even possibly zero entropy. Zero entropy is perfect order. The spiritual realm is perfect order and eternal.

We speculate that from the eternal order of heaven comes the impermanent order of space and time. This implies that the non-physical that comes out of the spiritual realm is "broken" and unstable. Some of it devolves into the not-so-physical, and finally, some devolves into the physical. This is consistent with what we have learned from physics and discussed earlier in the book.

Using the insights from this top-down model, we should be able see traces of the non-physical in spacetime matter and energy in the form of not-so-physical entities. Of course, this corresponds to what has happened as discussed in the earlier chapters and in Appendix A.

Up until now, the physical and the spiritual have been viewed as two separate realms, yet some scientists and some theologians have crossed over into in each other's disciplines. FAM offers a new paradigm for how the spiritual and physical are part of one reality and gives us a holistic view of theological and scientific inquiries.

We believe that truth is truth and is not different in each discipline but that each discipline sees a different aspect of that

same underlying reality. That reality consists of the physical, the not-so-physical, and the non-physical. We just need to be careful to let physics do physics and theology do theology with no more and no less for each discipline.

The concept that the physical universe emerged from, and is part of, a larger, non-physical realm has been around for centuries. Hinduism, many other religions, including some Christian mystics, and modern thinkers have proposed different versions of this concept. Given the developments of modern physics, it's time to look at it again.

FAM is completely different from these earlier versions because it is consistent with both science and Scripture. Not only that, but FAM also provides insights into many of the mysteries in science and Scripture. Some of these insights are discussed in the next chapter.

Chapter 9

FAM and Deeper into the Mysteries

"Something deeply hidden had to be behind things."
—*Albert Einstein*

Scientific theories are judged by how well they can predict the outcomes of experiments. They are not judged on how intuitively pleasing they are in themselves. Quantum mechanics and relativity are perfect examples of this. They are both very counter intuitive, but they make correct predictions. On the other hand, paradigms, or worldviews about the basic nature of reality, cannot be tested by actual physical experiments. They can only be judged by their ability to provide insights into the mysteries about reality that we know from science and Scripture. Nevertheless, like scientific theories, they should not be discarded out-of-hand because they seem strange or unrealistic at first glance. In this chapter, we make the case that the paradigm, based on the physical, not-so-physical and non-physical categories combined with FAM, offers new and deeper insights into many of these mysteries.

In Chapter 1, we mentioned several mysteries that come from science and Scripture. We pointed out that the two common worldviews, or paradigms, are not giving new insights in-

to these mysteries. Adherents in the first paradigm, materialism, claim that only the physical is real. Adherents in the second paradigm believe in the reality of the physical, but also believe in the reality of a separately-created, non-physical, spiritual realm.

In this book, we introduced two ideas that, when taken together, result in a new, third paradigm. This paradigm suggests that the reality of this universe consists of physical, not-so-physical, and non-physical entities. The not-so-physical entities have both physical and non-physical attributes or behaviors. This paradigm further suggests that our observable universe began because of non-physical (in this case spiritual) entities becoming unstable and evolving as described by science. This paradigm further suggests that this instability came from the fall of the angels which we learn about from Scripture.

Note that the current two paradigms have been around for centuries and there seems to be a well-established, but unstated, assumption that no other paradigms are possible. People are reluctant to discuss new paradigms. After all, what else could there be? The materialists say only the physical is real. Believers add a non-physical reality for the human soul and the spiritual realm. Doesn't that cover all the possibilities? No, it doesn't.

The not-so-physical category of physics and FAM suggests an addition to the existing paradigms. Accepting the reality of the not-so-physical, only means accepting what is demon-

strated in the experimental results uncovered by modern physics. For over a hundred years we have been observing "particles" that show some physical and some non-physical attributes and behaviors.

Scientists and theologians do not have a way to discuss the underlying reality of these, part physical and part non-physical, particles. That's not surprising because these particles don't fit in either of the existing paradigms. Of course, it is always very difficult to consider changes to existing paradigms. However, the time has come to explore a new, third paradigm that includes the category of the not-so-physical to better understand the mystery of what physics theories and experiments have revealed.

In this chapter, we will summarize some of the key points made in the earlier chapters and show how adopting the not-so-physical FAM paradigm can give new insights that take us deeper into these mysteries. The first five mysteries discussed below come from science and the final three come from Scripture (and accepted interpretations of Scripture).

The basic nature of our physical universe — Modern physics experiments have demonstrated over and over that the fundamental "particles" of nature have both physical and non-physical attributes and behaviors. Obviously, materialism cannot explain this, but neither can the other existing paradigm. The idea of the not-so-physical is simply an acceptance that what the physicists have found is correct. Nature is what it is, not what we want or expect it to be.

The Complex Numbers and Quantum Mechanics — We mentioned in Chapter 3 that, if we correlate the "real" axis with the physical and the "imaginary" axis with the non-physical, we gain insights into the mysteries of complex numbers and why they are so useful in quantum mechanics. This discussion is provided in Appendix A10.

The nature of the very early universe — Scientists have developed an amazingly detailed description of the universe, but also have uncovered many mysteries. One of the most mysterious findings is that the very early universe had perfect or near-perfect order, much like a perfect crystal. Something "broken" or fallen from the spiritual realm, as described by FAM, is consistent with this initial high order.

The source of the very early universe — An unstable universe that evolves from a non-physical, or nearly non-physical, beginning is consistent with the idea that it came from an undetectable non-physical event. It would look to us as if it came from nothing. The fall of the angels could be the source of that non-physical event.

The fine-tuning issue — Scientists also tell us that many of the constants of nature have values that, if slightly different, would result in a universe that could not evolve life and consciousness as we know it. For most people, this is an obvious indication of design. However, as in the broken vase example, the design could be of something more holistic than simply the individual pieces. With FAM, there is a holistic perspective where the "pieces" come from a non-physical realm of life and

consciousness. Therefore, it should not be a surprise that these pieces have something within them that allows a path back to life and consciousness.

The scientific method — We pointed out in Chapter 3 that scientists are now developing some theories that cannot be scientifically verified. The mystery is that this contradicts the very basis of the scientific method. Scientists are being forced to do this because the underlying reality itself is not-so-physical, perhaps even in some cases undetectable. We feel that the categories of physical, not-so-physical, and non-physical are the logical place to start addressing this increasingly important issue.

The fallen angels —-FAM provides insights into the fall that relate it to the creation and evolution of our universe.

The material body and the immaterial soul — The most accepted explanation of the evolution of the human body that is consistent with religious belief is that God infuses an undetectable, immortal soul into each human being. The mystery is how can a non-physical entity (the soul) affect a physical entity (the body). The current paradigm which completely separates the non-physical from the physical provides for no connection or interface. The concept of the not-so-physical can help with this mystery. With this view, one accepts as reality that the body is made-up of molecules and atoms, which are themselves made-up of not-so-physical, fundamental particles. Perhaps the non-physical soul can interact

with the non-physical aspects of the fundamental particles in the body. This is consistent with everything we are presenting.

Where did evil come from? — We cover this mystery and the new insights that FAM has to offer in the next chapter.

Chapter 10

The Mystery of Where Evil Came From

The mystery of where evil came from, given a good God as creator, is one of the most difficult mysteries of all.

Scripture tells us that God created the universe and everything that He created was good. However, there is the mystery that the universe is full of suffering, death, and evils of all kinds. Grappling with the problem and source of evil is a serious pastoral issue as explained here:

> More people have abandoned their faith because of the problem of evil than for any other reason. It is certainly the greatest test of faith, the greatest temptation to unbelief. And it's not just an intellectual objection. We feel it. We live it. That's why the Book of Job is so arresting.
>
> The problem can be stated very simply: If God is so good, why is his world so bad? If an all-good, all-wise, all-loving, all-just, and all-powerful God is running the show, why does he seem to be doing such a miserable job of it? Why do bad things happen to good people?" — Peter Kreeft, The Catholic Education Resource Center —https://www.catholiceducation.org/en/culture/catholic-contributions/the-problem-of-evil.html

Atheists argue that the problem of evil proves there is no God.

> The problem of evil is the greatest emotional obstacle to belief in God. It just doesn't feel like God should let people suffer. If we were God, we think, we wouldn't allow it.
>
> The atheist philosopher J. L. Mackie maintained that belief in God was irrational, for if God were all-knowing (omniscient) he would know that there was evil in the world, if he were all-powerful (omnipotent) he could prevent it, and if he were all-good (omnibenevolent) then he would wish to prevent it. The fact that there is still evil in the world proves that God doesn't exist, or if he did, that he must be "impotent, ignorant, or wicked." — Matt Fradd, Catholic Answers
>
> —https://www.catholic.com/magazine/online-edition/the-problem-of-evil

An initial insight into this mystery of evil comes from St. Thomas Aquinas: "For evil is the absence of the good, which is natural and due to a thing." — St. Thomas Aquinas, *Summa Theologica*, Vol I (Q. 49 A 1). In other words, evil is not a "thing." It is a lack of something needed, or something broken, e.g., a broken leg. That is an example of a physical evil. Our world is full of physical evils like this which involve suffering and death.

Moral evil results from freely chosen conscious acts that are not in accord with God's will. Creatures with free will necessarily have the ability to choose evil or they are not really free.

God created these angels of light, as He created everything to be 'good'. Yet He also created them to be free, because only free creatures can experience love. Love cannot be coerced, or it ceases to be love. — Scott Hahn, *Joy to the World: How Christ's Coming Changed Everything,* New York: Image, 2014 (p. 84; this is part of an earlier quote from Scott Hahn that was presented in Chapter 8.)

Scripture speaks of a sin of these angels. This "fall" consists in the free choice of these created spirits, who radically and irrevocably *rejected* God and his reign. We find a reflection of that rebellion in the tempter's words to our first parents: "You will be like God." The devil "has sinned from the beginning"; he is "a liar and the father of lies." — *Catechism of the Catholic Church* (CCC 392).

God created man a rational being, conferring on him the dignity of a person who can initiate and control his own actions. "God willed that man should be "left in the hand of his own counsel," so that he might of his own accord seek his Creator and freely attain his full and blessed perfection by cleaving to him" *Genesis* 17: *Sir* 15:14. "Man is rational and therefore like God; he is created with free will and is master over his acts. — St. Irenaeus, *Adv. haeres.* 4.4.3: PG 7/1, 983. — *Catechism of the Catholic Church* (CCC 1730).

The issue of physical evil is addressed in *The Catechism of the Catholic Church.*

> But why did God not create a world so perfect that no evil could exist in it? With infinite power God could always create something better. But with infinite wisdom and goodness God freely willed to create a world "in a state of journeying" towards its ultimate perfection. In God's plan this process of becoming involves the appearance of certain beings and the disappearance of others, the existence of the more perfect alongside the less perfect, both constructive and destructive forces of nature. With physical good there exists also physical evil as long as creation has not reached perfection. *Catechism of the Catholic Church* (CCC 310).

In the FAM paradigm, connections can be made that correlate physical evil with the free will action of the fallen angels. With FAM, everything God creates is good, namely the spiritual realm and the angels with free will. FAM provides the insight that the fall of the angels could have resulted in the beginning of the evolving universe. As pointed out above, one would expect an evolving universe to be a trial-and-error process full of suffering, death, and evil.

Appendix A

Physics and the Not-So-Physical

Appendix A1

The Electron

"The electron, as it leaves the atom,
crystallizes out of Schrödinger's mist like
a genie emerging from his bottle."
—Sir Arthur Stanley Eddington

Everything we touch and feel is made up of atoms. What we actually physically touch are the electrons and their fields. We do not touch the inside of an atom.

If waves pass through two narrow, parallel slits they will produce a particular interference pattern at a distance from the slits. This is true for all waves, whether they're light waves, water waves, or sound waves. When single electrons are sent through a double slit apparatus an interference pattern builds up as the screen records each individual electron impact. They show both wave and particle behaviors.

In the Davisson–Germer experiment (1923-1927), an electron beam was reflected off a surface of a crystal of nickel metal and displayed a diffraction pattern. In other words, it demonstrated that the electron beam behaved in a particle-wave manner.

There are two conceptually different ways for physicists to interpret the mystery of the wave-particle duality of small particles such as the electron. Both interpretations, however, ultimately require the electron to behave in ways that are not-so-physical because its behavior cannot be described before measurement. Both interpretations also involve an inherent randomness in the motion and the ability to predict trajectories is only probabilistic.

The most common of the particle interpretations is called the Copenhagen Interpretation. In this case, the electron is associated with a mathematical entity called the wave function. With this view, the "particle" is not-so-physical because it does not actually have a defined position or a defined velocity as it moves along.

Physicists use a mathematical equation of the wave function to calculate the probability of where the moving particle will be measured. At the time of the measurement, the mathematical wave function "collapses" and then it is certain where the electron encountered the measuring device.

The uncertainty principle of quantum mechanics applies to the electron. It states that the position and momentum of any quantum particle cannot simultaneously be known with complete accuracy. Also, unlike the photon, since it has mass, it can be at rest. But it never is exactly at rest. There is always a blur in exactly where it is and how much momentum it has. According to the quantum field theory interpretation, it is not really a particle, but an excitation in the electron field. The

wave collapse is non-local because the collapse happens faster than the speed of light. Non-local is described in Appendix A4.

In the quantum world, the electron cannot be directly measured in a purely straightforward physical manner. The uncertainty principle must be taken into account for the specific meaning of a measurement. Quantum mechanics can only predict the probability of where the electron will be and the measurement itself is subject to the uncertainty principle.

The electron and all its configurations in all the various elements make up our contact with the everyday world. Atoms have specific shells of energy with a specific number of electrons. Atoms make up molecules, and molecules make up everything we call physical.

Yet the concept of the electron is blurry because physics cannot describe its behavior as a particle before measurement, and as a wave it has a non-local aspect in the wave collapse.

Appendix A2

The Aharonov-Bohm (AB) Experiment

The AB experiment demonstrated the real existence of a mysterious field, called the vector potential. It is a "real" field, i.e., effects of its presence can be detected in the laboratory. However, its actual strength cannot, in principle, be measured, and it behaves internally, according to Aharonov and others, in a non-local manner.

The vector potential and its effect in this experiment clearly illustrates the boundary of the physical and not-so-physical.

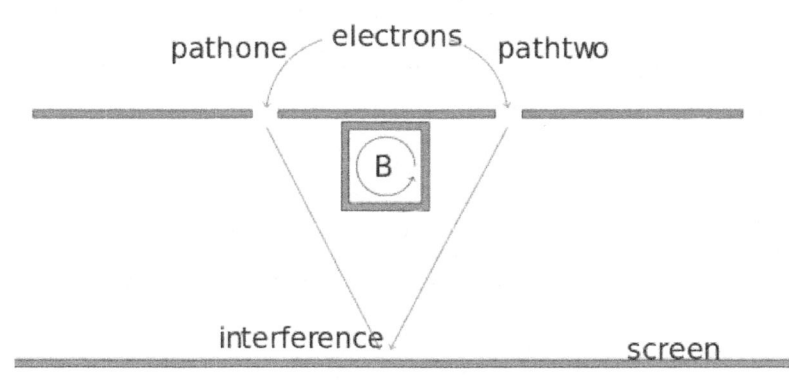

Figure A1. The Aharonov-Bohm Effect (a)

We explain this experiment in a very simplified manner. The solenoid in the illustration in Figure A1 is completely shielded, as indicated by the box in this figure, to ensure that there is no magnetic field outside of the solenoid. Then, the beam of electrons is split, and two electron beams are sent past the shielded solenoid. Then the two beams are recombined into one beam. When there is a magnetic flux present inside the solenoid the electrons exhibit a wave interference pattern on a detector screen as predicted by quantum mechanics. This wave interference pattern depends on the phase difference of the two electron wavefunctions.

Action at a distance in physics refers to one object affecting another object separated in space without actual physical contact between them. It appears that the magnetic field is acting at a distance. That it is somehow reaching out beyond the shield around the solenoid and affecting the beams.

To understand the AB effect, physicists attribute the interaction of a field called the *vector potential* with the electron wave functions. This field changes the phases of the electron wave functions to produce an interference pattern.

Before this experiment was actually performed, the vector potential was not considered a real field; rather, it was understood to be a mathematical property used to describe and simplify the calculations of the Maxwell equations describing electromagnetic theory.

In 1959, Yakir Aharonov and David Bohm proposed an experiment to demonstrate the potential terms mathematically

present in the Schrödinger equations would do what we just described.

To explain the results of this experiment, it is necessary to choose between action at a distance from the magnetic field inside the shielded solenoid or conclude that the vector potential is a real field acting on the electron wavefunction. As a real field, it is detectable only in an indirect way. The vector potential is not a classical force field. The AB effect is a quantum effect.

We provide this quote from the famous physicist Richard Feynman.

> Feynman [13] has discussed the 'reality' (his quotation marks) of the vector potential. He gives two different definitions of reality (a) a real field is a mathematical function we use to avoid the idea of action at a distance. His second definition is (b) a real field is the set of numbers we specify in such a way that what happens at a point depends only on the numbers at that point. —A.M. Stewart arXiv2014v5 25/4/14 Page 7 of 12.
> —https://arxiv.org/ftp/arxiv/papers/1209/1209.2050.pdf

This is a quantum mechanical effect, and the apparatus has to be carefully set up to demonstrate the physics. Figure A2 is an illustration that shows the essence of the experiment.

The Aharonov Bohm effect describes a field that is real, detectable, but not measurable and has non-local properties. It

is not measurable because its actual value has no physical significance. Only changes in the field over distance or time can be detected or measured. To study the non-local aspect, we provide a link to a paper by Yakir Aharonov, Eliahu Cohen, and Daniel Rohrlich.

— https://arxiv.org/abs/1502.05716

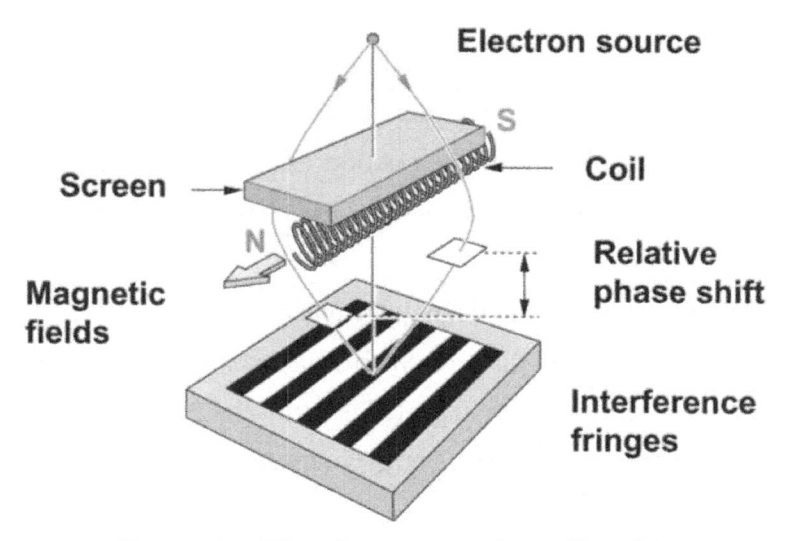

Figure A2. The Aharonov-Bohm Effect (b)

— https://www.ncbi.nlm.nih.gov/pmc/articles/PMC4323049/

The above link is to an excellent article that explains the AB effect research and results. These experiments illustrate a blur between the physical and the not-so-physical. The vector potential is real, but not-so-physical.

Appendix A3

Virtual Particles, Hypothetical Beables, and the Quantum Soup

When two particles collide, they can annihilate one another and create a new and different pair of particles. The mysterious "virtual particle" can be understood as mediating this interaction. It is not a "real" particle, but is transitory, short-lived, and undetectable.

We can think of the virtual particle as a short-lived disturbance in the underlying field. Such a disturbance is not as permanent as the fundamental particles themselves and only exists long enough to transfer the energy and momentum of an interaction.

Throughout this book, we have made a distinction between what is "real" and what is "physical." The virtual particle, the temporary disturbance, is real in the sense that it works in the calculations and can be understood as a disturbance of the underlying fields. However, since it's not detectable, it satisfies our definition of being not-so-physical, and perhaps even non-physical.

Physicists are currently exploring concepts that so far cannot be verified experimentally. They are interesting because they may be pointing towards future insights into the nature of

physical existence. They definitely are pointing in the direction of the not-so-physical, and maybe the non-physical.

Sometimes, we run out of words trying to explain the entities of the quantum domain. We cannot escape the fact that the exact nature of the particle or the field cannot be pinned down. When we get to this point, it is difficult to stay in physics and to not drift into philosophy.

The term "beable" in theoretical physics can have many meanings. Just the very idea that it might be real gets it the label beable. It may exist for a very short time or under only very constrained conditions. It may be indistinguishable from other beables that are defined in a particular way.

Here are a few hypothetical beables/particles/fields:

a) Right after the Big Bang, cosmologists proposed there was an inflation period when the universe appears to expand very rapidly. We can see in the ultra-deep space photo taken by the Hubble telescope a mind-boggling density of galaxies. Through computer modeling, we can study the strands and fibers of the overall three-dimensional structure of the galaxies' locations. To help explain inflation, cosmologists consider the idea of an inflationary field. The quanta of this field are called inflatons.

b) A *tachyon* is a hypothetical particle that always moves faster than light.

c) The *axion* is proposed as a possible component of dark matter.

d) Weakly interacting massive particles *(WIMPs)* are hypothetical particles that are thought by many to constitute dark matter.

e) The *graviton* is a hypothetical elementary particle that mediates the force of gravitation in the framework of quantum field theory. The recent discovery of gravitational waves confirms the not-so-physical field nature of spacetime. Here are some references that detail the experiments:

https://brilliant.org/wiki/gravitational-waves/

https://www.scientificamerican.com/article/is-gravity-quantum/

https://www.quantamagazine.org/gravitational-waves-discovered-at-long-last-20160211/

f) A possible non-physical beable is the Goldstone Boson.

In the Standard Theory of particle physics, one of the four major forces of nature, the weak force, obtains its mass through an interaction with the Goldstone Boson. Bosons are one of the two fundamental classes of particles, the other being fermions.

The Goldstone boson is defined as a massless, scalar field with zero spin. From this definition it is easy to ask: "Is the Goldstone boson actually physical?

From an often-quoted Quantum Field Theory text-book:

"The fact that this mass is gauge-dependent is a signal that the Goldstone boson is a fictious field, which will not be produced in physical processes."

— *An Introduction to Quantum Field Theory*, Peskin and Schroeder (p. 734).

Many other presentations state that massless scalar particles do not belong to any reasonable theory of nature. We do not observe such particles. However, Goldstone bosons must appear in the theoretical equations.

We see them in the equations, but because they are non-physical, we only see the results of their presence in the laboratory.

g) Supersymmetry is a theory that proposes that every type of particle has one or more "super partners." If supersymmetry is true, every type of elementary particle in the Standard Theory would necessarily have partners that we have not yet discovered. There are ongoing experiments at CERN that are searching for physics theories beyond the Standard Model.

https://home.cern/science/physics/supersymmetry

https://atlas.cern/updates/physics-briefing/edge-susy

Of course, none of the particles, fields, or mixtures we have been discussing exist in isolation. We can think of the collection of a volume of all these beables and fields to be some kind of "soup." It is a big bowl of interactions and in its entirety

a blended mixture of the not-so-physical and likely the non-physical.

> Isolated material particles are abstractions, their properties being definable and observable only through their interaction with other systems. —*Atomic Physics and the Description of Nature,* (1934) Neils Bohr

If we examine volumes of spacetime, some in matter-dense regions and others in near-vacuum regions, there will be self-field interactions and other field interactions. We will not be able to calculate the mixture of indistinguishable particles and all the possible kinds of superposition and entanglement of fields and their excitations. It would be an indescribable soup of not-so-physical existence. Julian Schwinger expresses the need for a holistic interpretation as follows:

> Is the purpose of theoretical physics to be no more than a cataloging of all the things that can happen when particles interact with each other and separate? Or is it to be an understanding at a deeper level in which there are things that are not directly observable (as the underlying quantized fields are) but in terms of which we shall have a more fundamental understanding? — *Quantum Mechanics - Symbolism of Atomic Measurements,* Julian Schwinger. https://www.goodreads.com/author/quotes/118871.Julian_Schwinger

Instead of trying to visualize one isolated quantum, we need to understand its existence in the context of its environment.

> This is all fiction, of course, due in part to the fact that bare particles are never seen in the physical world and can never be measured. — *Student Friendly Quantum Field Theory, Second Edition,* (2015) Robert D. Klauber (p. 318).

We discuss the early cosmology of the Big Bang in Appendix A9. The particle physics of the primordial soup of the unified fields at 10^{-43} seconds are being studied in the most powerful particle colliders in the world. See Figure A3 for a picture of The Large Hadron Collider (LHC).

Figure A3. A Picture of the Collision Section of The Large Hadron Collider (LHC) (CERN)

Now the most powerful particle colliders in the world are recreating this primordial soup by heating matter beyond 3.6 trillion degrees Fahrenheit (2 trillion degrees Celsius). The hope is that a better understanding of quark-gluon plasmas can shed light on the evolution of the universe.

—https://www.livescience.com/21715-big-bang-quark-gluon-plasma.html

We have reviewed some of the possible particles/beables/fields that can be incorporated into existing theories or used to develop new theories. The point we would like to make is that physicists need the not-so-physical beables to explain the blurry boundary that they would like to avoid. Of course, they would have preferred not talking about anything that is not physical, but they have to go where the physics takes them.

It is not wild speculation or some hidden agenda that brings us to this view. Physics itself is telling us that there are some not-so-physical, and perhaps non-physical, beables in their theories.

By including, rather than excluding, the other side of the physical boundary, we believe that it is possible to create new theories and insights that can lead to a deeper understanding of spacetime reality.

There is currently no complete theory which can keep track of the physical and the not-so-physical. It seems the more physicists press for clarity, the more they find "the blur."

Appendix A4

Non-locality and Entanglement

"The phenomenon of entanglement is the essential fact of quantum mechanics, the fact that makes it so different from classical physics. It brings into question our entire understanding about what is real in the physical world..."
—Leonard Susskind

What is meant in physics by non-local and entangled?

Imagine two particles separated by a large distance. What if we measure some value of one of the particles, which is undetermined until we measure it, and this allows us to instantly (or near instantly) know what the corresponding, previously undetermined, value of the other particle would be if we measured it? Since according to the laws of physics nothing can move faster than the speed of light, we would have a problem in figuring out the connection between them. However, quantum mechanics actually predicts that this will happen.

A faster than light interaction like this is referred to as a non-local effect. According to the laws of physics, two separate particles cannot interact like this. That would allow us to transfer information at a speed faster than light, and that is not possible according to current theories and never has been observed. However, according to quantum mechanics, "entangled" particles should be able to correlate quantum information between themselves this way. Unfortunately, however, we cannot use entangled particles to transmit information faster than light.

Entanglement is a quantum mechanical property that has to do with two particles interacting in such a way that they behave in many ways as a single particle. They are sort of mixed together and lose their individual properties.

An experiment to confirm the possibility of non-local effects between entangled particles was performed in 1982 by Alain Aspect. The experiment has been repeated with increasing accuracy many times since then. The results have always confirmed a non-local connection between the two entangled particles separated by a large distance. All attempts to explain this by saying that the variables actually have pre-existing values, but which are hidden from us, have been proven wrong.

At this point it is universally accepted that moving quantum particles do not have actual, specific values for position and momentum. There are also non-local effects that occur within an entangled pair of particles when a specific property of one these particles is measured.

In summary, the non-local effects of entangled particles that are predicted by quantum mechanics have been experimentally verified. These effects have been detected and measured many different times, but the non-local behavior itself cannot be completely described by physics. Entangled quantum particles are, therefore, not-so-physical according to the definition provided in Chapter 3.

Appendix A5

The Reality of the Not-So-Physical

As discussed in Chapter 3, the fundamental fields and particles of our universe, which have been discovered and are studied in physics, meet our description of being not-so-physical. We mentioned examples that include fields that are detectable, but not measurable, and the fundamental particles themselves, which behave in ways that cannot be completely described by the laws of physics.

By clearly describing the terms physical, not-so-physical and non-physical, we have established a distinction between "real" and "physical." There is a continuum among the physical, not-so-physical, and non-physical, but not between the real and the physical. Physical is real, but everything that is real need not be physical. That's one of the major points we are making in this book. The implications, three of which were addressed in Chapter 3, are very important. Making this distinction is only a natural and expected exercise because the world is having to come to terms with the blurry nature of reality.

There have been no new physics principles or laws developed or claimed here, but what is new is a labeling convention or description of the categories of not-so-physical and non-

physical, yet both are real. We go into more detail here about what it means to say: "cannot be described by the laws of physics." It simply means that the complete behavior of a system cannot be explained with known laws of physics given enough information about the starting conditions. Thus, if the outcome is, at best, only statistically predictable, then any given single "particle" is not following any known law of physics.

An example of this is when an atom absorbs a photon. We can only discuss the "likeliness" of the absorption event, not that it will actually happen. The laws of physics for quantum mechanics deal with the probabilities and the statistical outcomes of events. Quantum mechanics is a very powerful tool, and even a macro-quantum system like a laser is very well understood by quantum physics. Yet down at the single quantum level, quantum mechanics can't predict which specific atoms will be involved in the lasing action with 100% certainty. Therefore, we call these quanta of matter and energy not-so-physical, but they are real. As stated earlier, a brief description of quantum mechanics is provided in Appendix A6.

Another example is the electron which is detectable and measurable. However, when passing through a double slit, there is no law of physics that can say which slit the electron will pass through or where it will land on the screen in the distance. However, the accumulation of particles is typically more important, and quantum mechanics is very good at giving this outcome. But again, down at the individual quantum level, it gives no certainty of any electron's individual path.

If it is a particle, then its path cannot be explained. If it is a spread-out wave, then its faster-than-light collapse to a point on the detector cannot be explained. Thus, even electrons can be said to be not-so-physical. However, electrons are real indeed.

These two examples can be contrasted with a baseball being hit with a baseball bat. As soon as the baseball leaves the bat, its entire trajectory can be described accurately with equations that predict which seat in the bleachers a home run hit will land. Another example of a predictable system is flipping a coin. It is commonly believed that if enough information is gathered about the initial velocity, rotation rate, air currents, floor roughness, etc., then it could be predicted whether a coin would land heads or tails. This is certainly NOT the case with quantum systems.

One consequence of accepting the reality of the not-so-physical is that it allows a reasonable, although necessarily not fully physical, explanation of the quantum experiments. A very short example is that the electron is a spread-out entity as it goes through both slits and then really does collapse in faster-than-light way at the detector. The full paper describing this interpretation is presented in Appendix B. It was originally developed in 1996 by one of the authors of this book after he realized that the electron has behaviors that are not-so-physical. It's called the ProWave Interpretation of Quantum Mechanics.

So, why hasn't it been necessary to make the distinction between "real" and "physical" until now? One of the main reasons for this is to keep the Standard Model of particle physics that the physics community in general has maintained for most of a century: Materialism is the law of the land. By blurring the line between real and physical, physicists are able to postulate all kinds of intermediate particles and force carriers but still shirk off any postulates of spirituality or non-physical reality because it can't be proven real. The discussions today have resolved not to discuss anything outside the current laws of physics such as the deepest meaning of the particle/wave duality. Confined to only dealing with macro-statistical behavior of quantum mechanical predictions, modern think-ing puts no effort into a discussion of the non-physical or of spirituality. This "material world" worldview, which is referred to as materialism, has not only been challenged by our clear logic in this book, but has been proven wrong and is no longer a valid position to hold.

There are non-physical fields and excitations of such fields that exist in reality. They are undetectable, unmeasurable and behave in ways that are beyond the laws of physics. However, they are part of the very foundation of the physical part of the universe and essential to the formulation of the Standard Model of particle physics.

Appendix A6

Quantum Mechanics and the Not-So-Physical

*"It is often stated that of all the theories
proposed in this century, the silliest is
quantum theory. In fact, some say that
the only thing that quantum theory has
going for it is that it is unquestionably
correct." —Michio Kaku*

There are many different ways to interpret the not-so-physical findings of modern physics. Almost everything that can be thought of has been tried, including trying to ignore the issue. However, the time of ignoring this issue has passed. In this appendix we'll look at a few of the more popular interpretations, and then suggest a path forward.

First, it will be very helpful to discuss the key postulates of quantum mechanics in a simple, most-accepted way.

- Every quantum mechanical system can be described by a mathematical "Schrödinger Wave Function" that evolves over time.

- The wave function depends on time, the positions of the entities in the system, and the forces acting on, and among, the entities. Note that the forces are actually embedded in the Schrödinger Equation in terms of potential energies.
- Only certain outcomes are possible, which are the specific matter wave solutions to the Schrödinger Equation. The outcomes are random for equal energy states, and the probabilities of these random outcomes can be computed by operating on the wave function at the time of the expected measurement.

The real postulates are more complicated than this, but this will suffice for our purposes.

Closely related to these postulates is something called the Heisenberg Uncertainty Principle, which states that you cannot know both the position and the velocity of a moving particle to arbitrary accuracy. In other words, the more you know about the position, the less you can know about the velocity (or momentum) and vice versa.

If you just use the postulates, and apply the appropriate mathematics, you can predict the statistical outcomes of experiments. Predictions using these postulates, and the associated mathematics, have been verified many, many times in all kinds of different experiments all over the world. The use of quantum mechanics is not controversial.

However, once the question: "What's going on before the measurement is made?" is asked, all kinds of disagreements

and different interpretations spring up. Let's look at three of the many available interpretations.

We'll consider the Copenhagen Interpretation because it is one of the original and perhaps still the most accepted interpretation. According to this interpretation, the particle does not have a specific position or velocity before measurement, and, in fact, it does not make sense to even ask the question. However, at the moment a measurement is taken, the mathematical wave function randomly "collapses" to one of the possible outcomes.

The de Broglie-Bohm Interpretation argues that there is a pilot wave, which deterministically guides the particle in a nonlocal way. Key to this approach is the quantum potential term which can be derived from the Schrödinger equation.

Finally, we will consider the ProWave Interpretation, which is in line with quantum field theory, written by one of our co-authors. This original interpretation argues that the mass and energy of the "particle" are spread out in a wave packet before the measurement. At the instant of the measurement, the wave packet collapses in a faster-than-light, nonlocal event to the location where the measurement is made. The key difference is that there is never an actual particle, but rather the experiment demonstrates the wave nature of the electron. (See Appendix B: The ProWave Interpretation by Dan R. Provenzano)

There are dozens of other interpretations with different descriptions, however, there is no universally accepted interpretation among physicists.

The important point is that ALL of the interpretations about the most basic elements of reality using quantum mechanics and quantum field theory include aspects that are not-so-physical. This observation leads directly to a conclusion.

The underlying reality of our observable universe is not-so-physical. This means that materialism is no longer a valid description of reality.

In other words, the findings of modern physics and the fact that there is no purely physical way to explain the underlying reality described by modern physics tell us that the underlying reality itself is not purely physical.

Yet another way to say this is that our "physical universe" is not completely physical. It emerged from not-so-physical fields and remains dependent on them for its very existence.

Note that the wave function is a mathematical representation that corresponds to the underlying reality. However, the wave function itself should not be considered a real, existing entity.

This is consistent with quantum field theory (QFT), which describes the reality underlying our physical world as fields. These QFT fields, in themselves, are not detectable. We can only detect the excitations of these fields, which are the fundamental "particles" of nature.

Rather than say fields that have non-measurable attributes and exhibit non-local behaviors have no real existence, or cannot be discussed, we prefer to say that they do have a real, but not a purely physical, i.e., a not-so-physical, existence.

We are making a distinction between "real" and "physical." In other words, it makes sense to say that since these fields with not-so-physical attributes are needed for us to predict the way the physical world behaves, they must have some kind of real existence in spacetime.

For many people, "real existence" and "physical existence" mean the exactly the same thing, and this is a deeply entrenched concept. This concept made much more sense when the universe was thought to be fully explained by classical physics. However, that is exactly the concept that is disproven by modern physics. Consider the Table A1 below, first presented in Chapter 3, to help clarify this distinction.

	Physical Existence	Real Existence
Physical Entities	*Yes*	*Yes*
Not-so-Physical Entities	*Partial*	*Yes*
Non-Physical Entities	*No*	*Yes*

Table A1. Kind of Entities vs. Types of Existence

Physical, Not-So-Physical and Non-Physical Entities correspond to the descriptions provided in Chapter 3. Physical Existence means actually exists, outside of our minds, in reality, and is (at least in principle) detectable, measurable, and can be described by the laws of physics. Real existence means actually exists, outside of our minds, in reality, whether or not it is detectable, measurable, or can be described by the laws of physics. Everything that has physical existence has real existence, but not everything that has real existence has physical existence.

The physical existence and real existence of physical entities is obvious. Scientific results make a convincing case for the real existence of not-so-physical entities (fields and excitations of fields) based on the actual experimental findings of modern physics. See Appendices A1 and A2. Examples of potential non-physical entities, typically fields or excitations of fields, are provided in Appendix A3.

The distinction between physical existence and real existence is simply an admission that our ability to detect, measure and describe is not what defines reality. Not only is modern physics pointing us in the direction of the real existence of not-so-physical and even non-physical fields, but it's even giving us ways to visualize and imagine aspects of these realms. According to quantum field theory, fields are the underlying aspects of all types of reality.

In summary, the real existence of not-so-physical and non-physical fields is just an open acceptance of what physics is

telling us and a willingness to see where it might lead us. This conclusion unlocks the door to new insights that have never been possible before. Some additional insights are provided in Appendix A10.

Appendix A7

Spiritual Time

Space and time as we know them were created at the moment of the Big Bang. Physics can start to explain the beginning of the universe at 10^{-43} seconds (Planck Time) after the Big Bang. The fields present at this time were unstable and their constant evolution is deeply connected with the passage of time.

Planck time is the time it would take a photon traveling at the speed of light to cross a distance equal to the Planck length. This is the 'quantum of time,' the smallest measurement of time that has any meaning in physics and is equal to 10^{-43} seconds. No smaller division of time has any meaning. Within the framework of the laws of physics as we understand them today, we can say that the universe came into existence when it had an age of 10^{-43} seconds.

— https://physlink.com/education/askexperts/ae281.cfm

As stated in Chapter 4, physicists cannot discuss a time "before" the Big Bang because time was created at the instant of the Big Bang.

The only way that we can conceive of God creating the universe is to think of God existing before and after He created it. These terms do not imply that God is somehow inside of

time as we know it. He created time as we know it. So, when we say "before" the Big Bang, we are referring to God's time or some kind of "spiritual time." When we say "time," we are referring to time as we know it in physics, the regular time that's part of our spacetime universe.

There's not a lot we can say about spiritual time, but we can make some distinctions between the two kinds of time. We live in the physical world with its four known space-time dimensions of length, width, height (or depth), and time. God dwells in a different realm—the spiritual realm—beyond the natural perception of our physical senses. In the spiritual realm, the underlying structures are stable, but there is a sequence of conscious, intentional events. However, there is not necessarily any passage of spiritual time between these events. God is not limited by the physical laws and dimensions that govern our world (Isaiah 57:15). He is spirit (John 4:24).

God exists independently of time: "But there is one thing, my dear friends, that you must never forget: that with the Lord, a day is like a thousand years, and a thousand years are like a day" (2 Peter 3:8).

Appendix A8

Fine-Tuning Issue

*"If everyone is thinking alike, then
somebody isn't thinking."*
—George S. Patton

Science has found that a lot of "coincidences" related to the values of the fundamental constants of nature are needed in order for life and consciousness as we know them to have evolved. The coincidence topic was originally named the Anthropic Principle but is now more often called the Fine-Tuning Argument. The facts are not controversial, but the interpretations are very controversial.

Some of the facts that make up this issue are the following:

- The ratio of the mass of the proton to the mass of the electron must be very close to what it is for atoms to hold together;

- The charge of the proton and the electron are equal;

- The relative strengths of the nuclear and magnetic forces must be very close to what it is for atoms to hold together;

- The unique properties of water (ice floats);

-The expansion rate of the universe. If the expansion rate were much less than the actual value, the universe would have collapsed before life could have formed. If it were much greater, the formation of stars, which are needed for life, could not have formed;

- The list of coincidences goes on and on....

The point is that if any of these properties of nature were only slightly different—matter, life, and consciousness as we know them could not have evolved. Clearly, these coincidences seem to imply that our universe was somehow designed or tuned to produce life and consciousness.

Those who believe in God tend to be happy with this discovery and many have used it to argue that God must have directly designed the physical universe. However, if that is the case, then God is responsible for all the evil, suffering, and death in the universe. That problem is discussed in Chapter 10. Furthermore, as a method of producing life and consciousness, it is certainly not very efficient given the billions of galaxies in the universe.

Those who do not believe in God have had a lot of difficulty with this discovery. Their only argument is that there are an infinite number of separate universes. Each universe has a different combination for the values of the constants. Therefore, there has to be at least one universe that would have this seemingly "tuned" values for the constants. Since we have evolved, we must be in that universe. The other universes are not detectable. This is called the multiverse solution. Obvious-

ly, this is a philosophical solution, not a physics solution, because we can't test it experimentally.

William of Ockham was a philosopher who lived in the fourteenth century. He is most famous for a principle he developed called "Ockham's Razor." According to this principle the solution with the fewest assumptions is probably the correct solution. The multiverse solution has to be the greatest violation of Ockham's Razor in the history of philosophy. What could have more assumptions than needing to assume an infinite number of undetectable universes to make a position hold together?

The bottom line is that Fine-Tuning certainly shows essentially unarguable evidence of design in the physical universe. However, we believe that the design is at a higher, non-physical level. This new way of considering design at a higher level is part of the Fallen Angel Model (FAM) and is described in Chapter 8.

Appendix A9

Big Bang Cosmology

"Gravity explains the motions of the planets, but it cannot explain who sets the planets in motion."
—Isaac Newton

The Big Bang Theory is the most accepted cosmological theory about how our spacetime universe began and evolved. Nevertheless, it seems like the more we learn, the more we encounter new mysteries.

According to the Big Bang Theory, the universe began about 13.8 billion years ago as an expansion of space and time. Cosmologists believe that it started as a single "Superforce" in a very small volume. The four fundamental forces of nature: electromagnetic, gravity, the weak and strong forces were somehow contained in this Superforce. There were no elementary particles present. This Superforce was highly ordered but very unstable and almost immediately started to expand and evolve. The expanding fields of the universe produced matter, stars, and eventually all the elements in the periodic table, and everything else we see in the universe today.

To focus on the earliest instant of time, we refer to a time called the Planck duration of time, or Planck's epoch. It lasted only a tiny, tiny part of a second.

Note: This extremely short period of time that starts at the beginning and lasts only 10^{-43} second (which looks like this: 0.0000000000000000000000000000000000000000001 second). Just to give you an idea of how short this duration of time is, there are a lot more Planck durations in one second than there have been seconds since the Big Bang.

The end of Planck's epoch is where cosmologists can begin to describe things. This is as far back towards the origin as cosmologists and physicists can consider. The period starting at this time is called the Grand Unification epoch and lasted only a very brief time. At the beginning of this time, the universe is thought to have been in a state of very low entropy. The special state of zero entropy represents no disorder. During this period, the four fundamental forces of nature, namely, the electromagnetic, weak, strong, and gravitational, were still united in a way that it would be impossible to individually distinguish them.

Inflation came next and very greatly expanded space in a tiny fraction of a second.

During these first three periods there were no particles. After inflation, electrons, quarks and the elementary particles started to form. The evolutionary process continued, eventually producing the universe we see around us today.

The photo in Figure A4, called the eXtreme Deep Field (XDF), was assembled by combining ten years of NASA Hubble Space Telescope photographs. They were taken in a very small patch of sky. Realize that we will see images like this in every direction we look. We are surrounded by an estimated one hundred billion galaxies. We encourage you to "fly through" the XDF at the NASA link, available online at https://youtu.be/odprMkzOst8.

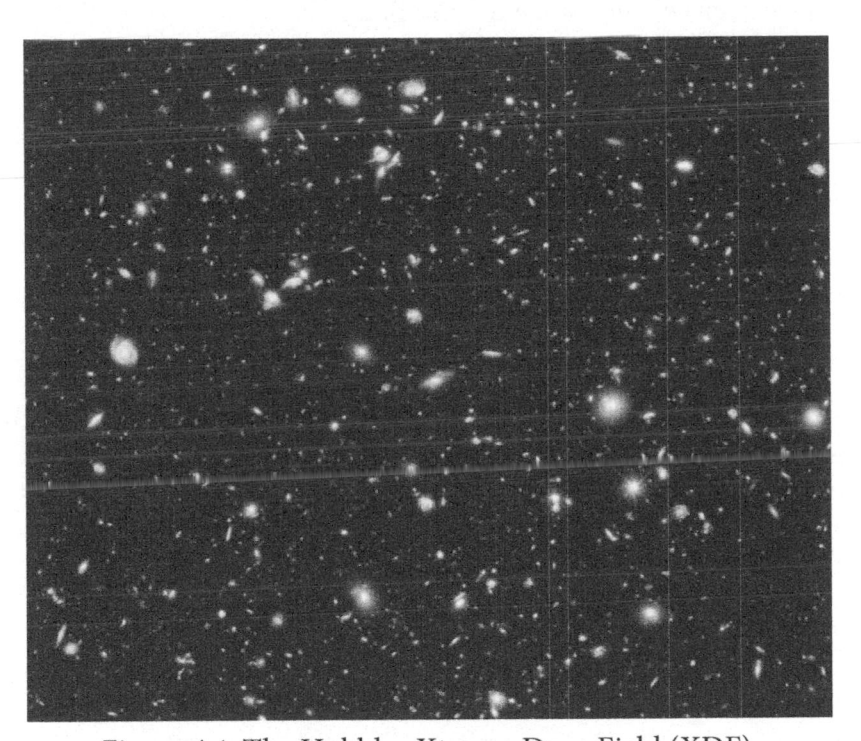

Figure A4. The Hubble eXtreme Deep Field (XDF)
https://www.nasa.gov/mission_pages/hubble/science/xdf.html

As we observe the cosmos today, the galaxies are accelerating away from one another. Cosmologists still do not have a clear answer about the physical reason for this, but the most accepted explanation is something called "dark energy." It acts as a repulsive force, pushing the universe apart, causing it to pick up speed. Astronomers can only detect it indirectly, for instance, by measuring the distance between galaxies. There needs to be a lot of it. Dark energy is thought to comprise roughly 68% of the known matter/energy in the universe.

Similarly, physicists have had to postulate something else that is not detectable to account for the way the galaxies form and hold together. This time it's an attractive force like that produced by normal matter, but it's not visible. They call it "dark matter." Again, there needs to be a lot of it. The amount of dark matter needed is about 27% of the matter/energy in the universe. Combined together, this means that 95% of the matter/energy in the universe is unknown and can't be explained.

The important point from this appendix is that the fields in the early universe meet our definition of non-physical. They can't be described by the laws of physics because the laws themselves weren't even formed yet. It makes no sense to even talk about detecting or measuring these fields in a way that could be experimentally verified. Also, this early universe "Superforce" was at a very low entropy state. The story of the history of the universe as told by modern cosmology is a story of how the non-physical fields evolved into not-so-physical

fields and finally into the physical universe we see around us today.

It's very important to note that, since we can't detect non-physical fields, it would look to us like the universe popped into existence from nothing. That's exactly the way it does look to us.

The amazing scientific discovery that our "physical" universe evolved from non-physical fields to the physical universe we see around us today deserves a lot more attention and thought than it has been given.

With the understanding that there was evolution from non-physical fields to not-so-physical fields to physical objects, we should expect to see traces of the not-so-physical remaining today. This is exactly what has happened. Finding traces of the not-so-physical is an understatement. Physics has actually discovered that the fundamental particles of nature, e.g., protons, electrons, and particles of light are, in fact, not-so-physical.

Appendix A10

The Mysteries of Complex Numbers and the Not-So-Physical

"The best that most of us can hope to achieve in physics is simply to misunderstand at a deeper level."
— *Wolfgang Pauli*

In this appendix we will show how correlating the categories of the physical, non-physical, and not-so-physical with the arithmetic of complex numbers provides insights into the mysteries of complex numbers. We will then present what others have said about the necessity of using complex numbers in quantum mechanics.

We also discuss how these three categories can help explain why complex numbers are necessary in quantum mechanics. We suggest that this representation is reflected in the complex phase of the quantum wavefunction and is an essential part of the foundations of quantum physics.

Let's begin with how complex numbers are defined.

$$c = a + bi$$

where a and b are real numbers. The number a is called the "real" part, b is called the "imaginary" part, and

$$i = \sqrt{-1}.$$

The first complete description of complex numbers with rules for their mathematical operations was published in 1572 by the Italian mathematician Rafel Bombelli. He did not use the word "imaginary." It is commonly believed that Rene Descartes first used the term "imaginary," and that he meant it in a derogatory manner. He said that we imagine these kinds of numbers, but they really don't exist. Of course, he had no way to know that they would become necessary in the development of the theories that describe the results of modern experiments. See *A Short History of Complex Numbers* by Orlando Merino for an article with more details.

— http://www.math.uri.edu/~merino/spring06/mth562/ ShortHistoryComplexNumbers2006.pdf

Obviously, complex numbers are somewhat of a mystery in themselves. However, a bigger mystery is why they are not only so helpful in quantum mechanics but are actually needed in this theory. The following quote is from Professor Leonard Susskind: "The need for complex numbers is a general feature of quantum mechanics...." *Quantum Mechanics, The Theoretical Minimum*, Leonard Susskind and Art Friedman, Basic Books, 2014 (p. 44).

Some originally thought that what is really needed in quantum mechanics is just a pair of numbers. However, physicists quickly realized that in order to do the needed mathematical

operations with a pair of numbers, rules are needed. The needed rules turn out to be the same as the rules for complex number operations. More discussion on this issue and some references are provided in the latter part of this appendix.

Let's now address the purpose of this appendix which is to show how adopting the concept, or paradigm, of the reality of the not-so-physical, along with the reality of the physical and the non-physical, can provide new insights into the mysteries related to complex numbers.

We'll start with the positive real numbers. The positive integers were most likely the first numbers used. Eventually, fractions, transcendentals, and the rest of the real numbers were being used. Somewhere in this process, we expanded the real number line to include negative real numbers. When we did this, we had to make sure that addition, subtraction, multiplication, and division between real numbers always produced real numbers. The issue of multiplication between two negative numbers needed to be either a positive or a negative number. Positive was chosen based on the logic that if a number is not, non-positive, then it is positive. The minus sign can be thought of as an operator that turns a positive real number into a negative real number and vice versa. The same solution was chosen for division.

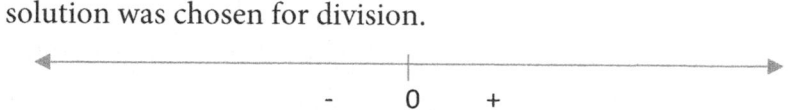

Figure A5. The real number line.

We have made the case that the strange results of the double-slit experiment and the other quantum results are telling us that our "physical" universe is not-so-physical after all. Within this paradigm, it follows that the "real" numbers, i.e., those that correspond with what we detect, measure and explain in physical terms could more accurately be called the "physical" numbers. These numbers are not able to describe what is going on when an electron is in a superposition of quantum states while moving between the double slits and the detector. Given this paradigm, it is reasonable that we would need a number system that allowed for states that contained non-physical and not-so-physical attributes and behaviors in addition to physical attributes and behaviors.

The complex numbers fit this situation perfectly. The imaginary axis is orthogonal (in a mathematical, not a space-like sense) to the real axis and complex numbers are part real and part imaginary. If we think of the real axis as corresponding to the physical aspect of reality and the imaginary axis as corresponding the non-physical aspect of reality, we see that a complex number can be interpreted as part physical and part non-physical.

$$c = a + bi$$

where a is the physical (P) part and b is the non-physical (NP) part. The number c fits our description of a real quantity that has both physical and non-physical aspects, and both really exist in nature. Note if $b = 0$, then c is a purely physical num-

ber, if $a = 0$, then c is a purely non-physical number. If both a and b are non-zero, then c is a not-so-physical (NSP) number. With the concept that the non-physical really does exist, maybe it's time to rethink using the word "imaginary" for this axis.

In quantum mechanics, equations with complex numbers are used to describe the system between measurements. However, at the point of the measurement, the equations produce probabilistic predictions of observables such as position, and these observables are always physical numbers.

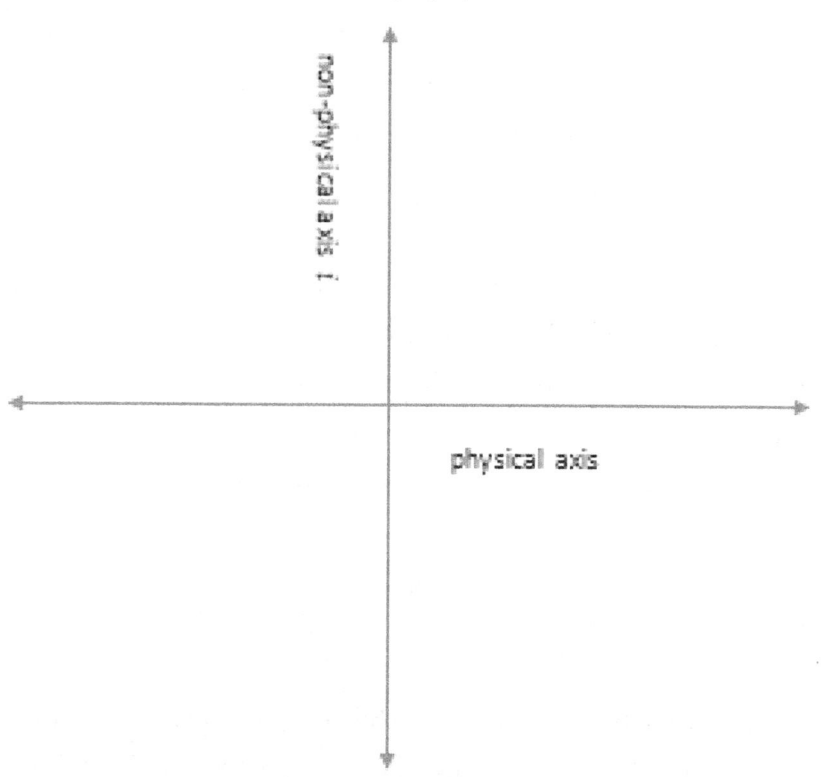

Figure A6. The complex plane with both axes considered to be real; one axis is physical and the other is non-physical.

We know that with complex numbers:

$$i = \sqrt{-1}.$$

But an interesting question is: Can we get some insights into why this is the case?

First, we know that i can't be a physical number because then $a + bi$ would be a physical number, and we would be back to physical numbers only. It has to be some kind of "non-physical" or "imaginary" number. In other words, it can't directly add, subtract, multiply or divide with physical numbers. It needs to be orthogonal to the physical numbers.

Let's apply the same criteria as we did for multiplication with negative real numbers. Let's require that the four standard processes in arithmetic on complex numbers must all produce numbers in the complex space. Addition and subtraction are easy; just add or subtract the physical and non physical parts separately. The key is multiplication. Using "NSP" as a not-so-physical number we ask the question: What does i have to be in the equation below to keep NSP in the complex space?

$$NSP = (a + bi)(c + di)$$
$$NSP = ac + (ad + bc)i + bdi^2$$

The first two terms are in the complex space. The third term, which contains i^2, is like a minus times a minus, or think of it as not, non-physical. So, if it's not, non-physical, it is

reasonable to think of it as physical. We're just using the same line of thinking as for the negative numbers. In other words, we can think that multiplying by i is an operator that turns a purely physical number into a purely non-physical number and vice-versa. So, let's make it physical and see what the implications are for i.

$$i^2 = k, \text{where } k \text{ is physical,}$$
$$i = \sqrt{k}.$$

Note that k must be < 0 because if it's not, then i would be real, and we would collapse the space into purely physical numbers. Now let k have an absolute value of 1 because k is like a unit vector in the non-physical "direction." So,

$$i = \sqrt{-1}.$$

This also works for division. It can be easily shown that the result of the division of two complex numbers results in a number that is in the complex space.

For a complete and rigorous presentation of complex numbers, see the *Feynman Lectures on Physics, Volume 1: Algebra Ch. 22*

— https://www.feynmanlectures.caltech.edu/I_22.html

It might seem that just using a pair of numbers for the physical and non-physical would be sufficient for quantum

mechanics. However, physicists quickly realized that in order to do the needed mathematical operations with a pair of numbers, rules are needed. The rules turn out to be the same as the rules for complex number operations as discussed in the two references immediately below. The first is an abstract from a physics paper by Goyal, Knuth, and Skilling:

Complex numbers are an intrinsic part of the mathematical formalism of quantum theory, and are perhaps its most characteristic feature. In this paper, we show that the complex nature of the quantum formalism can be derived directly from the assumption that a *pair* of real numbers is associated with each sequence of measurement outcomes, with the probability of this sequence being a real-valued function of this number pair. By making use of elementary symmetry conditions, and without assuming that these real number pairs have any other algebraic structure, we show that these pairs must be manipulated according to the rules of *complex* arithmetic. We demonstrate that these complex numbers combine according to Feynman's sum and product rules, with the modulus-squared yielding the probability of a sequence of outcomes.

— *Origin of Complex Quantum Amplitudes and Feynman's Rules*, by Philip Goyal, Kevin H. Knuth, and John Skilling. https://arxiv.org/pdf/0907.0909.pdf

Another example is provided in the following abstract from an article in the *American Journal of Physics,* written by Ricard Karam.

Complex numbers are broadly used in physics, normally as a calculation tool that makes things easier due to Euler's formula. In the end, it is only the real component that has physical meaning or the two parts (real and imaginary) are treated separately as real quantities. However, the situation seems to be different in quantum mechanics, since the imaginary unit *i* appears explicitly in its fundamental equations. From a learning perspective, this can create some challenges to newcomers. In this article, four conceptually different justifications for the use/need of complex numbers in quantum mechanics are presented and some pedagogical implications are discussed.
— https://aapt.scitation.org/doi/10.1119/10.0000258

One of the key places where complex numbers enter quantum theory is in the phase of a particle's wave function. As discussed in Appendix A6, wave functions are an integral part of quantum mechanics and are associated with each particle's movement. These wave functions have complex phases that are not observable. A very good description of this situation is given by Suzanne van Dam:

There are two ways to interpret the unobservable nature of the complex phases. In one interpretation it is concluded that states described by a different complex phase are physically the same and differ only in mathematical description. Another way to look at it is that the states are observationally indistinguishable, but are nevertheless physically different. *PhySci Archive Spontaneous Symmetry Breaking in the Higgs Mechanism,* Suzanne van Dam — http://philsci-archive.pitt.edu/9295/

Actually, there is third way, which is what we have proposed in this book. Limiting the interpretations to these two ways is a result of the traditional implicit assumption that the words "physical" and "real" mean exactly the same thing. By accepting that the complex phase actually exists in nature, but it is "not-so-physical" we have an insight into why the complex numbers are needed in quantum mechanics. With this approach, the complex, unobservable phase is considered to have a part that is non-physical.

Complex numbers are also used in the foundations of quantum theory. Here's an example:

1.1 First Postulate

At each instant the state of a physical system is represented by a **ket** $|\psi\rangle$ *in the space of states.*

Comments

• The space of states is a vector space. This postulate is already radical because it implies that the *superposition* of two states is again a state of the system. If $|\psi_1\rangle$ and $|\psi_2\rangle$ are possible states of a system, then so is

$$|\psi\rangle = a_1|\psi_1\rangle + a_2|\psi_2\rangle,$$

Where a_1 and a_2 are complex numbers. ...
— SUPPLEMENTARY NOTES ON DIRAC NOTA-TION, QUANTUM STATES, ETC. — R. L. Jaffe, 1996 — http://web.mit.edu/8.05/handouts/jaffe1.pdf

With the insight that complex numbers can be seen to represent or correlate to the non-physical and not-so-physical categories, one can see that these categories are present in the formulation of the quantum postulates.

In summary, considering that the fundamental particles of nature have physical and non-physical aspects provides a new insight into why the complex numbers are not only useful but are needed in quantum mechanics. All we have done is to con-sider the real axis as corresponding to the physical aspect of reality and the imaginary axis as corresponding to the non-physical aspect of reality. We have not suggested any actual changes to the physics or to the mathematics.

Appendix B

The ProWave Interpretation
of Quantum Mechanics

Dan R. Provenzano

July 27, 1996

Abstract

It is widely accepted in Quantum Mechanics that measurements reveal the particle nature of elementary quanta, but there are many interpretations on how these "particles" move from the emitter to the point of measurement. This paper introduces in the ProWave (for "Propagating Wave") Interpretation of Quantum Mechanics. The basic idea is that elementary quanta always *exist* in the form of a wave, and always *travel* in the form of a wave, described by Schrödinger evolution, but are always *measured* each at a single location. This concept replaces all interpretations based on quanta traversing a particle path with the notion of a propagating wave coupled with a new concept of "Quantum Energy Localization." It is argued in this paper that the ProWave Interpretation explains all known experimental results in a "realistic" way that would have pleased Einstein, Schrödinger, deBroglie and all those who are currently looking for a sensible way to understand the implications of Quantum Theory. As

examples, the 2-slit experiment, and EPR experiment, and a quantum eraser are interpreted in the ProWave picture.

Introduction

Classroom education on Quantum Mechanics (QM) concerns the various quantum phenomena and how to deal with them mathematically. In the laboratory, we use QM as a tool to predict measurement statistics. The experiments are repeatable, and the results are not in dispute. But when it comes to the interpretation of the theory of QM, there is much discomfort in the community. Sure, quantum phenomena are so removed from our daily experiences, and in many aspects are so counter intuitive, that it might seem only natural that our interpretation of the theory and corresponding view of reality must reflect that. Furthermore, the Complementarity Principle simply states that the elementary quanta are neither particles nor waves, but some entity that transcends both of their natures and only displays one of these attributes at a time. This principle is merely a statement of our conceptual difficulties with QM but doesn't really attempt a solution.

A semiclassical interpretation was put forth by Schrödinger who suggested that the wavefunction for matter waves is analogous to the field variables in electromagnetic waves. This interpretation was rejected long ago due to its intrinsic "nonlocality problems." However, the Bell Inequality [2] and its numerous experimental verifications have since dictated the

need for a nonlocal interpretation of quantum theory. Thus, we can start with Schrödinger's original idea, and build on it to provide an understanding as to what happens during a measurement or "collapse of the wavefunction."

The ideas for the ProWave Interpretation resulted from desperately trying to make some sense out of the various experiments and connecting them with accepted quantum theory. We now think it is possible to (at least) conceive of how these bizarre quantum effects could come about in a sensible way.

The Experiments

To date, quantum theory has been overwhelmingly confirmed by physical experiments. The need for such a theory in the first place began as the experimental results of the early 1900's could not be explained by contemporary theories. For compactness, I will describe only the quantum interference effects of photons but note that electrons and neutrons have been observed to display quantum interference as well. Below is a review of three interesting experiments, our understanding of which is controversial. These provide a good survey of the weirdness of QM. In Sections 5 and 7, the ProWave Interpretation is applied to these experiments.

A) The infamous two slit experiment involves passing light through two slits and allowing the radiation from both slits to

diffract and overlap on a distant screen. The interference fringes that are observed are attributed to the wavelike and coherent nature of the photons as they emerge from the slits. If the flux of photons is low enough such that one photon is present in the system at once, then each photon (event) produces only one localized detection at the screen. By integration of many such events, an interference pattern emerges, as predicted by the probability distribution of the wavefunction. Note that if the screen were placed sufficiently close to the slits so as to prevent overlap of diffracted waves from the slits, then each event induces local detection corresponding to the photon having been present at one of the two slits. In this case, the system probability is determined by an incoherent mixture of quantum states, where the quantum states refer to slit passage. The philosophical question raised by this whole experiment is: Does the photon pass through only one slit, or both, or can we even ask this question?

B) The Einstein, Podolsky, Rosen (EPR) Paradox [1] has been the subject of many discussions on quantum interpretations. In 1985, Alain Aspect et. al. measured the polarizations of two correlated photons at various rotation positions of his detectors [3, 4, 5]. Their *coincidence count* violated Bell's Inequality and experimentally verified that the nonlocal nature of quantum theory is real. The main question here is: How can two particles apparently "instantaneously" communicate with

each other while being physically separated by an arbitrary distance?

C) In one type of quantum eraser experiment, polarization-correlated photon pairs are emitted in opposite directions [11]. (Refer to Figure 3 later in Section 6.) They are allowed to recombine and interfere at a 50% beam splitter, with detectors at each output port. The apparatus is set up and phase controlled such that both photons of each pair are detected by the same detector, as predicted by QM. Now, a half-wave plate is inserted in one of the paths so as to rotate the polarization by 90° with respect to the other path. This removes the guarantee of interference at the beam splitter, and it becomes possible to get one "click" at each detector from a pair of correlated photons. Building on this further, inserting linear polarizers at 45° (with respect to each photon path) directly in front of each detector returns the original interference results. It is amazing that we no longer see the effect of the half-wave plate. We have essentially <u>erased</u> its effect. The deepest question raised by this experiment seems to be: Can we affect the nature of the photons in the past by manipulating the present?

Current Interpretations

The myriad of interpretations of quantum theory are all attempts to explain the meaning of reality consistent with what we know about how the quantum world behaves. All popular

interpretations are consistent with quantum theory and experimental results, and acceptance of any given interpretation implies acceptance of certain consequences regarding objective reality. We will mention a few of the more popular ones, but others can be found in the references.

1. The Copenhagen Interpretation denies any deep physical reality. Since elementary quanta cannot have simultaneous values for non-commuting observables, reality itself cannot be defined until a measurement is made.

2. The Many Worlds Interpretation accepts the existence of an infinite number of universes (complete with physical energy like our own). Several new ones are created every time a quantum system is forced into one of its eigenstates after previously existing in a coherent superposition of any basis states.

3. The Many Histories Interpretation establishes that trajectories taken by elementary quanta are obtained by "summing over the possible histories." For example, in the quantum erasure experiment, the linear polarizers have changed the set of possible histories of the photons' behaviors, thus affecting the possible outcomes of the experiment.

4. The Transactional Interpretation supports the notion that the emission and absorption of energy quanta is an indivisible, fundamental event. The nature of these

events, such as when and where, are determined a priori outside of time and before the transaction takes place. Note that under this interpretation, a photon absorbed by your skin from a star 1 million light years away was a predetermined event, 1 million years ago.

5. The Neorealist Interpretation maintains that the world is made up of ordinary objects as we are used to but permits that some of these objects move faster than the speed of light. Consequences of this interpretation include the possibility of reverse causality.

6. The No Collapse Interpretation maintains that the wavefunction describing a quantum system never collapses. We only observe and "think" that it has collapsed, while all the other non-measured states of the wavefunction are forever inaccessible. After the measurement, the continuing wavefunction no longer describes the probability of what can be measured. As an aside comment: the mathematics used in this interpretation begins with wavefunctions with several vector spaces involved, such as a measuring apparatus. Classical correlations emerge when one only studies the states of the apparatus. A major problem is that the mathematics needs to assume "collapse" theory to even begin writing down an initial wavefunction. Otherwise, each quantum has an incredibly complex past wavefunction whose components in each space are likely to possess orthogonalities, destroying quantum inter-

ference. In short, this interpretation contains initial conditions which seem inconsistent with its conclusions.

All of these interpretations require belief in realities beyond the scope of scientific experiment. This is the price paid for claiming that the formal theory of QM describes all physical processes. The ProWave Interpretation pushes quantum weirdness back into the realm of physics, and therefore does not force us to postulate and philosophize about inaccessible realities.

The ProWave Interpretation

ProWave makes no assumption of localization of the photons before measurement. In fact, it rejects the common notion of wave-particle duality. Recent teaching by laser physicist W.E. Lamb Jr. supports this line of thinking [13]. Maintaining any sort of particle nature of elementary quanta is what has led us into trouble, philosophically. Let's start with a list of the assumptions made in the ProWave Interpretation:

1. Elementary quanta of matter and energy exist as their wavelike behavior suggests (wave packets), always.
2. Their time evolution is described by the Schrödinger equation (or better yet, by the Heisenberg equation of motion for the density operator).

3. Energy transfer, in quantum amounts, takes place locally. Thus, when a photon is absorbed and measured, its energy is <u>transferred</u> at only one point in space (Basically, this is only a defining property of "quantum").

Assumption (2) deals with propagation, which is a nonlocal, wavelike phenomenon, and Assumption (3) deals with the creation and destruction of quanta, which is a local phenomenon. These assumptions eliminate the ambiguity of what the electrons and photons do while we don't measure them. They are quantum waves: Electrons orbiting atoms are standing waves of matter-energy, photons are wavepackets of electromagnetic energy, etc. Also, we accept that a photon passes through both slits if both are probable, and it was not already absorbed by the wall. The same goes for electrons. In this way, we can reinstate physical reality which is dismantled in any wave-particle duality interpretation. The physical reality is simply that described by the wavefunctions and density matrices of a system, no matter how quantum entangled the states may be. It may be difficult to imagine the states in classical terms, but they are states nonetheless in which these very simple elementary quanta can exist. And they propagate according to the laws described by the mathematics of quantum mechanics.

As the quanta propagate and interact with the macroworld, two separate types of interactions occur. The first is defined as

a partial interaction: This interaction reorganizes or redirects the wavefunction designated by a unitary transformation matrix. Examples of such are beamsplitters and magnetic fields. The other type of interaction is defined as a complete interaction: This is designated by the destruction (and creation) of a quantum of energy, for example a bound electron absorbing a photon.

Before applying ProWave to the experiments described earlier, here it's quickly shown that ProWave can add insight into how a cloud chamber can measure the particle-like nature of matter waves. As, say, an electron traverses its ``path" in the cloud material, it is constantly being forced into localized positions by partial interactions with the material. Thus, the matter wave is being reorganized constantly and not really allowed to diffract much before collapsing repeatedly. The result is a clearly drawn path that was previously believed that only a particle could make.

The ultimate challenge for ProWave is to explain how a spread-out wave can collapse and deliver its energy locally upon absorption. It is helpful to envision wave evolution analogous to blowing up a balloon. Upon measurement, that balloon pops. The collapse (also pertains to reconfiguring the wave's energy) is probabilistic, like not knowing where a balloon will pop first. But once a measurement has been taken (or perhaps the quantum is destroyed) the wave collapses everywhere nonlocally and passes its energy to the absorber as one quanta. Likewise, when a balloon pops, the entire surface

of the balloon is quickly affected by the loss of tension in the rubber, however time elapses before the surface collapses. This collapse (for the quantum) need not be instantaneous but must be faster-than-light to ensure that nonlocality still applies. The phenomena of energy absorption and reconfiguration (quantum state changes) are inherently quantum uncertain events and cannot be pinned to "instantaneous"- only for practical purposes do we assume so. This is not a problem physically because the nature of this collapse is very poorly understood. In fact, I am suggesting the possibility of a more general theory that reduces to QM when the time of the collapse is considered small, in the same way that QM reduces to classical mechanics under certain conditions. This is typically the way physics advances; I don't see this potential for the other, far less intuitive, interpretations.

Explanation of the Experiments

ProWave offers new insights into the experiments involving quantum phenomena, and how nature can produce the results that it does. It is worthwhile to describe how the experimental results mentioned above can make sense given the ProWave view of reality. A deeper, more mathematical description of the experiments is found in the Appendix which follows with ProWave providing a consistent, realistic explanation.

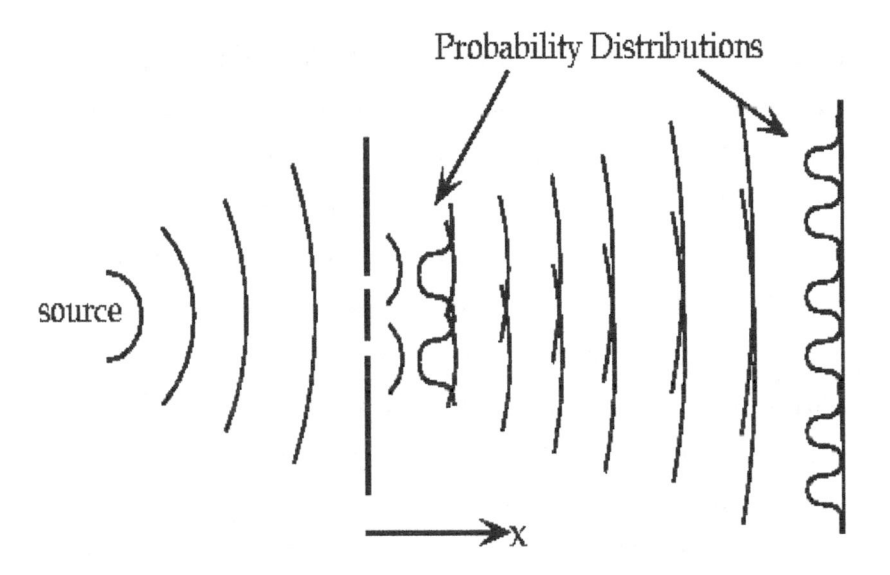

Figure 1: A typical 2 slit experiment showing probability distributions at different distances from the slits.

In the two-slit experiment (Fig. 1), a photon enters the two slits as a single, expanding wave. At the wall, its instantaneous probability of impacting on the surface of the wall is quite high. In the event that it makes it through the slits, the wave at the walls disappears and all the energy is collected and passes through the slits. This is governed by the quantum mechanical probability of absorption of the wall. As the wave now interferes with itself upon passing through the slits and propagating some distance to allow overlap, the energy of the quantum is spread out according to its probability distribution function (Ψ^2). Absorption of the photon, now, is a local process governed again by probability. Once the probability distribution collapses, the "balloon pops" everywhere and the

quanta of energy localizes at the point of transfer. This localization need not occur instantaneously, and it makes sense to conceive of it occurring on the timescale of energy absorption. As of today, this notion does not violate any laws of physics because there currently is no description of how a photon's probability distribution collapses upon absorption.

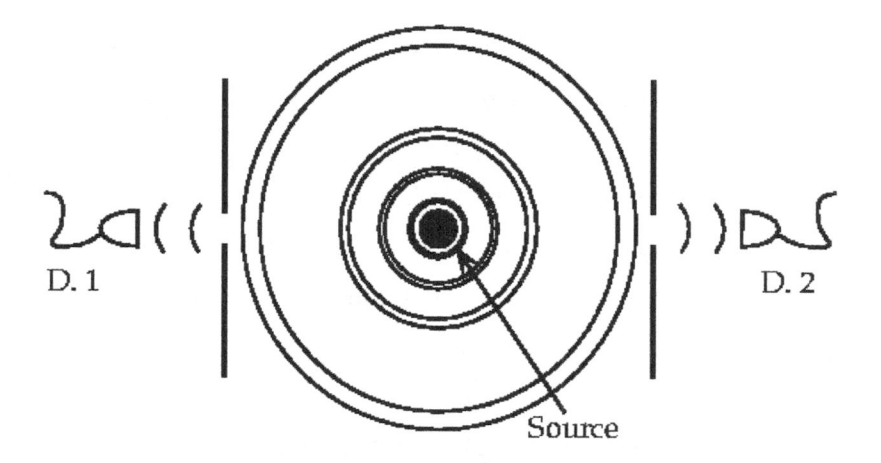

Figure 2: An experiment with EPR correlated particles.

I think the key to understanding any of the EPR correlations (Fig. 2) is to forego the idea that two distinct particles are emitted from some source in opposite directions. Quantum mechanics treats them as indistinguishable and as both being emitted in both directions, so let's treat them that way physically. The sources typically do not prefer a direction upon emission, making the correlated photons themselves spherical waves propagating, overlapping each other (one field). Any effect on one wave has a direct effect on the other

wave as well. Thus, say, if a particle is measured at one location (a photon was absorbed locally), then its partner snaps into a state opposite the source and resumes propagation. Analogously, imagine two balloons expanding together with the same radius. If one balloon pops, that causes the other to reconfigure as well. The reconfiguring of the second photon could be conceived of to have occurred instantaneously, but the final act of localization for energy transfer need not be. Again, this is consistent with what is known from QM about spin, polarization, and momentum correlations.

The quantum erasure experiment (Fig. 3) described in Section III is nothing other than a "directional interference" effect. No future activities or consciousness effects are needed to explain this experiment. The correlated pair is emitted as two quanta overlapping each other. They interfere at the splitter and the effects are detected. When one path undergoes polarization rotation, we no longer observe the interference of the two paths. This is no surprise because one path has polarization x and one has polarization y, and these are orthogonal. However, both x and y polarizations have a component of polarization in the z direction. These z-components do interfere at the beam splitter and the effect can be observed by putting in a linear polarizer oriented in the z direction directly in front of each detector. Note that the z-polarizer effectively filters out the orthogonal ($\bar{z}$) interference which can cancel the z-component interference. In essence, all of these interference effects are present until the complete

interaction. The type of interference that is manifested and becomes visible is a function of how the detectors are set up.

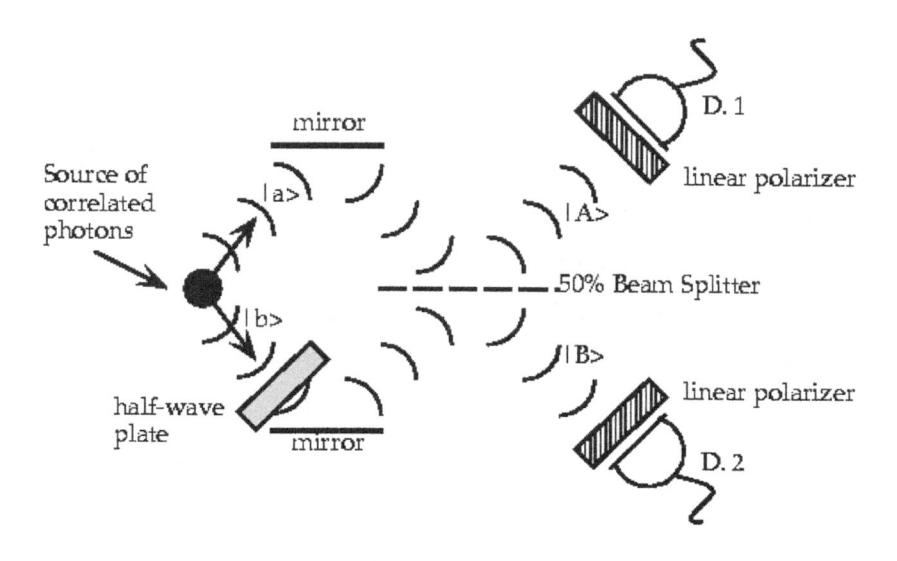

Figure 3: The quantum eraser experiment.

Summary

Photons, electrons, and all other elementary building blocks of our physical world represent simplicity in nature and existed long before complex structures like humans existed. Reality is quite real for all forms of matter, although admittedly, it is not always intuitive to rationalize the nature of this simplicity. What is meant by "simplicity" here is that just because we need strange quantum mechanical language to describe these systems, quantum mechanics can describe quite

accurately their behavior, for example, "spin up" and "spin down" states. In contrast, to accurately describe a more macro structure such as a group of several molecules, a hopelessly more complex calculation is needed. Thus, the quantum world represents simplicity, not complexity.

Whether in the form of leptons or photons, individual quanta of energy are passive creatures and propagate as waves, interfering as expected. These effects are observed only by carefully controlling the "directions" (e.g., spin projection, and polarization) in which we choose to observe the waves. The mystery of quantum behavior occurs in the waves' ability to collapse into eigenstates upon absorption or possibly a partial interaction with other matter. There is no wave-particle duality. There are no point particles, only localized energy transfers. The ProWave Interpretation of quantum mechanics is the alternative to the myriad of unpalatable existing interpretations. The building blocks of matter and radiation exist in only one world, and they have only one history.

Appendix

This section contains mathematical descriptions of the experiments discussed in the text. The ProWave Interpretation is consistently applied here and offers an intuitive way to digest the equations.

A) To better describe the double slit experiment, we will need to consider the quantum state of the slits (measure which slit through which the photons pass). It is generally understood that when the particular slit of passage is known regarding each photon, the interference pattern disappears. In the right operating regime, with the screen up close, there is no interference, with the screen far away, there is interference, as seen in the two probability distributions in Fig. 1. Consider the state of a perfect transmission:

$$|\Psi_1\rangle = \frac{1}{\sqrt{2}}(|1\rangle + |2\rangle)$$

where state vectors $|1\rangle$ and $|2\rangle$ refer to the slit number. Consider now the effect of the wall containing the slits, which tells us a number based on the slit passed by the photon. The state of this system is written as

$$|\Psi_2\rangle = \frac{1}{\sqrt{2}}(|1\rangle |1_A\rangle + |2\rangle |2_A\rangle)$$

where A = Apparatus. Thus, to describe a partial effect of the apparatus, a density matrix is needed to describe the system. There is uncertainty in the wavefunction itself, as the screen is positioned at various distances from the slits.

$$\rho = \sum_i P_i(x) |\Psi_i\rangle \langle\Psi_i| = \begin{bmatrix} \frac{1}{2} & c(x) \\ c(x) & \frac{1}{2} \end{bmatrix}$$

where $c(x)$ represents the degree of coherence between the [slit] states for the wave. Using the language of QM, but with simplified equations, let our observable $= B =$ the "interference operator." Let $a =$ "propagation not guided by interference" and $b =$ "propagation guided by interference." We define B to have the following expectations:

$$\langle 1 \,|\, B \,|\, 1 \rangle = \langle 2 \,|\, B \,|\, 2 \rangle \equiv a$$

$$\langle \Psi_1 \,|\, B \,|\, \Psi_1 \rangle = \frac{1}{2}((\langle 1| + \langle 2|)B(|1\rangle + |2\rangle)) \equiv b$$

The matrix

$$B = \begin{bmatrix} a & b - a \\ b - a & a \end{bmatrix}$$

has these properties. Now, using the state $\rho(x)$ we take a measurement:

$$\langle B \rangle = Tr[\rho B] = (1 - 2c)a + (2c)b$$

which provides us the expectation by which many quanta produce fringes. The coefficient of "b" indicates the relative amount of interference present at the screen.

Consider the two extreme cases:

1. <u>Near Field</u>: Diffraction of the waves has not caused significant overlap. $c(x) \sim 0$, and there is no interference.

2. <u>Far Field</u>: Waves from the two slits (but the same quantum) have a large amount of overlap at the screen. $c(x) \sim \frac{1}{2}$ gives rise to the quantum coherence and so interference fringes emerge.

Interpretation: It is the present state of the system which describes the possible outcomes, not our conscious "knowledge" of anything regarding, say, the "path taken by the particle." In this particular set-up, any photon not hitting the wall containing the slits passes through both slits. Note, a partial interaction between matter and a quantum of energy puts that quantum into a state we cannot adequately conceptualize (i.e. a reconfiguration of the energy in the wave packet), but we can only intelligently discuss probabilities of likely outcomes upon a complete interaction with matter in the case of photons.

B) Many EPR experiments involve the generation of correlated pairs of photons in an entangled state. Without loss of generality, consider as an example, the singlet state

$$|\Psi_0\rangle = \frac{1}{\sqrt{2}}(|x_L\rangle |x_R\rangle + |y_L\rangle |y_R\rangle)$$

Where x,y refer to orthogonal polarization states, and L,R label the left and right paths. The results of these experiments pioneered by Alain Aspect in 1982 confirm nonlocal effects. All the mathematics confirms this as well, but it has also been proven that these effects cannot be used to change the statistical averages of observables over distances faster than light could propagate a signal [7]. Any observable, B, which acts on one of the two sides treats this state as if each particle were in a mixture of states and not quantum correlated. Only after bringing together the data from both detectors can the patterns of quantum interference be observed. Neither side will exhibit quantum interference on its own, for example, measure any observable B on the left side:

$$\langle B_L \rangle = \langle \Psi_0 \mid B_L \mid \Psi_0 \rangle = \frac{1}{2}(\langle x_L \mid B_L \mid x_L \rangle + \langle y_L \mid B_L \mid y_L \rangle)$$

The interference terms with inner products involving both x and y disappear from the orthogonality of $\langle x_R | y_R \rangle = 0$. As Fig. 2 suggests, these quanta are waves propagating and overlapping in space. Thus, they are both present at both detectors. The measurement of one quantum (by probabilistic means) forces the other to reconfigure opposite to the first one. When the first quantum undergoes annihilation and transfers its energy locally, the other quantum reconfigures as well, governed by the quantum correlation (which includes conservation laws). Based on the equation above, by measuring

the polarization of the photon on the left, we can determine what the polarization of the photon on the right will be if measured in the x-y basis, but we cannot use this knowledge to send information faster-than-light.

C) The Quantum Eraser Experiment can be understood in terms of following the state functions of the correlated particles. First, let's understand how the interference is observed without the polarization rotator. With the rotator removed, the state can be expressed as

$$|\Psi_0\rangle = \frac{1}{\sqrt{2}}(|a_1\rangle |b_2\rangle + |b_1\rangle |a_2\rangle)$$

where a,b refer to the two different paths described in (Fig. 3), and 1,2 index the quanta. The beam splitter performs a unitary transformation into the A,B basis according to

$$U = \frac{1}{\sqrt{2}} \begin{bmatrix} 1 & 1 \\ 1 & -1 \end{bmatrix}$$

where U acts on each a,b state (and each photon) separately giving

$$U\,|a\rangle = \frac{1}{\sqrt{2}}(|A\rangle + |B\rangle)$$

$$U\,|b\rangle = \frac{1}{\sqrt{2}}(|A\rangle - |B\rangle).$$

Thus, upon leaving the beam splitter, the 2-photon state is

$$|\Psi\rangle = U_1 U_2\,|\Psi_0\rangle = \frac{1}{\sqrt{2}}(|A_1\rangle\,|A_2\rangle - |B_1\rangle\,|B_2\rangle)$$

which indicates that the only two outcomes of a measurement are both quanta appearing at the first detector, or both at the second detector. ProWave asserts that at this point, both photons are still present at both paths A and B, like the wave function suggests, until the energy is actually transferred to the detector. This is because there is quantum coherence between these states.

Now, if we insert the polarization rotator in the "b" path, the system acquires an additional degree of freedom and is described by

$$|\Psi_1\rangle = \frac{1}{\sqrt{2}}(|aP_+\rangle_1\,|bP_-\rangle_2 + |bP_-\rangle_1\,|aP_+\rangle_2).$$

Where P_+ and P_- represent orthogonal polarization states. Next, we use this state to propagate through the beam splitter, obtaining

$$|\Psi'\rangle = U_1 U_2 |\Psi_1\rangle$$

$$|\Psi'\rangle = \frac{1}{2\sqrt{2}} (|AP_+\rangle_1 |AP_-\rangle_2 - |AP_+\rangle_1 |BP_-\rangle_2$$
$$+ |BP_+\rangle_1 |AP_-\rangle_2 - |BP_+\rangle_1 |BP_-\rangle_2$$
$$+ |AP_-\rangle_1 |AP_+\rangle_2 + |AP_-\rangle_1 |BP_+\rangle_2$$
$$- |BP_-\rangle_1 |AP_+\rangle_2 - |BP_-\rangle_1 |BP_+\rangle_2).$$

With all these terms present, it is no surprise that this state generates all combinations of detector clicks (with repeated events, of course). Each term in this state has equal likeliness of emerging upon detection.

With this same state, $|\Psi'\rangle$, consider putting in the two linear polarizers in front of the detectors, oriented at 45° to both beams for simplicity. These polarizers let pass the polarization state $|P_0\rangle$ and absorb the orthogonal state $|\overline{P_0}\rangle$ and are related to the original polarization basis by

$$|P_+\rangle = \frac{1}{\sqrt{2}} (|P_0\rangle + |\bar{P_0}\rangle)$$

$$|P_-\rangle = \frac{1}{\sqrt{2}} (|P_0\rangle - |\bar{P_0}\rangle).$$

To find out what effect these have on the state of the system, project onto the polarizers' basis, and drop all terms that don't lead to coincidence counts (2 photon counts). The new wavefunction now has only P_0 terms and is not normalized because of the dropped terms.

$$|\Psi''\rangle = \frac{1}{2\sqrt{2}}(|A_1\rangle\,|A_2\rangle - |B_1\rangle\,|B_2\rangle).$$

Thus, we have recovered the same interference effect as before by treating the wavefunction as the actual energy carried by the photons right up to the point of their demise in the detector. The state of the photons is the reality we seek, and it describes all interactions and interferences we observe with a causal relationship. The interference along all directions was always present, up till the final interaction which destroyed the photons.

Acknowledgments

I thank all the members of our "quantum lunch" group: Joe Provenzano, Erann Gat, Joe Kahr, and Rich Doyle for our stimulating discussions.

Dan Provenzano
Thu Jan 15 19:33:34 PST 1998

References

1. Einstein, B. Podolsky, and N. Rosen, Phys, **47**, 777 (1935).

2. J. S. Bell, Physics (N.Y), 1, 195 (1965).

3. Aspect, P. Grangier, and G. Roger, Phys. Rev. Lett. **47**, 460 (1981).

4. Aspect, P. Grangier, and G. Roger, Phys. Rev. Lett. **49**, 91 (1982).

5. Aspect, P. Grangier, and G. Roger, Phys. Rev. Lett. **49**, 1804 (1982).

6. J. Horgan, Sci. Amer. July, 1992.

7. G. C. Ghirardi, A. Rimini, T. Weber, Lett. Nuovo Cimento, **27**, 293 (1980).

8. D. Mermin, Am. J. Phys. **49**, 940 (1981).

9. D. Mermin, Phys. Today, Apr. 1985.

10. J. Pykacz, Phys. Lett. A. **171**, 141 (1992).

11. P.G. Kwiat, A.M. Steinberg, and R.Y. Chiao, Phys. Rev. A. **45**, 7729 (1992).

12. N.J. Cerf and C. Adami, "Quantum Information Theory of Entanglement," Phys. Comp. 96. (1996).

13. W.E. Lamb, Jr., Appl. Phys. B. **60**, 77 (1995).

1

introduction

In a recent provocative essay Fawcett (1970:1) has remarked: "A population is made up of people, and psychology is the study of people. Yet, there have been few historical intersections between demography, the science that studies populations statistically, and psychology, the science that studies people behaviorally." His monograph reviews the scarce population psychology literature existing up to 1970—for example, KAP studies, clinical and psychoanalytic studies of childbirth, personality factors in fertility surveys, persuasive communications, psychological factors in the acceptance of contraception and abortion, modernity and fertility, and psychological consequences of family size and population density. Fawcett characterizes the studies as dealing only with certain specific aspects of human reproductive behavior. Together, he asserts, they fail to provide a comprehensive framework for explaining the underlying causal mechanisms governing individual fertility behavior, which in turn affects group fertility, a central demographic problem.

Thus, a pertinent issue for psychologists is not the superficial measurement of people's attitudes and behavior that are evident in traditional KAP and fertility surveys, but rather analysis of the genesis of their motivation for childbearing and how actual fertility planning and behavior are conceived in relation to their daily lives or their goals of self-actualization. In this connection, it becomes necessary to study in a broad framework the personal values that directly or indirectly influence fertility. Fertility behavior may also arise in part from a deep substratum of consciousness that dominates thought and feeling, with influence on such practical behaviors as marriage, contraception, and the rearing of children.

It is likely that individual values and behavior may differ across groups, being affected to a certain extent by one's sociocultural and environmental milieu. For example, values toward children held by people of upper socioeconomic status are likely to be different from those held by people of lower socioeconomic status; people's attitudes toward contraception may also vary depending upon their socioeconomic milieu (e.g., urban middle-class or rural). What kinds of relationships exist between these factors? To investigate these relationships in an interdisciplinary and comprehensive manner is the purpose of the Value of Children investigation.

However, before describing the study and discussing the results, it is pertinent to introduce the conceptual scheme of human values used in the investigation, and to consider how these values contribute to the underlying process of human fertility behavior, contraception, and other related population phenomena in general.

Values defined

Value can be defined as one's personal regard for certain objects, persons, or events. The degree to which one regards a certain object can be expressed in terms of weight, importance, respect, worth, or merit. We call a state of personal feeling "value." Thus a value is a feeling accompanied by perceiving, imagining, or thinking about that object. In a mode of one's consciousness, such a feeling can be organized into a system of structures: a hierarchy of values.

The investigation of values goes back to the German philosopher Eduard Spranger (1928), who insisted that at least six major values operate in the conduct of people's lives: theoretical, economic, political, aesthetic, social, and religious values. Everyone is supposed to have these six values in a hierarchical order, and one value is supposed to be supreme. A person's striving is thus governed by a system of values dominated by a specific one (political, for example), which in turn determines one's choice of career. It is not the purpose of this report to evaluate the validity of Spranger's thesis, but one can say at least that such a system of values may in fact determine one's way of living. An attitude toward objects can thus be viewed within such a hierarchy of one's system of values: money, children, maintenance of peace, scientific curiosity. A number of objects and events can be classified according to one's value system, which is itself a manifestation of a structural relationship between objects and events. If a person were asked to classify health, affection, peace, welfare, and staple foods in order of their importance, his ordering would reflect his value system at the time. Moreover, if we question a person about a specific object and ask him about this thing from different angles, his responses will reflect his value system.

A value can also be concrete. It can exist in object-means or goals-instrumental relationships. Affection, for example, may be regarded as one index of the maintenance of interpersonal relations, and thus it can be classified as an abstract interpersonal value. To love children is a specific manifestation of affection, and thus it can be regarded as concrete. It can also be seen that one way to experience affection is to love children. Therefore children may be regarded as a means or instrument for the realization of affection (goal or object). Thus a value or mode of feeling toward an object can operate in a very complex relationship—concrete at one time and abstract at another, goal or object at one time and means or instrument at another—depending on how it evokes a special meaning within one's system of values, which itself may develop and change from time to time.

Aims and content of the study

This report investigates parents' values regarding children. While setting aside the complex process and nature of the value problem, let us first focus on the objects to be studied: children and parents. Children are complex living organisms. Always changing, they are influenced by their milieu and sociocultural setting, and by behavioral norms and practices. Parents are the roots of their offspring. They enable their children to survive during the course of the children's becoming. If we stress the side of the parents and study their conceptions about children, we should analyze the underlying process to see how conceptions about children operate under certain conditions. What constitute the value components of children? In what conditions are these components organized?

Our central concern is with the individual makeup of parents, how they perceive children as "valuable objects." It is conceivable that values are concerned with the conditions of living organisms coping with an environment and thus determine our way of looking at things. Applying this situation to parental action toward children, we find that parents plan for, embrace, reject, praise, or scold children, depending on how they value them. Our concern will focus on analyzing parents' motivations. How are motivations toward children aroused and maintained under specific conditions? How do they influence attitudes toward bearing or rearing children?

Relying on the above conceptual framework, the present investigation explores various dimensions of values attached to children by parents. While deferring a more detailed theoretical discussion for the final chapter, I believe it is worthwhile mentioning here at least three general dimensions of values that may be conceived to reflect individual and group values. They are psychological-affective values, utility values, and combined and complex values of costs and benefits, all of which are composed of positive and negative aspects.

The questionnaire used to explore these dimensions in the Value of Children (VOC) Study consisted of about 400 items, including open-ended questions and structured or semi-structured items.[1] The strategy was to use multiple methods of measurement for the same or related variables to assess the validity of the findings. Unstructured questions were generally posed early in the interviews, so that answers to them would not be influenced by the structured items. The following value dimensions of respondents were investigated.

Value-of-children dimension

1 Advantages of having children compared with not having children
2 Disadvantages of having children compared with not having children
3 Reasons why most people want children
4 Importance of having at least one daughter and at least one son
5 Reasons for wanting daughters and sons (both personality and utility dimensions)
6 Strength of boy preference (the combined value of personality and utility dimensions)
7 Reasons for wanting another child (17 structured items, all describing positive fertility motivations)
8 Reasons for not wanting another child (nine structured items that describe negative fertility motivations)
9 Beliefs about children and childbearing (Likert-type attitude scale consisting of 45 positive and negative items)

Several items were directly concerned with utility dimensions of the value of children:

10 Economic and practical help expected from sons and daughters
11 Expectation of children as a source of financial support in the future

---

1 See Appendix A in Arnold et al. (1975) for the English version of the core questionnaire used in all six countries.

12 Expectation of living with children in the future
13 Perceived cost of children: whether children are seen as an economic benefit or cost; number of children respondent could raise before suffering a heavy financial burden; effect of doubled income on wanted family size; effect of free education on wanted family size; perceived burden of educational costs
14 Perceived changes in the functions of children: whether there are generational changes in children's willingness to give money to parents, live with parents, support parents in old age, help with chores or business

Family-size dimension

The questionnaire included items reflecting the combination of affective-psychological and utility values, as well as societal beliefs and values formed in particular sociocultural contexts. These items were:

1 Number of additional children wanted
2 Reasons for not wanting fewer children
3 Reasons for not wanting more children
4 Ideal number of boys and girls
5 Ideal ordering of sex of children
6 Definition of a small and a large family
7 Beliefs about the effects of large or small family size on the child

Moderator dimension

The moderator dimension reflects external or environmental constraints that serve to facilitate or control respondents' fertility motivations by influencing, directly or indirectly, their attitudes, beliefs, and values about having and rearing children. The items used in the questionnaire concerned:

1 Attitudinal modernity
2 Mass-media exposure
3 Ownership of consumer durables
4 Communication with spouse about family size
5 Communication with spouse about contraception
6 Relative influence of husband and wife in decision-making
7 Which spouse had a stronger desire for children
8 Pressure from others regarding contraception, abortion, family size
9 Religion
10 Educational aspirations for children
11 Perceived adequacy of income and relative economic status

Birth control dimension

Several items explored respondents' attitudes toward fertility control:

1 Awareness of, knowledge about, and use of contraceptive methods
2 General opinion about contraception
3 Attitude toward use of contraception in specific circumstances
4 General opinion about abortion
5 Attitude toward use of abortion in specific circumstances

Respondent's status

Finally, approximately 40 items on such standard sociodemographic dimensions as age, marital history, education, occupation, income, urban and rural experience, education and occupation of parents, birth order, and number of own or adopted children were included in the questionnaire.

Our central concern was to assess the role of the value-of-children variables in respondents' childbearing decisions. How did these values function with special reference to respondents' background—e.g., age, education, social class, marital history, parity? Did the VOC variables influence—or were they influenced by—the moderator dimension (media exposure, educational aspirations, decision-making about family, cultural norms and practices)? Did they contribute to respondents' choice of a certain family size or conceptions about ideal or wanted family size?

For the purpose of the study, we made an ad hoc assumption about the underlying operation of these variables. Using a cause-effect model, we assumed respondents' background and social status to be independent variables, the family-size and birth control dimensions to be dependent variables, the value-of-children dimension to be intervening between the independent and dependent dimensions, and the moderator dimension also to be intermediate or influential variables.

Figure 1.1 illustrates the conceptual approach to the study. It is a simplified representation and does not show many interactions and feedback effects, but it is useful as a heuristic device. The general scheme it represents has guided the design of the research and our analysis of the data. The next chapter will describe the research methodology and the characteristics of the VOC sample in Japan. Subsequent chapters will present research findings and interpretation of the results.

Figure 1.1 Conceptualized relationships among sociodemographic factors, VOC variables, and fertility

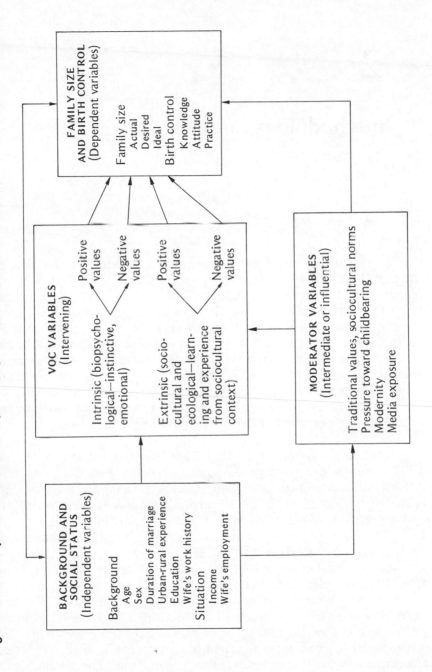

2

methodology and sample

Planning for the international Value of Children Study was initiated at the East-West Population Institute in Honolulu in late 1971. A core research group for Japan was organized in February 1972 at the invitation of the study's coordinator. Heading the Japanese research group were the author and Kiyoshi Shima of Musashino Women's College. Shoji Suzuki and Toshimi Nakajo participated as chief research staff members. In addition, a group of interviewers was organized on an ad hoc basis to conduct the field interviews. The research team included several coders who were responsible for data analysis. Representatives from an English language school translated the original questionnaire into Japanese. Secretarial help was provided by a member of Japan Marketing Education, Inc.

A workshop was held at the East-West Population Institute in April 1972 to design and plan the comparative research (see Fawcett, 1972). Afterward, communications were exchanged among the coinvestigators regarding the design of the questionnaire, method of interviewing, data coding, analysis of data, and format of the report. In July and August of 1972, a pilot survey was conducted with a pretest questionnaire, drafted for use in all six countries participating in the study. Ten urban and five rural couples were chosen for the pretest in Japan. Results from all of the pilot tests were tabulated and the questionnaire was revised. In November the revised questionnaire was translated into Japanese. To ensure the correctness of translation, a back-translation was performed. During the latter part of November, discussions were held with specialists concerning the field procedures to be used, in particular the hiring and training of interviewers and the sampling method.

In December, field interviews for the rural area were administered by 34 interviewers with the cooperation of local health personnel at municipal and prefectural offices. Interviews in the urban area were completed by 39 interviewers in January 1973. We first wrote letters requesting cooperation from each household in the randomly selected sample.

Responses to structured questions were coded in January and February; we used the standardized VOC coding instruction manual, which was translated into Japanese. A second workshop of project directors took place in Hong Kong late in February, at which coding schemes were devised for the open-ended questions. After the workshop, we coded the unstructured responses. A Japanese research assistant was sent to the East-West Population Institute to conduct further analysis of the data. We then constructed tables from the computerized data. In August, project directors of each country gathered at the East-West Population Institute to discuss the format for the final reports. The principal investigators then prepared the reports for their countries.

Interviews

Survey interviews were the basic means of collecting data for this study. The VOC questionnaire included items with diverse formats—open-ended questions followed by intensive probes, Likert-type attitude scales, and standard opinion and information items. To explore relationships of the various components of values ascribed to children, multiple measures were obtained of the same or similar dimensions.

The interviewers, mainly graduate students, were volunteers from the Tokyo University of Education, Tokyo Teachers' College, the University of Tokyo, Musashi University, and Musashino Women's College. These interviewers had at least some experience of interviewing in their major academic fields of psychology and sociology. Altogether, 65 were employed for the urban and rural surveys. Prior to the interviews, they received about ten hours of training. For the rural interviews three groups were organized, each consisting of 12 persons. Each interviewer was assigned two couples (four respondents) to interview per day. In the urban area, four interviewers on the average were assigned to each of 12 selected quarters in which each interviewer interviewed three couples (six respondents) within a week. The interview time per respondent averaged 80 minutes, but length of interviews ranged between one and two hours.

Interviews were scheduled at the convenience of respondents. For those working outside the home (mainly husbands), usually evenings,

Sundays, or Saturday afternoons were chosen. For those engaged in domestic duties (mainly wives), hours during the day were chosen when they were free. The first person interviewed was asked not to discuss the topic with the spouse who had not yet been interviewed. When both wife and husband were at home at the same time, they were interviewed separately by two interviewers. Thus every effort was made to prevent one spouse from influencing responses of the other.

The sample

Husbands and wives having at least one child were chosen as respondents for the study. Age of respondents ranged from 20 to 34 for wives and from 20 to 44 for husbands. The sample for each country included about 360 respondents, with 60 couples (120 respondents) from each of three socioeconomic groups: urban middle-class, urban lower-class, and rural. Comparable socioeconomic groups were selected in all six countries of the study to test the hypothesis that more affluent and particularly more urbanized respondents would manifest more modern attitudes toward children and fertility than less affluent and less urbanized respondents. Thus no attempt was made in this stage of the study to select a sample that would be statistically representative of Japan's population.

The following sampling procedures were followed in Japan. For the sample of agricultural households,[1] rural areas far from cities had to be selected. On the advice of statisticians in the Statistical Division of the Ministry of Health and Welfare, we selected three prefectures: Niigata (situated about 250 kilometers north of Tokyo on the Sea of Japan), Ibaraki (about 100 kilometers northeast of Tokyo), and Saitama (about 70 kilometers north of Tokyo). The population of the first of these prefectures is engaged mainly in rice agriculture, the second has about half rice and half dry-field agriculture, and the third has mainly dry-field agriculture. Within each prefecture, one or two villages were chosen on the advice of local health personnel. The villages were Koike and Kodaka near the city of Tsubame in Niigata Prefecture; Ami village, in the county of Inashiki, Ibaraki Prefecture; and Toyosato village, in Ohsato County, Saitama Prefecture. (See Figure 2.1 for the sample areas.) In each village, eligible respondents

1 Owing to Japan's high level of urbanization, finding purely agricultural households proved to be difficult, because many farmers operate businesses in addition to their farms. Such households were avoided in order to obtain a purely agricultural sample.

Figure 2.1 Locations of rural sample: Japan

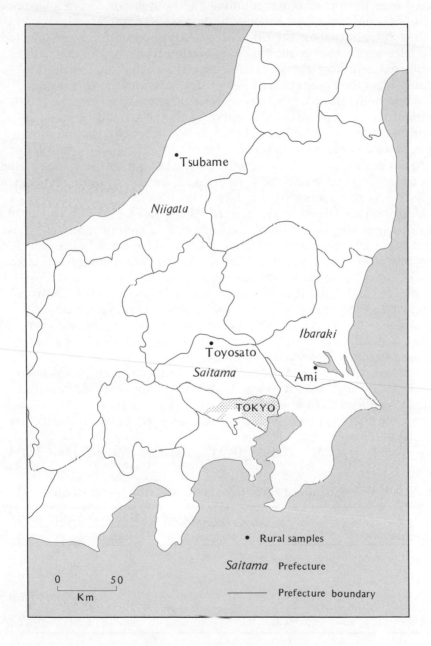

were selected from household registers. About 50 households were selected from each prefecture, totalling 142 households. From an average of 50 households, we aimed at obtaining 20 completed interviews
with couples in each of the three areas. After households were selected,
two letters were sent requesting cooperation from the prospective respondents, one from the VOC project staff and the other from the
Family Planning Federation of Japan. The interviewers then visited
the households three to five days after the letters were sent. In the in-
terim, the local health center telephoned the household to make ap-
pointments for the interviews. Through this procedure, actual interviews were completed with 66 couples (Table 2.1). In addition, there
were ten cases (one husband and nine wives) in which the spouse could
not be interviewed. Such cases are included in the aggregate analyses
of husbands and wives in this report.

Metropolitan Tokyo was chosen for the urban sample. Of the 23 old
city quarters, we randomly selected 12. Within each of these, we chose
50 households from voter registration lists, taking households suc-
cessively after a random start. The aim was to obtain completed interviews from 12 couples among the 50 households, for a total of 144
couples in the 12 quarters. No socioeconomic criteria were employed
in selecting the sample, but interviewers were instructed to skip any
households that were obviously of the upper class. Interviews were
completed with 119 couples, plus 15 husbands and 17 wives whose
spouses were not interviewed (Table 2.2).

Since adequate criteria for judging the socioeconomic status of respondents prior to the interview did not exist, we classified respondents as middle-class or lower-class after the interviews were completed,
during the analysis phase. This determination was based on the following criteria:
1. We asked respondents to identify their general income range. The

Table 2.1 Distribution of respondents by location: rural sample

Prefecture	Both spouses interviewed (number of couples)	One spouse interviewed	
		Husband	Wife
Niigata	19	0	1
Ibaraki	22	0	5
Saitama	25	1	3
Total	66	1	9

Table 2.2 Distribution of respondents by location: urban sample

Ward	Both spouses interviewed (number of couples)	One spouse interviewed	
		Husband	Wife
Chuo-ku	10	0	0
Shinjuku-ku	11	0	1
Koto-ku	11	0	1
Shinjuku-ku	12	0	0
Ota-ku	11	1	0
Setagaya-ku	6	5	4
Nakano-ku	10	1	1
Suginami-ku	8	2	4
Arakawa-ku	11	0	1
Nerima-ku	10	2	2
Katsushika-ku	6	3	2
Edogawa-ku	13	1	1
Total	119	15	17

cutoff point was at 1,500,000 yen (approximately US$5,000 at the time of the interviews). Those who checked this amount or the columns below it were classified in the lower income group; those who checked the columns above this amount were classified in the middle income group.

2. A further criterion was ownership of an automobile. Owners were considered middle-class; nonowners, lower-class.
3. The third reference was status of residence. Those who owned their homes were regarded as middle-class; those who rented were classified as lower-class.
4. The last criterion was husband's type of occupation. Those engaged in professional, technical, and managerial work were classified as middle-class; husbands engaged in all other occupations were classified as lower-class.

By combining these four criteria, we were able to divide the urban sample into two socioeconomic groups comprising 136 middle-class respondents and 134 lower-class respondents.

Profile of respondents

Nearly a third of the respondents were in the age group of 25–29 and about 44 percent were between the ages of 30–34 at the time of the interviews (Table 2.3). Nearly half of the wives were under age 30,

Table 2.3 Ages of respondents, by socioeconomic group and sex

Age group	Urban middle		Urban lower		Rural		Female		Male		All respondents	
Under 20	1	(0.7)	0	(0.0)	0	(0.0)	0	(0.0)	1	(0.5)	1	(0.2)
20–24	2	(1.5)	15	(11.2)	2	(1.4)	15	(7.1)	4	(2.0)	19	(4.6)
25–29	34	(25.0)	47	(35.1)	47	(33.1)	84	(39.8)	44	(21.9)	128	(31.1)
30–34	59	(43.4)	54	(40.3)	66	(46.5)	102	(48.4)	77	(38.3)	179	(43.5)
35–39	35	(25.7)	14	(10.4)	27	(19.0)	10	(4.7)	66	(32.8)	76	(18.4)
40–45	5	(3.7)	4	(3.0)	0	(0.0)	0	(0.0)	9	(4.5)	9	(2.2)
All age groups	136	(100.0)	134	(100.0)	142	(100.0)	211	(100.0)	201	(100.0)	412	(100.0)

NOTE: Percentage of sample is given in parentheses.

compared with one-fourth of the husbands. Urban middle-class respondents were somewhat older, on the average, than rural or urban lower-class respondents.

Monthly incomes among urban middle-class respondents ranged from 150,000 (US$495 at the 1972 conversion rate) to more than 300,000 (US$990) yen (Table 2.4). For the urban lower class, a monthly income range of 100,000 to 149,000 yen predominated. In the rural group, a wider and more evenly distributed range was observed.

Table 2.4 Monthly incomes of respondents
(Percentage of respondents)

Monthly income (thousand yen)[a]	Urban middle	Urban lower	Rural	All SES groups
Under 50	0.0	0.0	1.4	0.5
50–99	0.0	7.5	12.0	6.6
100–149	0.0	76.1	17.6	30.8
150–199	36.8	14.2	23.9	25.0
200–249	22.8	0.7	12.7	12.1
250–300	10.3	0.0	11.3	7.3
Above 300	29.4	0.0	9.2	12.9
No response	0.7	1.5	12.0	4.9
Total	100.0	100.0	100.1	100.1

NOTE: Percentages may not sum to 100 because of rounding.

a   100 yen was equivalent to about US$0.33 at the time of the interviews.

With regard to educational achievement, many of the urban lower-class and rural respondents had only the lower secondary (compulsory) level of education (Table 2.5). Roughly half of the respondents in each social class were educated at the high school (upper secondary) level. But whereas respondents with university education were fairly common in the two urban groups, especially among husbands, in the rural group this proportion was markedly small: 4.5 and 1.3 percent of male and female respondents, respectively.

Table 2.6 shows the occupational distribution of respondents. About 15 percent of the total were engaged in some kind of professional, technical, or managerial work. About 41 percent were clerical, sales, and service workers or craftsmen. About 18 percent were farmers

Table 2.5 Education of respondents
(Percentage of respondents at specified educational level)

Education	Urban middle	Urban lower	Rural
Wives			
Junior high school (8–9 years)	25.4	40.6	49.3
High school (10–12 years)	52.3	47.8	49.3
University (13–16 years)	22.4	11.5	1.3
Total	100.1	99.9	99.9
Husbands			
Junior high school (8–9 years)	15.9	32.3	46.3
High school (10–12 years)	43.4	44.6	47.8
University (13–16 years)	40.6	23.1	4.5
No response	0.0	0.0	1.5
Total	99.9	100.0	100.1

NOTE: Percentages may not sum to 100 because of rounding.

or farm managers. The distributions vary in expected ways by SES group. Although a majority of the wives held jobs outside the home, 39 percent were unemployed.

Over half (57 percent) of the sample was Buddhist, according to the respondents' own classification (Table 2.7). Twenty-seven percent had adopted no religion, and 16 percent had adopted a religion other than Buddhism. According to other data not shown in Table 2.7, however, 88 percent of the respondents actually held no strong religious beliefs, whereas 6 percent belonged to some Buddhist sect and 5 percent belonged to a new religion.

The mean number of living children our respondents had was 1.9. The mean number of children in the urban middle-class and rural groups was 2.02 and 2.04, respectively, whereas it was 1.58 in the urban lower-class group. Some 6.9 percent of the female respondents had had miscarriages, and about 0.5 percent had had stillbirths. We calculated that the abortion rate was about 13.2 percent. Over 70 percent of respondents had practiced some kind of contraception. These data and other findings related to fertility and fertility control are discussed in detail in Chapter 5.

In summary, it may be noted that the sample in Japan was more homogeneous than the samples in other countries in the VOC study, especially with respect to socioeconomic status. The rural group had

Table 2.6 Occupation of respondents
(Percentage of respondents)

Occupation	Urban middle	Urban lower	Rural	Female	Male	All re-spondents
Professional, technical, kindred workers	10.3	3.7	1.4	2.8	7.5	5.1
Managers, officials, proprietors (except farm)	21.3	6.7	2.8	3.3	17.4	10.2
Sales workers	5.9	5.2	2.1	5.2	3.5	4.4
Craftsmen, foremen, kindred workers	10.3	15.7	7.0	9.5	12.4	10.9
Clerical and kindred workers	16.9	23.1	7.7	13.3	18.4	15.8
Operatives and kindred workers	3.7	10.4	2.8	1.9	9.5	5.6
Service workers (except private household)	5.9	7.5	0.0	4.7	4.0	4.4
Farmers and farm managers	0.0	0.0	52.8	12.3	24.4	18.2
Laborers (except farm)	2.9	6.7	0.7	4.3	2.5	3.4
Other unclassifiable	0.7	2.2	0.0	1.9	0.0	1.0
Unemployed	19.9	17.9	22.5	38.9	0.5	20.1
No response	2.2	0.7	0.0	1.9	0.0	1.0
Total	100.0	99.8	99.8	100.0	100.1	100.1

NOTE: Percentages may not sum to 100 because of rounding.

Table 2.7 Religion of respondents
(Percentage of respondents)

Religion	Urban middle	Urban lower	Rural	Female	Male	All re-spondents
Buddhism	55.1	38.8	74.6	51.7	61.7	56.6
Other religion	17.7	19.4	11.3	15.1	16.9	16.0
No religion	27.2	41.8	14.1	33.2	21.4	27.4
Total	100.0	100.0	100.0	100.0	100.0	100.0

a mean of 10.6 years of education, for example, compared with 12.3 years for the urban middle-class, and most of the rural respondents had relatively high levels of income. Differences in fertility across groups were also slight, with the rural group having essentially the same family size (two children) as the urban middle class, despite a longer duration of marriage (8.2 years compared with 7.2 years). This homogeneity of the Japanese sample suggests that differences across groups in motivational patterns may be less striking than in other countries. As shown in the following chapters, however, some important differences were found, apparently reflecting situational factors and the extent to which modern value orientations have been adopted within various social groups.

3

advantages and disadvantages of children

This chapter describes major findings concerning general and specific values of children obtained from respondents' answers to questions about reasons for wanting and not wanting children. The first section summarizes responses to open-ended questions about the advantages and disadvantages of having childen as compared with not having children, and respondents' reasons for wanting or not wanting children under stipulated conditions. Next are described results obtained from structured items consisting of reasons for wanting and not wanting another child. A third section presents the results of a Likert-type attitude scale expressing positive and negative opinions about children and parenthood. The final section discusses similarities and differences of the results obtained from the three methodologies.

Open-ended questions

One major aspect of this study is its heavy reliance on respondents' unstructured, descriptive answers to the questions regarding the advantages and disadvantages of having children. To learn how respondents conceptualized their values, it was necessary to ask open-ended questions about this topic. Such questions appeared in several places in the questionnaire, notably toward the beginning. Six questions asked about advantages; four asked about disadvantages. Respondents' verbatim responses to each question were coded independently by several coders using predetermined coding categories. Most of the 60 coding

categories for advantages and 30 categories for disadvantages were
used in all six VOC countries; a few were added for country-specific
responses in Japan. General and specific coding categories are listed
in Exhibit 3.1.

Advantages of having children

Open-ended questions asked about the advantages of having children
in four contexts. The first concerned the advantages of having children as compared with having no children. Respondents were asked to
describe as many advantages as they could think of and then to rank
the most important and next most important items. The second question concerned respondents' perceptions of why others in the community wanted children. The third asked about the advantages of
having a specific number of children, and the fourth asked about the
advantages of having children of a particular sex.

General advantages

Among the first questions respondents were asked was the following:
"I would like to know what you think are some of the good things
or advantages about having children, *compared with not having children at all.* These might include the pleasure and benefits you get from
having children now and those that you expect in the future. What
would you say are some of the good things or advantages about having
children, compared with not having children?" Table 3.1 summarizes
the responses, which were coded into eight general categories. The
most frequently mentioned advantage was the happiness, love, and
companionship offered by children; less salient were childrearing satisfactions, personal development of parent, benefits to the family unit,
economic benefits and security, kin group benefits, and social or religious influences.

Happiness, love, and companionship were almost equally salient to
the three SES groups. The rural group, however, cited childrearing
satisfactions more frequently than the two urban groups, whereas the
two urban groups mentioned benefits to the family unit and personal
development of the parent more frequently than the rural group. Another interesting finding is that economic benefits and security and
kin group benefits were mentioned more frequently by rural than by
urban respondents. Tradition and security associated with children
were apparently salient values to the rural group, although emotional
benefits were much more salient.

Wives mentioned more frequently than husbands personal develop-

Exhibit 3.1 Advantages and disadvantages of having children: major and specific code categories derived from content analysis of responses

ADVANTAGES

Happiness, love, companionship

Companionship, avoidance of loneliness

Love, affection

Play, fun with children; avoidance of boredom

Relief from strain, distraction from problems

Happiness for individual parent (general)

Happiness for family

Uniqueness, specialness in parent-child relationship

Personal development of parent

Character development, responsibility, maturity, morality

Incentives to succeed, striving to provide for children

Fulfillment of self, completeness as person

Extension of self

Learning from experience of childrearing

Motherhood, fatherhood; adulthood

Childrearing satisfactions

Pride in children's accomplishments

Children to carry out parent's hopes, aspirations

Opportunity to teach, guide, instill values

Satisfaction in one's childrearing ability, accomplishments

Satisfaction in providing for children

Economic benefits, security

Economic help in old age

Companionship, comfort, care in old age

Unspecified help in old age

Economic benefits, security *(continued)*

Economic help (old age not mentioned)

Comfort, care (old age not mentioned)

Help in housework, family chores; practical help

Help in family business, farm

Help in taking care of other children

Unspecified help (old age not mentioned)

Benefits to family unit

Children as bond between spouses

Children as family life; complete, closeknit family

Kin group benefits

Continuity of family name

To increase strength, power of kin group

To satisfy desires of other kin

Social, religious influences

Conformity to social norms

Children as benefits to society

General, intrinsic value of children

Children as treasure, wealth, assets

Instinctive, natural to have children

General wanting, liking children

Country-specific advantages

Children as prime value in life, source of encouragement and liveliness

To preserve one's youthfulness

Personality formation of other siblings

Exhibit 3.1 *(continued)*

DISADVANTAGES

Financial costs

Educational costs

General financial costs

Emotional costs

Responsibility of parenthood

Discipline, moral behavior

Health problems of children

Concern over children's future success, happiness

Concern about satisfying children's present wants

Noise, disorder, nuisance

General rearing problems

General emotional strain

Physical demands on parents

Health hazard of pregnancy; maternal health

Physical work, tiredness caused by children

Restrictions on alternative activities

Restrictions on time

Restrictions on travel

Restrictions on social life, recreation

Restrictions on job, career

Restrictions on personal wants

Restrictions on privacy

General lack of flexibility, freedom

Marital problems

Less time, interaction between spouses

Disagreements over children

Country-specific disadvantages

Deterioration of childrearing environment; pollution and accidents

Housing problems

Schooling problems

Economic and material aspects of social security inadequate for childrearing

Concern over age differences between children, age balance

Dislike of children

More children a cause of more associations and possible trouble with neighbors and relatives

Futility of raising children; no security to parents in old age

Table 3.1 General advantages of having children
(Percentage of respondents who mentioned specified advantage categories)

General advantage	Urban middle	Urban lower	Rural	Female	Male	All respondents
Happiness, love, companionship	61	69	63	66	63	64
Childrearing satisfactions	37	36	46	38	41	40
Benefits to family unit	28	35	14	28	23	26
Parent's personal development	29	21	17	26	18	22
Economic benefits, security	7	9	19	14	9	12
Kin group benefits	3	4	11	3	9	6
Social, religious influences	4	1	1	1	2	2
General, intrinsic value of children	1	2	3	1	3	2

ment of the parent and the economic benefits and security that children provide, but husbands mentioned childrearing satisfactions and kin group benefits slightly more frequently. These results are reasonable in the sense that mothers learn more about themselves through their direct contact with children in the course of raising them. Wives were also more likely than husbands to anticipate needing economic support from their children because fewer wives were in the labor force. Male respondents may have regarded their children as extensions of themselves and put more stress than women on the kin group benefits of children since in Japan children take the father's surname.

Breaking these frequencies into specific categories produced the results shown in Table 3.2. Happiness for the family was the most frequently mentioned specific advantage of children for the sample at large. Next was children as a source of encouragement and liveliness,[1] followed by pleasure from growth and development of children, chil-

---

1 This item was one of the country-specific categories, the original word given by respondents being *ikigai*. It is literally translated "enjoyment of life" through sustained work. While there are similar English expressions, such as "goals and incentives from children" and "parenthood satisfactions," no identical expression is found in English. *Ikigai* is a culturally loaded word that for the Japanese has a direct experiential appeal within the context of strenuous Japanese life.

Table 3.2 Specific advantages of having children
(Percentage of respondents who mentioned specified advantage categories)

Specific advantage	Urban middle	Urban lower	Rural	Female	Male	All respondents
Happiness for family	41	49	46	47	47	46
Prime value in life	35	41	42	38	39	39
Pleasure from growth and development of children	24	19	22	24	19	22
Children as bond between spouses	22	27	10	21	18	19
Children to carry out parent's hopes, aspirations	14	14	23	14	19	17
Companionship, avoidance of loneliness	11	14	12	10	15	12
Children as family life, complete or close-knit family	10	16	7	12	19	11
Happiness for individual parent (general)	10	11	10	15	5	10
Satisfaction in providing for children	10	5	11	8	9	9
Character development, responsibility, maturity, morality	12	7	3	6	9	7

dren as a bond between husband and wife, and children to carry out the parent's hopes and aspirations. Less frequently mentioned were companionship, avoidance of loneliness; children as family life, complete or close-knit family; happiness for individual parent; satisfaction in providing for children; and character development or responsibility, maturity, morality.

Urban respondents mentioned more often than rural respondents the advantages of children as a bond between spouses and as a source of family life. The middle-class group mentioned more than other groups character development or responsibility, maturity, morality; the rural group was most inclined to mention children to carry out parent's hopes and aspirations. The lower-class group least frequently mentioned satisfaction in providing for children and pleasure from children's growth and development, but it mentioned happiness for the family, children as a bond between spouses, and children as family life more frequently than the other two SES groups.

More female than male respondents mentioned pleasure from children's growth and development and the happiness that children bring the individual parent. For male respondents, children to carry out parent's hopes and aspirations, companionship or avoidance of loneliness, children as family life, and children to complete the family were relatively more salient.

After naming all the advantages of children they could think of, respondents were asked to rank them in order of importance. The results are presented in Table 3.3. For the sample as a whole, happiness for the family and children as a prime value in life far outweighed the other advantages. Ranking by importance and by frequency of mention (salience) roughly correspond except that companionship/avoidance of loneliness, which ranked sixth in salience, ranked eighth in importance.

Table 3.3 Most important advantages of having children
(Percentage of respondents who ranked specified advantage categories first in importance)

Advantage	Urban middle	Urban lower	Rural	Female	Male	All respondents
Happiness for family	20	29	21	24	22	23
Prime value in life	19	19	26	23	20	21
Pleasure from growth and development of children	10	4	6	8	6	7
Children as bond between spouses	8	5	1	6	4	5
Children to carry out parent's hopes, aspirations	3	5	6	2	7	5
Children as family life, complete or close-knit family	3	8	2	3	5	4
Happiness for individual parent (general)	2	4	3	3	2	3
Companionship, avoidance of loneliness	3	3	3	2	3	3
Satisfaction in providing for children	6	1	2	2	3	3
Character development, responsibility, maturity, morality	4	2	1	2	3	3

   Regarding subgroup differences, the following points should be
noted. First, prime value in life was more important to the rural group
than to the two urban groups. Second, pleasure from children's growth
and development, children as a bond between spouses, satisfaction in
providing for children, and character development were somewhat
more important to the middle-class group than to the other SES
groups. Third, the lower-class group placed more importance than the
others on happiness for the family and children as family life. And
fourth, more male than female respondents ranked as most important
children to carry out parent's hopes and aspirations and children as
family life, whereas more women than men gave first ranking to
happiness for the family, prime value in life, pleasure from growth,
and children as a bond between spouses.

   One can conclude from these spontaneous responses to questions
about the general advantages of children that for Japanese respondents
the dominant value dimensions associated with children were psychological-affective: happiness for the family, the experience of childrearing (pleasure from growth and development, children to carry out
parent's hopes), and benefits to the family unit (affection bonds, children as family life).

Why people in the community want children

A projective open-ended question probed respondents' perceptions of
others' childbearing motivations: "In your opinion, what are the main
reasons why people around here want children?" Nearly a fifth of the
respondents mentioned happiness for the family and having children
as heirs (Table 3.4). Mentioned with slightly less frequency was prime
value in life. Some respondents were unable to hazard a reason, while
one in ten indicated that most people have an instinctive, "natural,"
or general desire for children—a response that did not appear in the
question about advantages of children. Two other reasons that were
not mentioned when respondents talked about their own motivations
were conformity to social pressures and a desire to continue the family name, although neither was mentioned with much frequency.

   Rural respondents and men emphasized the kin group benefit of
having children as heirs. These respondents seemed to subscribe to the
traditional view that children are needed to inherit the family wealth
and to satisfy desires of the kin group. The lower-class and rural
groups mentioned happiness for the family somewhat more frequently
than the middle class. Prime value in life was mentioned most frequently by the rural group and women. The lower-class group had the

Table 3.4 Perceived reasons why people in the community want children
(Percentage of respondents who mentioned specified reasons)

Reason	Urban middle	Urban lower	Rural	Female	Male	All re-spondents
Happiness for family	16	21	22	17	17	19
To have heirs	14	10	32	14	20	18
Prime value in life	15	10	22	17	9	15
Having children is instinctive, natural	14	13	3	10	9	10
No reason given/don't know	7	15	6	8	10	9
General desire for children	9	15	4	8	9	9
Companionship	10	7	11	10	7	9
Children as family life	14	5	2	6	8	7
Conformity to social norms	2	7	5	3	7	5
Children as bond between spouses	8	5	3	4	7	5
Continuity of family name	4	3	6	3	6	4

NOTE: Only the first two reasons mentioned by each respondent were included in analysis.

highest frequency of "general wanting" and "don't know" responses, but slightly more middle-class than lower-class respondents mentioned "instinctive" or "natural" behavior; in contrast, few rural respondents gave these answers. Slightly more lower-class and rural than middle-class respondents mentioned pronatalist social pressures.

Advantages of having a specified number of children

Respondents were asked how many children they wished to have and why they would not want fewer than that number. The assumption was that fewer would be viewed as disadvantageous. The results are shown in Table 3.5. A desire to provide companionship for other children was the predominant reason, mentioned by about a third of the respondents in each subgroup. This response suggests that the desired number of children was not considered of value to the parents themselves but rather to their existing children. Another salient advantage, especially to lower-class and female respondents, was to foster the

Table 3.5 Reasons for not wanting fewer than desired number of children
(Percentage of respondents who gave specified reasons)

Reason	Urban middle	Urban lower	Rural	Female	Male	All re-spondents
Companionship for other children	30	36	36	36	34	35
To foster character development of children	30	51	10	49	29	33
Good number to have, want that number	23	15	12	16	17	16
To avoid having an only child	12	15	9	14	12	13
Anxiety over infant mortality	7	5	28	14	13	13
Companionship, avoidance of loneliness	11	5	9	10	6	8
Happiness for family	12	1	5	3	8	6
Want more boys	4	5	9	5	7	6
Want certain combination of boys and girls, balance	5	5	7	7	2	4
Want more girls	9	1	3	8	1	4

character development of children already born. The other reasons were to avoid having an only child ("an only child would be lonesome"), fear that existing children might die, a desire for companionship or happiness for the family, and the desire for a particular combination of boys and girls, for children of both sexes, or for more children of one sex or the other. Some respondents (16 percent) gave a tautological response, saying that the number they desired was a "good" number to have, or that they simply wanted that number.

The middle-class group gave the response "good number to have" and cited companionship, happiness for the family, and a desire for more girls more frequently than the other groups. Avoiding an only child was more salient to the two urban groups than to rural respondents, whereas anxiety over infant mortality was mentioned mostly by rural respondents.

In addition to concern about the character development of their children, female respondents gave relatively more emphasis than males to companionship and avoidance of loneliness, desire for a certain combination of sons and daughters, and desire for more girls. Male respondents gave relatively more emphasis to happiness for the family and desire for more boys.

Reasons for wanting children of a particular sex

As the reasons given for wanting a particular number of children reveal, parents' motives for wanting children are often related to sex preferences. A parent may want girls because of their personality traits, for example, or because there are no girls in the family. VOC respondents were asked whether it was important to have at least one daughter or one son and, if so, why it was important. Their reasons are summarized in Tables 3.6 and 3.7.

The three most salient reasons for wanting girls were to provide companionship for the mother, the behavior or personality of girls, and expected help with housework and family chores. Differences among the subgroups in some cases were substantial, however. The middle-class group mentioned most frequently the behavior or person-

Table 3.6 Reasons for wanting a daughter
(Percentage of respondents who mentioned specified reasons)

Reason	Urban middle	Urban lower	Rural	Female	Male	All respondents
Companionship, closeness with mother	42	54	41	62	13	42
Desirable behavior or personality of girls	48	40	34	25	41	38
Help in housework, family chores	14	18	30	18	17	19
Parent's preferred sex ratio	11	6	5	1	12	7
Mixture of sexes for benefit of children	14	4	4	2	11	7
Satisfaction in providing for children	5	4	8	4	6	5
Companionship, comfort, care in old age	3	7	7	8	2	5
Happiness for family	6	2	5	1	8	4
Children to carry out parent's aspirations	2	1	2	2	2	2
Unspecified help in old age	0	0	4	1	1	1

ality of girls, followed by companionship for the mother, help with housework, a mixture of sexes for the children's benefit, and the parent's preferred sex ratio. The lower-class group most frequently mentioned companionship for the mother, followed by the behavior or personality of girls and help in housework. Similarly, for the rural group the most salient reasons, in order, were companionship for the mother, girls' personality traits, and help in housework. Women mentioned much more frequently than men the companionship of girls, their closeness to the mother, and the comfort that daughters provide. Men, on the other hand, gave relatively more stress to the personality traits of girls, wanting girls to achieve their desired sex ratio, having a mixture of sexes for the benefit of the children, and happiness for the family. Of interest are the negligible percentages of respondents who mentioned help in old age even among the rural group.

The main reasons given for wanting boys (Table 3.7), in order of salience, were to have heirs, the behavior or personality traits of boys, companionship for the father, unspecified help from sons (old age not

Table 3.7 Reasons for wanting a son
(Percentage of respondents who mentioned specified reasons)

Reason	Urban middle	Urban lower	Rural	Female	Male	All respondents
To have heirs	27	19	64	34	36	36
Desirable behavior or personality of boys	29	53	18	28	26	31
Companionship, closeness with father	23	32	10	11	24	20
Unspecified help (old age not mentioned)	3	15	7	9	4	8
Continuity of family name	12	6	5	8	6	7
Parent's preferred sex ratio	9	3	4	6	4	5
Help in old age	5	2	8	7	4	5
Children to carry out parent's aspirations	1	8	6	2	6	5
Help in family business	2	2	5	3	3	3
Mixture of sexes for benefit of children	4	3	2	3	3	3

mentioned), and continuity of the family name. (To have heirs was not among the first ten most frequently cited reasons for wanting girls.) Many more rural than urban respondents mentioned this reason for wanting sons. Like girls, boys were desired for their behavioral traits by substantial percentages of all subgroups.

But differences among subgroups are noteworthy. The lower-class group mentioned the behavior or personality of boys much more frequently than middle-class or rural respondents. Companionship for the father was most salient to the lower-class group and men, least salient to rural respondents. Unspecified help for parents was mentioned by more lower-class and female respondents than others, whereas help in old age was relatively more salient to rural and female respondents than to the other groups (though the percentage of respondents mentioning this reason was small). More middle-class respondents than others mentioned continuity of family name. Children to carry out parent's hopes and aspirations predominated as a reason among lower-class, rural, and male groups.

In summary, respondents expressed somewhat different motivations for wanting girls and wanting boys. For girls, the reasons tended to be related to psychological rewards such as companionship for the mother and the behavior or personality of girls. In addition, girls' contribution to housework and family chores was a salient motivation. For boys, practical reasons were prominent: boys can be heirs, can continue the family name, and may help their parents both as children and later as adults. The personality of boys and the companionship they provide, especially to the father, were also salient reasons for wanting sons.

Disadvantages of having children

General disadvantages

As with advantages, respondents were asked an open-ended question about the disadvantages of having children: "Now I would like to know about some of the difficulties or disadvantages connected with having children *compared with not having children at all.* These might include, for instance, various problems or stresses related to raising children, or things that you cannot do or have to give up because you have children. What would you say are some of the difficulties or disadvantages connected with having children, compared with not having children?" Their responses, along with those of VOC respondents in other countries, were content-analyzed and coded into general and specific disadvantage categories (Exhibit 3.1). The general disadvantages as perceived by the Japanese sample are shown in Table 3.8.

Table 3.8 General disadvantages of having children
(Percentage of respondents who mentioned specified
disadvantage categories)

General disadvantages	Urban middle	Urban lower	Rural	Female	Male	All re-spondents
Restrictions on alternative activities	57	54	33	56	40	48
Emotional costs	38	49	45	49	38	44
Financial costs	23	20	24	19	26	23
Physical demands on parents	6	9	5	9	5	7
Marital problems	12	2	3	5	6	6
Kin group costs, problems of inheritance	0	0	1	1	*	*
Societal costs, over-population	0	0	1	1	*	*
Other disadvantages	0	0	2	1	1	1

* Less than 1 percent.

The dominant categories for the sample as a whole were, in order
of salience, restrictions on alternative activities, emotional costs, and
financial costs. Somewhat less salient were physical demands on parents and marital problems caused by children. Fewer than 1 percent
of the respondents mentioned societal costs such as overpopulation,
but this may have been due to the way the question was phrased.

Subgroup differences are of interest. Urban respondents and women
in particular felt the restrictions on their alternative activities, over
half of these groups mentioning this disadvantage. The urban lower-class, rural, and female groups mentioned emotional costs of children
somewhat more frequently than the other groups. For financial costs,
the third category, differences among SES groups were minor, but
somewhat more husbands than wives mentioned this disadvantage. As
expected, physical demands on parents were more salient to women
than to men; physical demands were also more salient to lower-class
respondents than to the other SES groups. Marital problems were
mentioned by more middle-class respondents than others.

The frequent mention by urban respondents of restrictions on alternative activities may be taken to mean that urban life exposes people to many activities as they adapt to rapid changes in their daily environment, whereas rural life remains slow and monotonous. Thus children become a hindrance to parents engaged in these alternative activities in the city but do not seriously disturb a quiet rural life.

The frequent mention of emotional strain by the urban lower-class and rural groups implies that they suffer from physical and psychological burdens caused by their unsatisfactory surroundings. The financial costs of children mentioned especially by the middle-class and rural groups may signify their greater sacrifice in raising children at the expense of their standard of living.

The physical demands mentioned in particular by the lower-class group probably include travel to a distant job, shortage of nursery schools, and the like. Middle-class couples could probably afford to leave their children in nursery schools, and rural couples were probably able to rely on grandparents for childcare. The difference between female and male respondents in the salience of physical demands of children on parents may be explained by the fact that mothers usually have responsibility for the physical rearing of children, whereas fathers usually have financial responsibility for the family's support.

The relatively high frequency with which middle-class respondents mentioned marital problems suggests that because of the busy activities of each spouse, the marital bond may be weakened by having children.

When the major disadvantage categories shown in Table 3.8 are broken down into specific disadvantages, the results shown in Table 3.9 are obtained. The specific disadvantage mentioned by the greatest proportion (a fourth) of respondents was restrictions on time, followed by general financial costs. Health problems of children were also salient to the sample as a whole. Mentioned less frequently but by at least a tenth of all respondents were the general emotional strain caused by children; noise, disorder, and nuisance; restrictions on the parent's job or career; general lack of flexibility and freedom; and restrictions on social life.

Restrictions on time, lack of flexibility and freedom, and restrictions on personal wants were mentioned more frequently by the two urban groups than by the rural group. Apparently urban life requires more alternative activities in adapting to daily life than does a rural existence, and therefore rearing children becomes much more of a burden and more time-consuming for urban parents. A further difference between urban and rural respondents is found in the salience of health problems. Rural parents tended to worry more about the health of their children than urban parents, probably because of their relative lack of knowledge about health care and shortages of medical services in rural areas. Noise, disorder, and nuisance caused by children were

Table 3.9 Specific disadvantages of having children
(Percentage of respondents who mentioned specified
disadvantage categories)

Specific disadvantage	Urban middle	Urban lower	Rural	Female	Male	All respondents
Restrictions on time	27	29	16	29	17	24
General financial costs	21	21	22	18	23	21
Health problems of children	15	19	23	19	18	19
General emotional strain	16	13	13	16	11	14
Noise, disorder, nuisance	9	13	13	13	10	12
Restrictions on job, career	10	13	12	13	9	11
General lack of flexibility, freedom	12	13	9	12	9	11
Restrictions on social life, recreation	13	8	8	11	10	10
Restrictions on personal wants	10	9	6	11	5	8
General rearing problems	3	12	8	8	6	7

more frequently mentioned by the urban lower-class and rural groups, probably because of their lack of a suitable childrearing environment. Restrictions on social life were more salient to the middle class than to the other two SES groups, whereas general childrearing problems were least salient to this group, probably because of the abundant information and resources available to them. All SES groups mentioned the financial costs of children with nearly equal frequency.

With regard to differences between the sexes, more women than men mentioned restrictions on their time (29 percent as against 17 percent), the general emotional strain of having children, restrictions on their jobs and careers, lack of flexibility and freedom, and restrictions on personal wants. More men than women mentioned financial costs of children (23 percent, compared with 18 percent). These responses are understandable. Women usually take the chief responsibility for rearing children, whereas men have primary financial responsibility for supporting the family.

When respondents ranked specific disadvantages according to importance, restrictions on time and health problems of children were predominant (Table 3.10).[2] Urban respondents were more likely to

2 A similar finding was obtained from a country-specific question about fears and anxieties associated with childrearing (see Appendix, p. 104). Using a five-

Table 3.10 Most important disadvantages of having children
(Percentage of respondents who ranked specified
advantage categories first in importance)

Disadvantage	Urban middle	Urban lower	Rural	Female	Male	All re-spondents
Restrictions on time	14	19	8	19	7	14
Health problems of children	10	13	15	13	12	13
General financial costs	7	7	8	5	9	7
General emotional strain	7	6	4	7	4	6
General lack of flexibility and freedom	9	8	1	6	5	6
Restrictions on job, career	5	5	6	7	4	5
Restrictions on social life	6	5	1	6	2	4
Noise, disorder, nuisance	2	6	4	2	4	4
Restrictions on personal wants	4	4	3	3	3	3
General rearing problems	1	5	4	3	3	3

cite restrictions on their time as most important, and more women
than men gave first ranking to this category. Across all subgroups,
health problems of children ranked second. The two urban groups
cited general lack of flexibility and freedom much more often than
the rural group. Restrictions on social life were ranked first by more
urban and female respondents than others, whereas noise, disorder,
and nuisance were cited in particular by the lower-class, rural, and
male groups.

Disadvantages of having more than desired number of children

Respondents who wanted more children were asked why they would
not want more than the number given as their desired family size. As
Table 3.11 shows, the financial burden of additional children was the
major reason, mentioned by a fourth of all respondents. To raise another child would pose a financial problem for these Japanese couples.
The urban lower-class group perceived this problem more keenly than

---

point scale to rate eight items selected as the source of parents' anxiety, 54 percent of the urban and 33 percent of the rural respondents rated health problems of children as causing great anxiety. Receiving the highest rating, however,
was fear of accidents. The cost of raising children was rated fifth or sixth in anxiety level. The discrepancy between these results and the present findings may
be due to differences in conceptual focus and methodology.

Table 3.11 Reasons for not wanting more than desired number of children

(Percentage of respondents who gave specified reasons)

Reason	Urban middle	Urban lower	Rural	Female	Male	All respondents
General financial burden	23	31	23	20	30	25
General rearing problems	5	5	9	6	7	6
Housing problems	5	10	1	6	5	5
Responsibility of parenthood	5	4	1	3	4	3
Health hazard of pregnancy; maternal health	4	2	3	5	1	3
Already have number of children wanted	0	5	5	4	2	3
Spouse doesn't want more children	2	1	3	1	2	2
To have correct number for childrearing, ease of handling, happiness	0	4	1	2	2	2
Educational costs	1	1	3	2	1	2
Physical demands	4	1	0	2	1	2

other groups, as did male respondents, who were chiefly responsible for financial support. Other reasons, mentioned by much smaller percentages of respondents, were general rearing problems, housing problems, the responsibility of parenthood, and concern about the mother's health. Concern about the housing problem was peculiar to Japanese respondents. The urban lower-class group mentioned this category more frequently than other groups, a finding that may reflect the crowded urban housing conditions in present-day Japan. Female respondents were particularly concerned about the hazards of another pregnancy and their own health.

Reasons for not wanting more children

Respondents who said they did not want more children were asked why not. As Table 3.12 shows, the financial burden again predominated. The second most common "reason" was that the respondent already had the number wanted, a response that provides no useful information; then came concern about pregnancy and maternal health, general rearing problems, and housing problems.

Table 3.12 Reasons for not wanting more children
(Percentage of respondents who gave specified reasons)

Reason	Urban middle	Urban lower	Rural	Female	Male	All respondents
General financial burden	11	20	19	16	17	17
Already have number of children wanted	10	5	16	11	9	10
Health hazard of pregnancy; maternal health	8	5	9	11	3	7
General rearing problems	2	4	12	8	4	6
Housing problems	10	5	0	6	3	5
Restrictions on job, career	5	2	4	5	2	3
To have correct number for childrearing, ease of handling, happiness	1	3	3	0	4	2
To retain desired balance of sexes	2	1	1	2	1	2
General emotional strain	1	1	3	2	1	2
Spouse doesn't want more children	1	2	2	0	3	2

The financial burden of another child was most often mentioned by the urban lower-class, rural, and male groups—although the difference between male and female respondents on this reason was slight. More rural respondents than others said they already had the number of children they wanted; more in this SES group also mentioned problems related to pregnancy or maternal health and rearing problems. The middle class mentioned general childrearing problems least often but frequently mentioned the effects of another child on the mother's health, housing problems, and restrictions on job or career. For women general rearing problems, the hazards of another pregnancy, and restrictions on job or career were particularly salient.

When one compares Table 3.12 with Tables 3.9 and 3.10, the main difference is that in identifying general disadvantages of children, respondents more frequently mentioned psychological and affective problems like restrictions on time, anxiety about health, general emotional strain, and noise and disorder, whereas when asked to give reasons for not wanting more children, they mentioned physical and economic problems like the financial burden, rearing and housing problems, and restrictions on job or career.

Discussion of open-ended responses

With regard to response frequencies, respondents mentioned more advantages of having children than disadvantages. About three advantages were cited for every two disadvantages. Urban middle-class respondents mentioned the greatest number of disadvantages; the rural group mentioned fewer disadvantages than either of the two urban groups.

For the question on the advantages of having children, the dominant categories mentioned were happiness, love, and companionship (love and affection; play, fun with children; happiness for the family), the dimension of childrearing satisfactions (pleasure from children's growth and development, children to carry out parent's hopes and aspirations), personal development of parent (incentives to succeed, fulfillment of self), and benefits to the family unit (children as a bond between husband and wife). Less salient were economic benefits and security (economic help in old age, unspecified help), kin group benefits (continuity of family name), and social and religious influences.[3]

When respondents were asked about the advantages of children to others in the community rather than to themselves, their responses became more general and conventional.

The most salient disadvantages of having children were restrictions on alternative activities (restrictions on time, on social life, on job or career, and general lack of flexibility and freedom). Other salient disadvantages were emotional problems (such as the emotional strain caused by children, childrearing problems, health problems of children, noise, disorder, and nuisance), financial problems, and physical demands on parents.[4]

The questions about advantages and disadvantages of having children tended to elicit general responses. When asked more specific questions about their rationale for wanting or not wanting children—e.g., why

---

3 It is worth noting that for Japanese respondents in Hawaii (all of whom were urban), the most salient specific values were companionship and avoidance of loneliness, pleasure from children's growth and development, and children as family life. In Hawaii, furthermore, respondents tended to value children more for their contribution to the individual parent's happiness than for their contribution to happiness for the whole family (Arnold and Fawcett, 1975:42–43).

4 For Japanese respondents in Hawaii the most salient disadvantages were general lack of flexibility and freedom, financial costs, emotional strain, restrictions on job and social life, general childrearing problems, disciplinary problems, and physical demands (Arnold and Fawcett, 1975:49). The difference between the response patterns of the two samples may be due to differences in their socio-cultural contexts.

they would not want fewer or more than a certain number of children—respondents gave more concrete and realistic answers. The question about why they did not want fewer than the desired number was intended to reveal a threshold value for wanting children. That is, respondents might consider there to be disadvantages to having fewer than the desired number of children. Interestingly, respondents gave reasons for not wanting fewer that were mainly for the benefit of children, not of the parents. In other words, the threshold value led to an empathetic attitude toward children, which became an instrumental value to respondents.

With regard to sex preferences for children, psychological-affective values such as companionship for parents or the personality traits of girls and boys generally ranked higher than such practical values as help with housework or satisfaction in providing for children. Psychological-affective value dimensions were mentioned in relation to girls more frequently than boys. Boys were also valued as heirs.

Structured items

The preceding section has dealt with unstructured questions probing respondents' perceptions of the advantages and disadvantages of children. The VOC questionnaire included structured items intended to reveal values that might not have surfaced with nondirective probing. They consisted of a list of 17 reasons that "people sometimes give for wanting another child" and a similar list of nine reasons sometimes given for not wanting another child. Respondents were asked to rate these reasons as very important, somewhat important, or not important. Tables 3.13 and 3.14 present the percentages of respondents who considered each item to be either very important or somewhat important.

For the whole sample, important reasons for wanting another child were that children are fun to have around the house (87 percent), they help one to learn about life and oneself (83 percent), respondents wanted a companion for their children (77 percent), and they wanted the special feeling of love that exists between parent and child (74 percent). These reasons are more or less concerned with the value dimension of love and affection. Reasons regarded as unimportant were concern with religious duties (7 percent), pressure from relatives to have more children (13 percent), children as a source of economic help (17 percent), desire for help in old age (29 percent), and to carry on the family name and traditions (36 percent). These reasons are related to social and instrumental values for having children.

Table 3.13 Important reasons for wanting another child
(Percentage of respondents who considered specified
reasons to be very important or somewhat important)

Reason	Urban middle	Urban lower	Rural	Female	Male	All respondents
Fun to have children around house	87	91	85	90	85	87
To help me learn about life and myself	83	81	83	88	77	83
Want companion for my child/children	78	79	77	74	84	77
For special feeling of love between parent and child	69	77	76	79	69	74
Enjoy caring for, raising children	54	54	69	64	54	59
Spouse wants more children	49	54	48	60	54	59
Want a boy/another boy	59	61	51	49	65	57
Enjoy having small baby	49	54	59	61	47	54
To have enough children survive to adulthood	44	44	56	52	44	48
Want a girl/another girl	48	47	46	52	42	47
To share what I have and know with children	41	37	47	40	44	42
To make my marriage stronger	32	40	44	43	34	39
To carry on family name, traditions	27	31	51	33	40	36
To have child to help me in my old age	15	20	51	33	25	29
One more person to help family economically	7	12	32	19	15	17
Relatives feel I should have more children	13	10	16	14	12	13
My religious duty to have children	2	2	16	10	4	7

When the response frequencies are analyzed by socioeconomic status and sex, the following trends are observed. In the rural group, higher scores were given to the importance of family name and tradition (51 percent versus 27 and 31 percent for the middle class and lower class, respectively), help in old age (51 percent versus 15 and 20 percent), economic help (32 percent versus 7 and 12 percent), religious duty (16 percent compared with 2 percent for the other groups), and pressures from relatives (16 percent versus 13 and 10 percent). Wanting a boy was more important than wanting a girl for all subgroups except female respondents.

Reasons for not wanting another child that respondents regarded as important (Table 3.14) were the financial burden to the family (56 percent), the emotional strain (50 percent), not being able to give enough attention to children already born (45 percent), and the restriction of freedom to do other enjoyable things (41 percent). These results roughly correspond to those obtained from the open-ended questions (Tables 3.8 and 3.9). Reasons that respondents considered relatively unimportant were concern about overpopulation (16 percent), problems and strains between spouses that another child would

Table 3.14 Important reasons for not wanting another child
(Percentage of respondents who considered reason to be very important or somewhat important)

Reason	Urban middle	Urban lower	Rural	Female	Male	All respondents
Would be financial burden to family	47	63	58	55	56	56
Would be emotional strain for me	43	51	55	57	42	50
Not able to give enough attention to other children	37	46	51	50	39	45
Would restrict my freedom to do other things I enjoy	48	43	34	53	29	41
Spouse does not want more children	38	34	47	35	44	39
Would be a lot of work, bother for me	36	31	44	46	27	37
Could not spend as much time with spouse	24	25	25	27	22	25
Would cause problems, strains between spouse and me	18	18	33	25	21	23
Concerned about overpopulation	25	15	8	12	20	16

cause (23 percent), and not being able to spend as much time with spouse (25 percent). Respondents' unconcerned attitude toward over-population was an unexpected finding, in view of Japan's population density.

More urban lower-class respondents (63 percent) than others con-sidered the financial burden of another child to be important. The emotional strain of another child and not being able to give enough at-tention to other children were more important to women and the rural and lower-class groups than to men and the middle class. Restriction on freedom was less important for males and the rural group than for the other groups. Strain between spouses was regarded as important by less than a fifth of the two urban groups but by a third of the rural group, who were also more concerned about work and bother. The middle- and lower-class groups attached relatively greater importance to concern about overpopulation than the rural group as a reason for not wanting another child (25 percent and 15 percent, compared with 8 percent); males showed more concern than females (20 versus 12 percent).

The results from Tables 3.13 and 3.14 suggest that traditional rea-sons for wanting children persist—especially among the rural group, who emphasized the importance of family name, old-age and eco-nomic help, and boy preference. On the other hand, the financial bur-den and emotional strain of another child were important to a major-ity of lower-class and rural respondents and to nearly half of the mid-dle class. As expected, more women than men were concerned about the emotional burden of a larger family, but men and women placed nearly equal importance on the financial burden.

Why did so few respondents regard overpopulation as an important reason for not wanting another child? If overpopulation in present-day Japan were considered to be a cause of poverty as it is in most develop-ing countries, the Japanese VOC respondents might have attached more importance to it. This result should be taken to mean that al-though they felt the pressure of overpopulation in Japan, their per-sonal lives were not disturbed by it. The Japanese have a high standard of living owing to their economic achievements, and their reasons for not wanting children derive from other, more personal sources than overpopulation, which is generally considered to be a social phenome-non. Thus the lack of importance attached to overpopulation by our respondents may be taken to signify their unconcern about social problems that do not affect their personal economic wellbeing.

The preceding paragraphs have described results of the structured items for the total sample. The results were also analyzed separately for those who replied that they actually wanted another child and those who replied that they did not. Results for the two groups are shown in Tables 3.15 and 3.16. The differences in mean scores indicate which items may be most significant in actual childbearing decisions.

As Table 3.15 indicates, respondents who wanted more children generally had higher mean scores on reasons for wanting than those

Table 3.15 Mean scores on reasons for wanting another child, by those wanting and not wanting more children

Reason	Wanting more (N = 199)	Not wanting more (N = 189)[a]
Enjoy having small baby	1.7	1.8
To carry on family name, traditions	1.5	1.5
Want boy/another boy	2.2	1.7*
Want girl/another girl	1.8	1.6*
Relatives feel I should have more children	1.2	1.1
To have child to help me in my old age	1.4	1.4
My religious duty to have children	1.1	1.1
To have one more person to help family economically	1.2	1.2
To make my marriage stronger	1.6	1.4*
To provide a companion for my child/children	2.6	1.9*
Enjoy caring for, raising children	1.9	1.6*
Spouse wants more children	1.9	1.5*
Fun to have children around house	2.6	2.2*
Raising children helps me to learn about life and myself	2.4	2.2*
To have special feeling of love between parent and child	2.2	2.0†
To share what I have and know with children	1.6	1.5
To have enough children survive to adulthood	1.8	1.7

NOTE: Possible scores range from 1 (not important) to 3 (very important).
* Significant at .001 level.
† Significant at .01 level.
a   Twenty-one respondents were uncertain.

who did not want more, and for nearly half of the items the scores showed significant differences between the two groups of respondents. Differences between the two groups on wanting a boy, wanting a girl, to make marriage stronger, to have companion for other children, enjoy caring for children, spouse wants more children, fun to have children around house, to learn about life and self, and special feeling of love were all significant at the .001 or .01 level. Desire for children of a particular sex and expected emotional benefits appear to have been dominant reasons for wanting another child. Differences in the responses of the two groups should be taken to mean that respondents who wanted more children were able to imagine the described benefits more realistically than others and to respond to them in congruence with their desires.

Differences between the two groups in mean scores were smaller for reasons for not wanting another child (Table 3.16). Only one item, emotional strain, showed a difference significant at the .001 level. A less significant difference ($p = .05$) emerged for financial burden, insufficient attention for other children, and problems between spouses.

Table 3.16 Mean scores on reasons for not wanting another child, by those wanting and not wanting more children

Reason	Wanting more ($N = 199$)	Not wanting more ($N = 189$)[a]
Would be financial burden to family	1.7	1.8†
Spouse does not want more children	1.7	1.6
Would restrict my freedom to do other things I enjoy	1.6	1.5
Would be a lot of work, bother for me	1.4	1.5
Could not spend as much time with spouse	1.4	1.2
Concerned about overpopulation	1.2	1.2
Would be emotional strain for me	1.6	1.8*
Not able to give enough attention to other children	1.5	1.7†
Would cause problems, strains between spouse and me	1.2	1.4†

NOTE: Possible scores range from 1 (not important) to 3 (very important).
* Significant at .001 level.
† Significant at .05 level.
a   Twenty-one respondents were uncertain.

Attitudes toward children

Forty-five Likert-type items were used to assess respondents' attitudes concerning children and childrearing. Respondents were asked to score these items on a six-point scale ranging from strong agreement (7 points) to strong disagreement (1 point). (Items toward which respondents felt neutral were scored as 4.) Our expectation was that analysis of responses to these structured items might reveal dimensions of values associated with children that could not be obtained from responses to other types of questions.

For convenience of comparison, individual items were organized into nine clusters, based on the results of an aggregate factor analysis of the scores of 2,591 respondents from six countries (see Arnold et al., 1975:49–64). These nine factors were found to describe the following dimensions of the value of children: continuity, tradition, security (VOC Scale 1); parenthood satisfactions (Scale 2); role motivations (Scale 3); happiness and affection (Scale 4); goals and incentives (Scale 5); social status (Scale 6); external control (Scale 7); costs of children (Scale 8); and decision-mindedness (Scale 9). Mean scores for the nine scales and for each attitude item are given in Table 3.17. Examination of the table shows that the scales of goals and incentives, role motivations, and parenthood satisfactions had the highest mean scores, with nearly all items within these scales eliciting strong to moderate agreement and none having scores of 4.0 or less. The other scales had substantially lower mean scores and in some cases extreme variability of mean scores for items within the scales.

Two of the items clustered under happiness and affection (Scale 4) —"A person who has no children can never really be happy" and "The family with children is the only place in the modern world where a person can feel comfortable and happy"—had negative mean scores, whereas in open-ended responses to the unstructured questions happiness and affection emerged as important values. This apparent discrepancy in the findings might be explained by the fact that in the case of the unstructured questions about the advantages of having children, respondents were free to compose their own replies, but in answering structured questions they were required to react to others' statements and therefore to conform in some way to an attitude structure the investigators had in mind.

Under external control (Scale 7), the item "It isn't right for a couple to interfere with nature by deciding to limit the number of children they will have" elicited moderate agreement. When translated into Japanese, this statement conveyed nuances of ideological and moral

Table 3.17 Mean scores on 31 VOC attitude items, by nine subscales
(Scales based on aggregate factor analysis for all countries)

Scale and item	Mean score
Goals and incentives (Scale 5)	6.2
Having children gives a person a special incentive to succeed in life	6.7
Having children around makes a stronger bond between husband and wife	6.2
One of the highest purposes in life is to have children	5.8
Role motivations (Scale 3)	5.6
After becoming a parent, a person is less likely to behave immorally	6.1
It is only natural that a woman should want children	6.0
It is only natural that a man should want children	5.9
A girl becomes a woman only after she is a mother	5.4
A boy becomes a man only after he is a father	4.4
Parenthood satisfactions (Scale 2)	5.5
Just the feeling a parent gets of being needed is enough to make having children worthwhile	5.6
A person who has been a good parent can feel completely satisfied with his achievements in life	5.5
One of the best things about being a parent is the chance to teach children what they should and should not do	5.4
Decision-mindedness (Scale 9)	4.4
A couple ought to think seriously about the inconveniences caused by children before they have any	5.8
The first thing a couple should think about when deciding to have children is whether or not they can afford it	5.1
Before having a child, a couple should consider whether it would interfere with the wife's work or not	4.2
Before having a child, a couple should consider whether they would rather use their money for something else	2.5
Happiness and affection (Scale 4)	4.1
It is only with a child that a person can feel completely free to express his love and affection	5.8
A person who has no children can never really be happy	3.6
The family with children is the only place in the modern world where a person can feel comfortable and happy	2.9
Costs of children (Scale 8)	4.1
Children limit you in what you want to do and where you want to go	4.5

Table 3.17 *(continued)*

Scale and item	Mean score
Having children causes many disagreements and problems between husband and wife	3.0
Raising children is a heavy financial burden for most people	4.8
When you have children, you have to give up a lot of other things that you enjoy	4.3
Continuity, tradition, security (Scale 1)	4.0
A person can feel that part of him lives on after death if he has children	4.8
It is important to have children so that the family traditions will live on	4.7
One of the best things about having children is the true loyalty they show to their parents	4.1
A man has a duty to have children to continue the family name	4.0
A good reason for having children is that they can help when parents are too old to work	2.7
External control (Scale 7)	4.0
It isn't right for a couple to interfere with nature by deciding to limit the number of children they will have	5.1
Considering the pressures from family and friends, a person really doesn't have much choice whether or not to have children	2.8
Social status (Scale 6)	2.8
A person with children is looked up to in the community more than a person without children	3.0
A young couple is not fully accepted in the community until they have children	2.5

beliefs to the Japanese respondents and they were therefore more susceptible to it. As we shall see in Chapter 5, however, the Japanese respondents reported positive attitudes toward contraception and high rates of contraceptive practice. Such an apparent contradiction may be explained by the reasoning that ideal opinions such as that expressed here do not always lead to corresponding practice. In other words, the respondents may have agreed that in an ideal situation it is wrong to interfere with nature but felt compelled to interfere because of economic or other circumstances.

The two items clustered under social status (Scale 6) "A young

couple is not fully accepted in the community until they have children"
and "A person with children is looked up to in the community more
than a person without children"—received from Japanese respondents
the second lowest rating (2.5 and 3.0, respectively) of the six countries
sampled (Arnold et al., 1975:58). Only the Japanese in Hawaii rated
them lower. The low scores on this scale imply that having children
does not enhance one's social status in the modern Japanese community.

Other attitude items that received high scores (above 6.0) but did
not fall within any of the clusters of empirically derived scales were
affirmative statements about the affectionate bond, the benefits of
children, and love, loyalty, and companionship. Items that obtained
low scores (below 3.0) were those describing children as economic
benefits, obligations, or a means of help in old age.

When the scale scores are broken down by SES group (Table 3.18),
relatively small differences across groups are observed. The rural group,
however, scored notably higher than either of the urban groups on
continuity, tradition, and security, as expected. The rural group also
scored higher on happiness and affection and lower on costs of children.

Scores on the 45 items were also factor analyzed separately for the
Japanese respondents, by means of principal components analysis with
varimax rotation. Six factors were derived by this method. To interpret the meaning of the six factors, items with loadings over .40 were
identified and grouped together within each factor, and their factor
scores as well as means were compared. The factor structures are presented in the Appendix Table. Fourteen, or about one-third, of the 45
items clustered in factor I. Of these 14 items, four stress parental goals
and incentives, three are concerned with role motivations, two are related to parenthood satisfactions, and the rest are concerned with the
dimension of happiness and affection. Since the dominant value dimensions of this cluster are parental goals/incentives and role motivations (nine of the 14 items), an appropriate label for this factor is
parental incentives and role motivations.

Factor II contains nine items with loadings above .40, of which six
stress continuity, tradition, and security, two are concerned with happiness and affection, and one is unclassified. This factor is therefore
designated as *continuity, tradition, and security.*

Four of the six items clustered under factor III are concerned with
financial and emotional burdens of raising children and the other two
emphasize decision-making in relation to parenthood. This factor has
accordingly been labeled *costs of children.*

Table 3.18 Mean scores on nine VOC attitude scales, by socioeconomic group

Scale	Urban middle	Urban lower	Rural
Goals and incentives (Scale 5)	6.0	6.2	6.3
Role motivations (Scale 3)	5.4	5.6	5.7
Parenthood satisfactions (Scale 2)	5.2	5.3	5.7
Decision-mindedness (Scale 9)	4.3	4.5	4.5
Happiness and affection (Scale 4)	3.9	4.0	4.6
Costs of children (Scale 8)	4.2	4.4	3.8
Continuity, tradition, security (Scale 1)	3.6	3.6	4.8
External control (Scale 7)	4.0	3.9	4.0
Social status (Scale 6)	2.7	2.7	3.0

Under factor IV, two items are concerned with the enhancement of social status, one item emphasizes role motivation, and the fourth is unclassified. This factor may therefore be called *social status.*

All three items under factor V stress the importance of weighing alternatives to children. Therefore an appropriate label for this factor is *alternatives to children.*

Of the items with high loadings under factor VI, one is related to parenthood satisfactions from children and the other, to happiness and affection. Because neither value dimension is dominant, the factor is not easily characterized. For this reason it has not been assigned a label.

A further interesting result of the factor analysis is the relationship between the loadings under the six factors and the mean scores of the attitude items. (See the Appendix Table.) Items with high factor loadings also received high mean scores, except for items under factors II and IV that emphasize costs of children and social status. None of the high factor loadings had negative signs.

Separate factor analyses for the subgroups of Japanese respondents (by SES and sex) revealed variations among subgroups in factor loadings. These analyses are not reported in detail in this volume. Nevertheless, certain consistencies of high factor loadings (over .40) among these subgroups, in comparison with the factor loadings from the factor analysis of the total sample described above, deserve comment. For the items in factor I (parental incentives and role motivations), for example, consistently high loadings were obtained for the middle-class and male groups. For items in factor II (continuity, tradition, and security) the male group showed consistently high factor loadings. For items in factor III (costs of children) the lower-class, female, and male groups showed consistently high factor loadings, while in factor IV (social status) the high loadings occurred among the rural, female, and male groups. For items in factor V (alternatives to children) only the rural group showed consistently high factor loadings.

In general, results of the factor analysis reveal that although the factor loadings are not so strong or consistent as in other VOC countries, the value dimensions extracted from the factor loadings are quite congruent with the dimensions obtained from the aggregated data from the six countries. Furthermore, consistently dominant factor loadings were obtained in the male and middle-class groups.

Differences among results

At this point, it may be useful to discuss differences in results obtained from the open-ended questions about the advantages and disadvantages of having children, the structured items about reasons for wanting and not wanting more children, and the nine scales based on aggregate factor analysis of the attitude items concerning children and parenthood. The responses given to the attitude items differed somewhat from those obtained from the open-ended questions and items about reasons for wanting and not wanting more children. The value dimensions reflecting strongest agreement in the attitude scales were goals and incentives from children, role motivations, and parenthood satisfactions, followed by decision-mindedness in childbearing and costs of children. The dimension of happiness and affection received an almost neutral mean score overall, although it was slightly positive for rural respondents. The scale on continuity, tradition, and security received a negative score for urban respondents, but a positive one among rural respondents. Items suggesting that children confer social status on their parents received negative scores among all subgroups.

As noted earlier, items on happiness and affection were highly salient in responses to open-ended questions, yet were relatively unimportant in responses to the attitude scales. How could such discrepancies among results be accounted for? It will be recalled that both the open-ended questions and the structured items on reasons for wanting or not wanting more children attempted to ascertain respondents' *direct motives* for having children. The attitude items, on the other hand, expressed *general opinions* about raising children. Responses to the attitude items thus did not reveal respondents' direct motives for having children but rather suggested certain value dimensions associated with children. Furthermore, the attitude items directed respondents' attention to attitudes expressed according to the investigators' intent and may therefore have created a response bias.[5] Because the discrepancies in the results may be accounted for by such methodological differences, these results should be interpreted with caution. Findings from the other five VOC countries reveal similar discrepancies in data obtained from the three different methodologies. For details see the introductory volume of this series (Arnold et al., 1975).

---

5 Stephan (1962:429) has pointed out the following pitfalls of attitude measurement in family planning research. Responses given to structured questions may represent a compromise among many motives. Researchers may erroneously infer from the responses that certain motives are primary. Thus, attitudes that are intended to be the object of measurement may not exist in individuals in crystallized form. Although the methods selected for the Value of Children Study were intended to explore the dimensions of the values associated with children by parents and were not used for family planning research, this warning may still be relevant to the apparent discrepancies in the results.

4

perceived economic costs and benefits of children

In the preceding chapter we examined respondents' opinions about having children as assessed by open-ended questions, structured questions, and attitude scales. The results showed that respondents associated economic as well as emotional costs and benefits with children. This chapter focuses on these economic costs and benefits, including utilitarian values of children. In the following chapter we will explore how perceived economic and psychological costs of children interact with favorable attitudes toward raising children in an effort to determine the relative influence of each on VOC respondents' childbearing decisions.

Economic costs

As we saw in Chapter 3, responses to both open-ended and structured questions indicated that the financial costs children entail were salient, important, and burdensome to many Japanese respondents. Two financial disadvantages of children were especially prominent, the general financial cost of raising children and the expense of children's education.

To probe further economic motivations in childbearing, the VOC questionnaire included several questions specifically about the financial burden of children. One of these was the following: "We would like to know how much of a financial burden it is to raise children, for a family in your circumstances. If you were to raise only *one* child, would it be fairly easy economically, somewhat of a financial burden, or a heavy financial burden? How about two children? Three children? . . . Six children?" Table 4.1 shows that, in their present circumstances, 71 percent of the respondents thought it would be fairly easy to raise one child, but more than a quarter (27 percent) thought it would be somewhat of a burden. Forty-seven percent thought raising two children would be fairly easy economically; almost as many (46 percent), however, thought two children would constitute somewhat of a financial burden. Only 21 percent of respondents thought raising three children would be easy, while 50 percent thought it would be somewhat burdensome and 29 percent said it would be very burdensome. When four children were mentioned, the largest proportion of respondents (65 percent) said raising them would be a heavy burden. These results provide a rough index of the financial burden of different family sizes as perceived by Japanese parents who, in many cases, indicated they had not completed their family building.

Respondents were also asked whether they would be economically better or worse off with more children: "Some couples feel that the more children they have, the better off the family will be economically. Others feel that having a lot of children will make their family less well-off. How do you personally feel about this?" As seen in Table 4.2, 64 percent of respondents said having more children would make the family worse off, whereas only 6 percent said the family would be better off with more children. (Thirteen percent said it made no difference and 11 percent qualified their answers by saying that a family with

Table 4.1 Perceived financial burden of raising different numbers of children

(Percentage distribution of respondents who considered raising specified numbers of children to be fairly easy economically, somewhat of a financial burden, and a heavy financial burden)

Number of children	Fairly easy	Somewhat of a burden	Heavy burden	All responses
1	71	27	2	100
2	47	46	6	99
3	21	50	29	100
4	7	27	65	99
5	4	10	86	100
6	2	4	93	99

NOTE: Percentages may not sum to 100 because of rounding.

Table 4.2 Family size and economic status
(Percentage of respondents who said more children make a family better or worse off economically)

Economic status	Urban middle	Urban lower	Rural	Female	Male	All re-spondents
Worse off	63	68	61	62	66	64
Makes no difference	16	10	13	13	13	13
Better off	5	6	6	5	7	6
Worse off at first, less so later	12	10	11	14	8	11
Depends	1	5	2	3	3	3
Other	1	0	5	2	2	2
No answer	2	1	2	1	2	2
Total	100	100	100	100	101	101

NOTE: Percentages may not sum to 100 because of rounding.

more children would be worse off at first, while the children were young, but less so later.) Differences among subgroups were negligible. If, as seems plausible, the respondents interpreted the question as applying to themselves, a clear majority believed they would be worse off with a large family.

What about respondents' perceptions of the cost of raising their children in relation to the family's resources? Respondents were asked to estimate how much money it had cost them to raise their children over the previous 12 months. Many understandably had difficulty answering this question, because expenditures on children for such things as food and housing are made as part of general household expenditures. Thus the estimates may not be realistic. Nevertheless, they indicate respondents' perceptions of the cost of children.

According to reported expenditures (Table 4.3), respondents spent an average of only 10 percent of their income on their children, or slightly over 5 percent per child. (It should be noted that the children of our sample were mostly of preschool age.) Middle-class respondents, with the highest average income, estimated spending the smallest proportion (8 percent) of income on their two children, whereas the rural group, with the lowest average income, estimated spending the largest proportion (16 percent)—though in absolute terms less income—on the same average number of children.

From these estimates and the fact that only 29 percent of the re-

Table 4.3 Estimated expenditure on children during past year
(Thousands of yen)

Item	Urban middle	Urban lower	Rural	All respondents
1. Average amount spent on all children	180.7	140.5	167.0	162.7
2. Mean family income	2,343.0	1,637.5[a]	1,024.0	1,668.1
3. Percentage of income spent on children (1/2)	8	9	16	10
4. Mean number of children	2.0	1.6	2.0	1.8
5. Percentage of income spent per child (3/4)	4	5	8	5

a   Mean family income of lower-class respondents exceeded 1,500 thousand yen (the cutoff point dividing the lower-class and middle-class groups) because other criteria in addition to income were used to identify the lower-class group (occupation, home ownership, consumer durables owned).

spondents said it would be a heavy burden to raise three children, the perceived economic cost of children, in relation to family income, does not appear to have been a major constraint to having more than two children. Responses to a related question bear out this inference. Respondents were asked: "Suppose your family income increased to double what it is now. Would that affect the number of children you want?" Eighty-one percent of respondents replied that they would not change their desired family size even if their income were doubled.

The acute housing shortage in Japan, mentioned earlier by some respondents as a reason for not wanting more than a desired number of children, may have contributed to respondents' desire to keep their family size small. The questionnaire did not contain a specific question on this topic, however, so we are not able to assess adequately the importance of living space in relation to other considerations.

In general, responses to the VOC questions discussed in this section suggest that perceived economic costs of children—or at least of large families—were of concern, but not of utmost concern, to the Japanese parents interviewed. Other factors, such as noneconomic costs associated with large families or noneconomic rewards ascribed to small families, would seem to have additional bearing on respondents' attitudes toward family size.

Economic benefits

Children are sometimes regarded as economic assets by parents, especially in traditional societies. Children can do household chores, help run family farms or businesses, support their parents in old age, and inherit family property. Children perform some of these functions as children, others when they get older; and parents may gain satisfaction from having children to fulfill these needs. How do contemporary Japanese parents regard such matters?

As reported in Chapter 3, expected help with housework and family chores was given as a reason for wanting a daughter by a fifth of respondents (Table 3.6) and unspecified help in old age as a reason by only 1 percent. Similarly, few respondents gave economic reasons for wanting sons—8 percent citing unspecified help, 5 percent mentioning help in old age, and 3 percent mentioning help in the family business (Table 3.7).

Later in the interviews, respondents were asked specifically whether they expected economic or practical help from their sons or daughters, either while the children were growing up or after they became adults. Twenty-five percent of the sample said they expected help from their sons, as compared with 62 percent who had no such expectations (Table 4.4). Even fewer respondents (14 percent) expected help from their daughters. A substantial majority of both urban groups did not expect economic help from their sons, compared with fewer than a fifth of both groups who did expect such help; but among rural respondents 43 percent anticipated some help from their sons. It is noteworthy that despite Japan's advanced modernization, such a traditional expectation of sons has survived among rural people.

Table 4.4 also shows respondents' anticipated reliance on children for financial support in old age. Sixty percent of the middle-class group and 57 percent of the lower class did not expect to rely on their children in old age. Only in the rural group did a majority (73 percent) have such expectations. For the total sample, slightly more females (48 percent) than males (41 percent) expected to be reliant on their children.

The general result seems to reflect a diffusion of modern thought. That is to say, most VOC respondents appeared to hold the view that after rearing their children their duties would be finished and their children would be independent, living independently from them. This attitude, which has probably been influenced by Western individualism, was quite unthinkable in prewar days. Elderly Japanese parents, those born in the Meiji period and prewar era, believe that children have a duty to take care of their parents in return for the sacrifices the parents endured in bringing them up (*oya-koko,* 'be loyal to parents'),

Table 4.4 Expected economic reliance on children
(Percentage distribution of respondents expecting economic or practical help from chidlren)

Reliance	Urban middle	Urban lower	Rural	Female	Male	All re- spondents
Expect help from boys						
Yes	15	17	43	28	23	25
No	74	66	47	58	66	62
Uncertain	11	16	11	14	11	13
No answer	0	1	0	1	0	0
Total	100	100	101	101	100	100
Expect help from girls						
Yes	9	12	21	19	9	14
No	83	77	66	71	80	75
Uncertain	8	10	13	10	11	10
No answer	0	1	0	1	0	0
Total	100	100	100	101	100	99
Expect to rely on children for financial support in old age						
Yes[a]	29	31	73	48	41	45
Not at all	60	57	17	40	48	44
Depends	8	9	9	7	10	9
Uncertain	2	2	2	3	2	2
No answer	0	2	0	1	0	1
Total	99	101	101	99	101	101

NOTE: Percentages may not sum to 100 because of rounding.

a   Category includes those who said they would rely a great deal plus those who said they would rely only a little.

that children should support their parents economically or psychologically.

Table 4.5 indicates changing opinions on this matter. A series of questions asked for opinions about whether children nowadays (compared with when the respondent was growing up) are more willing, just as willing, or less willing to live with their parents after marrying, to give part of their wages to their parents when they start earning, to support their parents in old age, and to help with chores around the house or in the family business. A majority of the VOC sample replied

Table 4.5 Perceived changes in the economic utility of children over time

(Percentage distribution of respondents who said children are more, less, or just as willing nowadays to assist parents)

Type of assistance	More willing	Just as willing	Less willing	Of those who said "less willing," percentage who disapproved of change
Live with parents after marrying	5	11	77	30
Give part of wages to parents	7	16	64	30
Support parents in their old age	2	18	72	45
Help with household chores	2	18	75	46

NOTE: Percentages do not sum to 100 because other responses ("depends" and "don't know") are not included.

that children are less willing than in the past to give these kinds of help to their parents. As shown in the last column of Table 4.5, a substantial minority of those who believed that children nowadays are less willing to assist their parents also believed that such a trend is unfortunate.

Respondents were also asked what means of financial support they might have when they got old. As shown in Table 4.6, most said they would rely on savings (54 percent). Other frequently mentioned sources of support were continuing to work (cited by 27 percent), children (26 percent), social security (25 percent), and investments (19 percent).

Although psychological and economic support from children over the long run might be considered as a potential benefit of having them, despite the economic and psychological costs of rearing children, most of the VOC respondents did not regard the possibility of such support as a benefit of parenthood. One cause of the decline in traditional expectations from grown children in Japan may be an increase in modern attitudes. Another may be that rapid growth of technological industries and the disappearance of small-scale and family enterprises have separated the work place from the living place. Employment outside the home has become commonplace. Children are no longer needed for family businesses. In addition, workers and old people are increasingly being taken care of by the government or employers through

Table 4.6 Types of financial support expected in old age
(Percentage of respondents expecting specified types)

Type of support	Percentage expecting support[a]
Savings	54
Continuation of work	27
Children	26
Social security	25
Investments	19
Insurance	10
National support to aged	10
Inheritance	8
Help from relatives	5
Other	11

a   Multiple responses allowed.

through work opportunities, life insurance, savings, pensions, and old-age homes. For younger people there are well-paying opportunities for employment and a variety of jobs to choose from. For a son to inherit his father's occupation or business is no longer considered as valuable as in the past. Children may go into the occupations they want, and parents allow them to do so.

Such a cool separation of children from the family for the sake of independence is not always regarded by parents as favorable, however. Most parents seek emotional ties with their children, even as they grow old. The extent to which parents expect to live with their children in their later years may be an indicator of emotional ties rather than economic dependence. As Table 4.7 shows, only 23 percent of the VOC respondents had no expectation of living with their children when the children were grown. Most of the others responding to this question said they expected to live with their children until death or only in their old age. Differences among the subgroups were substantial. Whereas 68 percent of the rural group expected to live with their children until death, only 12 and 14 percent respectively of the middle-class and lower-class groups expected to do so. In fact, 39 percent of the middle-class respondents said they would not live with their children at all, compared with only 6 percent of the rural group.

The emotional reliance on children implied by parents' anticipation of living with them is intimately related to the question of whether parents expect financial assistance in old age. To explore this relation-

Table 4.7 Expectation of living with children in old age
(Percentage distribution of respondents by expectation)

Expectation	Urban middle	Urban lower	Rural	Female	Male	All re-spondents
Not at all	39	24	6	21	24	23
Yes, only for a few years after marriage	4	5	1	1	5	3
Yes, only in my old age	16	22	10	16	16	16
Yes, until my death	12	14	68	33	31	32
Other	27	34	14	28	22	25
No answer	2	2	0	1	2	1
Total	100	99	99	100	100	100

NOTE: Percentages may not sum to 100 because of rounding.

ship further, we asked respondents whether they thought their children would give them some money from time to time after the respondents stopped working (Table 4.8). Thirty-seven percent did not expect any money from their children, but most of the others expected such support whether living with their children or not (22 percent), in the case of living with them (14 percent), or according to circumstances (24 percent). More rural respondents gave positive responses, both absolute and conditional, to this question than did the other SES groups (78 percent, compared with 45 percent for the middle class and 57 percent for the lower class). More than half of the middle class (52 percent) did not expect to receive money from their children under any circumstances, but this response was less common among the lower class (38 percent) and the rural group (22 percent). More wives than husbands expected money from their children regardless of the circumstances.

Discussion

The following points emerge from the results presented in this chapter:

First, respondents said that in their present financial circumstances they did not worry much about raising children. Most said they would not have more children than desired even if their incomes were to double, and they tended to believe that having more children would make their economic conditions worse. In other words, given their circumstances, most respondents considered two or three children to be optimal. This finding not only suggests that respondents were de-

Table 4.8 Expectation of money from children
(Percentage distribution of respondents by expectation)

Expectation	Urban middle	Urban lower	Rural	Female	Male	All respondents
Yes, whether I live with them or not	16	17	32	25	19	22
Yes, in the case of living with them	8	12	23	16	12	14
Not at all	52	38	22	32	42	37
According to circumstances	21	28	23	25	23	24
No answer	3	5	1	2	4	3
Total	100	100	101	100	100	100

NOTE: Percentages may not sum to 100 because of rounding.

liberately controlling their family size; it suggests also that they were doing so to minimize the economic and psychological costs of child-rearing.

Second, VOC respondents perceived a great reduction in the economic utility of children in recent years, a phenomenon that may be due to the diffusion of Western pragmatism and the separation of work place and residence. This decline in children's economic utility coincides with a decline in economic motivations for having children. However, many VOC respondents regretted the diminished willingness of modern Japanese children to support or assist their parents economically. In this respect they are probably representative of most Japanese parents, many of whom look back with nostalgia to the period when stronger emotional and economic ties existed between parents and their children, when small-scale industries and family enterprises were closely connected with family life. In contrast, the modern attitude toward childbearing is pragmatic: the economic and psychological costs of children are minimized, while the emotional rewards of children are maximized. Recognizing that children entail certain costs, however, Japanese couples are inevitably led to control their family size. In this connection, the role of family planning in modern-day Japan is of the utmost importance. In the next chapter we turn to decision-making about family size and the status of family planning.

5

family size
and family planning

It practically goes without saying that the number of children people consider to be ideal and the number they have in reality is likely to depend upon values ascribed to children by their society, the economic structure of that society, and its stage of development. Moreover, certain discrepancies can be expected between ideal and real family size, especially in less developed countries. As a country modernizes and its living level rises, such discrepancies tend to diminish. This is due to the widespread adoption of family planning, which goes hand in hand with socioeconomic development and enables couples to make their ideal family size a reality.

In Japan the ideal number of children per family is about three, more than half of Japanese couples considering this number as being ideal.[1] The two-child family is somewhat less favored, perhaps for the

---

1 The two-child family started to become common around 1960 as postwar economic growth began to accelerate. Earlier average family size in Japan had been much larger: 2.37 in 1955, 3.65 in 1950, and 4.71 in 1930 (Office of the Prime Minister, 1959:167). The family planning knowledge, attitude, and practice (KAP) survey conducted by the Mainichi Newspapers in 1959 found that the average number of children per family was just 2.0. This number increased somewhat in the 1960s (reaching 2.14 according to the survey of 1965), then began to decrease again (falling to 1.9 in 1971). The ideal number of children per family somewhat exceeded the actual number. According to the 1971 survey, for instance, 46 percent of those sampled wanted three children whereas 33 percent wanted two children. The most recent survey (1975) indicated no

reason that if one child dies only one other will remain; and a single-child family is considered unfortunate for both the parents and the child. Moreover, if couples have three children, they have a greater probability of having children of both sexes. Thus, three children are the ideal family-size norm among a substantial proportion of contemporary Japanese parents.

To investigate factors related to preferred and actual family size has been one of the main aims of the present study. The first section of this chapter reports VOC findings concerning family size—present parity, the number of additional children wanted, and ideal family size—and sex preferences of respondents. The second section presents findings related to family planning, including reasons for using or not using contraception, knowledge about contraception, spacing of births, and attitudes toward abortion.

Family-size preferences

As reported in Chapter 2, the mean number of living children for the total sample was 1.9, which is small relative to other countries in the VOC study. The average number for the middle-class and rural groups was about two (2.02 and 2.04, respectively), while that of the urban lower group was less than two (1.6). If respondents' current parity was equal or nearly equal to their completed parity, a drastic reduction of fertility had taken place in just one generation, for the average number of siblings that respondents in all subgroups reported having was about four and a half.

But current parity was not necessarily completed parity, for some respondents may have desired to have more children. In reply to a question on this point, slightly fewer than half of the respondents (48 percent) said they wanted more children, while a similar proportion (47 percent) said they did not want more. Slightly more husbands than wives wanted additional children (52 percent versus 45 percent), as did more urban respondents (58 percent) than rural respondents (40 percent).

Respondents who expressed a desire for more children were asked how many more. Table 5.1 shows that for the total sample the mean number of additional children desired was 0.9, and that the total number of children wanted was 2.8, on the average. This latter result was substantially less than respondents' ideal number of children, which

change in this trend since 1971: average number of children per family remained at 1.9, but 42 percent of respondents considered three children to be ideal and 40 percent considered two as ideal (Mainichi Newspapers, 1976).

Table 5.1 Selected measures of family size

Measure	Urban middle	Urban lower	Rural	Female	Male	All respondents
Mean number of living children	2.0	1.6	2.0	1.9	1.9	1.9
Mean number of additional children wanted	1.1	1.1	0.6	0.7	1.2	0.9
Total mean number of children wanted	3.1	2.7	2.6	2.6	2.9	2.8
Mean ideal number of children	3.2	3.2	3.0	2.9	3.3	3.1
Difference between ideal number and wanted number	0.1	0.5	0.4	0.3	0.4	0.3
Mean number of children in "typical" family in community	2.5	2.5	2.6	2.5	2.6	2.5
Difference between wanted number and "typical" number	0.6	0.2	0.0	0.1	0.4	0.3
Difference between ideal number and "typical" number	0.7	0.7	0.4	0.4	0.6	0.6

for the total sample was 3.1. The difference between ideal and wanted number suggests that, given an ideal situation in which all living conditions were satisfied, respondents would have preferred more children. That this difference was greater for the lower-class and rural respondents than for the middle class suggests that the two lower SES groups may have tended to suppress their wanted number of children more than middle-class respondents.

Interestingly, all subgroups wanted and idealized a larger number of children than the number they perceived to be typical of other families in the community, with the difference being greatest for the middle class. In fact, in our sample the middle class reported a substantially larger desired family size than the other two groups, a finding that is at variance with research in most developed societies. This too suggests that fertility motivations among the less affluent subgroups were suppressed by economic factors and other living conditions in Japan.

Table 5.2 shows sex preferences related to the first child. A slightly higher percentage of all respondents preferred a son for the first child

Table 5.2 Son-daughter preference for first child
(Percentage distribution of respondents)

Preference	Urban middle	Urban lower	Rural	Female	Male	All re-spondents
Son	39	43	51	32	58	45
Daughter	39	33	30	47	20	34
Doesn't matter	18	17	13	14	18	16

NOTE: Percentages do not sum to 100 because those who said "up to God, fate," etc. are omitted.

(45 percent versus 34 percent who preferred a daughter). A majority of male respondents (58 percent) and a substantial proportion of female respondents (32 percent) preferred a son for their first child, although a larger percentage (47) of women preferred a daughter. Son preference associated with the first child was evident among rural and lower-class groups, but not among middle-class respondents, among whom those having a sex preference were equally divided between sons and daughters. Taken together with reasons for wanting children of a particular sex as elicited by the open-ended questions, the relatively high percentages of rural and lower-class respondents expressing son preference may signify a desire for heirs—an indication, perhaps, of some persistence of traditional values related to children.

When asked about the sex composition of their ideal family, respondents having preferences tended to prefer a boy as their first child (45 percent, as against 36 percent who preferred a girl). Sex preferences for the second child were about equally divided between boys and girls (39 percent and 40 percent). When a third child was wanted the preference was again weighted toward boys, suggesting an ideal pattern of boy-girl-boy for the three-child family. There was also a slight indication of boy preference among the few respondents who wanted more than three children.[2]

What did respondents perceive to be a large or small family size? As Table 5.3 indicates, 97 percent of the respondents replied that one or

2 According to a study of birth-order preference by sex (Matsubara, 1964:105), the average Japanese couple desired the first child to be a daughter and second child a son. As the first child, a daughter can serve as a general helper by doing family chores, whereas a son, even as the second child, can be regarded as the successor of his family. Our findings, however, suggested a reverse pattern of sex preference by birth order. Wyatt (1967) discusses changes in parental motives for wanting sons and daughters in an ideal family, along with changes during the life cycle.

Table 5.3 Perception of small family size
(Percentage distribution of respondents by number of
children regarded as constituting a small family)

Number of children	Urban middle	Urban lower	Rural	Female	Male	All respondents
0	2	0	0	0	1	1
1	63	60	46	56	56	56
2	33	39	51	43	40	41
3	3	1	3	2	3	2
All numbers	101	100	100	101	100	100

NOTE: Percentages may not sum to 100 because of rounding.

two children constitute a small family. However, a slight SES difference in the perception of "small" is to be noted: 60 percent or more
of the middle class and lower class regarded a family with one child
as small, whereas a smaller majority (51 percent) of the rural group
regarded a family of two children as small. (In contrast, only a third
of the middle class and 39 percent of the lower class considered the
two-child family as small.)

Among all respondents, half considered a large family to comprise
four children, a fourth considered it to contain five children, and a
fifth regarded three children as constituting a large family (Table 5.4).
In all subgroups the largest percentages of respondents regarded the

Table 5.4 Perception of large family size
(Percentage distribution of respondents by number of children regarded as constituting a large family)

Number of children	Urban middle	Urban lower	Rural	Female	Male	All respondents
3	14	17	28	23	17	20
4	51	43	55	52	47	50
5	30	31	15	23	28	25
6	2	7	1	1	6	3
7	2	2	1	1	2	2
8	2	0	0	1	1	1
All numbers	101	100	100	101	101	101

NOTE: Percentages may not sum to 100 because of rounding.

four-child family as large; but nearly a third of the two urban groups viewed a family of five children as large and, somewhat unexpectedly, 28 percent of the rural group regarded three children as constituting a large family. More women than men viewed families of three or four children as large, whereas more men than women defined five- and six-child families as large.

Family planning knowledge, attitudes, and practice

Judging from the responses regarding small family size, it is not surprising that most of the VOC respondents knew about birth control, were in favor of it, and practiced it. Nearly all (99 percent) of those sampled indicated some knowledge of birth control methods, and 72 percent acknowledged practicing contraception at the time of the survey (Table 5.5).[3]

Table 5.5 Experience of contraceptive methods
(Percentage of respondents)

Experience	Urban middle	Urban lower	Rural	All respondents
Currently using a method	80	60	77	72
Ever used a method	93	86	88	89
Ever used pill, IUD, sterilization	16	11	21	16

Moreover, many respondents had used contraception even before the birth of their first child, although here we found striking SES differences: 47 percent of the middle class had used contraception between marriage and the first birth, compared with 34 percent of the lower class and only 15 percent of the rural group.[4] It is evident from these data that Japanese VOC respondents recognized the importance of birth control in marriage, for spacing as well as for stopping births.

Respondents were asked whether they knew about or had used par-

---

3 Our result accords closely with results obtained by the Twelfth KAP Survey conducted by the Mainichi Newspapers, which was carried out in May 1973 with a national stratified sample of 3,750 wives under age 50. The survey found that 81 percent of the women had practiced some kind of contraception. (See Mainichi Newspapers, 1976:296.)

4 The Twelfth KAP Survey of the Mainichi Newspapers found that 35 percent of the respondents had practiced contraception after having their first child (Mainichi Newspapers, 1976).

Table 5.6 Knowledge and use of specific contraceptive methods
(Percentage of respondents)

Method	Had heard about method	Knew how to use method	Had used method
Condom	96	94	82
Rhythm (Ogino) method	92	74	39
Withdrawal	73	62	23
IUD (Ota ring)	89	58	10
Pessary (diaphragm)	83	51	5
Pill	49	36	4
Tubal ligation	89	64	2
Vasectomy	87	62	1

ticular contraceptive methods. As indicated in Table 5.6, the condom was best known and most widely used. Its popularity may have been due to the fact that one can use it easily, without harm, whereas most of the other methods entail the use of chemicals or medical intervention, which might be distasteful or unpleasant. The rhythm method (developed by Kyusaku Ogino in 1924 and a popular method in Japan) and withdrawal were also quite popular among respondents. Only about half of the sample had heard about the pill and only 4 percent had actually used that method.

Attitudes toward contraception and abortion were also assessed. More than three-fourths of the respondents generally approved of married couples' using contraception (Table 5.7). Large majorities also approved of contraception to control the spacing or timing of births after the birth of the first child (86 percent) and to prevent further pregnancies after a couple has had all the children they want (90 percent). As for using contraception to delay the birth of the first child, however, fewer than half of all subgroups expressed approval. This finding suggests that respondents believed the birth of the first child should occur in the natural course of events, unless there is a specific reason to delay it.

With regard to abortion, slightly more than half of our respondents generally disapproved of a married woman's seeking an abortion to prevent an unwanted birth. When asked about specific situations in which a woman might choose abortion, however, at least 90 percent approved if a doctor said it would be dangerous for a woman to give

Table 5.7 Attitudes toward contraception and abortion
(Percentage of respondents who expressed specific attitudes)

Attitude	Urban middle	Urban lower	Rural	Female	Male	All respondents
Contraception						
Generally approve of married couples' using contraception	82	77	75	76	79	78
Generally disapprove of married couples' using contraception	5	4	10	8	5	6
Approve of contraception						
to delay birth of first child	47	36	38	37	42	40
to control spacing of births after first child	89	82	87	88	84	86
to prevent further pregnancies after having all the children wanted	90	89	92	92	89	90
Abortion						
Generally approve of a married woman's having an abortion to prevent unwanted birth	20	22	27	18	29	23
Generally disapprove of a married woman's having an abortion to prevent unwanted birth	53	57	46	60	43	52
Approve of abortion						
if doctor says it will be dangerous for woman to give birth again	99	94	89	92	94	93
if couple cannot afford to have another child	54	65	70	58	67	62
if pregnancy will interfere with wife's work or career	26	20	36	27	27	27
if pregnancy resulted from rape	90	91	92	89	91	90
Friends and relatives ashamed of abortion	36	37	37	43	30	37
Friends and relatives not ashamed of abortion	41	30	32	29	40	34

birth again or if the pregnancy resulted from rape, and 62 percent approved if a couple could not afford to have another child. Only 27 percent of all respondents approved of abortion if a pregnancy would interfere with a wife's work or career.

Substantially more rural and lower-class than middle-class respondents approved of abortion if a couple could not afford another child. A considerable difference was also noted among the three SES groups under the specified condition "if the pregnancy will interfere with the wife's work or career"; 36 percent of the rural respondents, 26 percent of the middle class, and only 20 percent of the urban lower class expressed approval of abortion under these circumstances.

Real experience of abortion reported by our sample—14 percent among all couples—is shown in Table 5.8, but this is probably not accurate. Because more than a third of the respondents said that their friends and relatives felt it was shameful to have an abortion (Table 5.7), it is likely that some respondents who had experienced abortion did not admit it. The Eugenic Protection Law, enacted in 1948 and revised in 1973, legalized abortion for health and economic reasons. According to Tietze and Murstein (1975:23), 732,600 legal abortions were performed in Japan in 1972 (the year of the VOC survey), representing an abortion rate of 353 per 1,000 live births. The Twelfth KAP Survey reported an abortion rate of 8.8 percent among couples responding to questionnaires simply left at their homes. The discrepancy between these findings and the VOC results may be explained by methodological differences, for the VOC study was based on direct interviews whereas most other surveys, including the Mainichi KAP study, used self-administered questionnaires. In addition, the characteristics of samples vary among studies.

Table 5.9 presents average birth intervals between marriage and first birth and between first and second births. The first birth interval was over a year and a half, on the average, and the second interval was

Table 5.8 Abortion experience
(Percentage of respondents reporting actual abortions)

Number of abortions	Urban middle	Urban lower	Rural	All SES groups
1	11	7	11	10
2	4	5	1	3
3	1	1	0	1

Table 5.9 Birth intervals in months

Birth interval	Urban middle	Urban lower	Rural	Female	Male	All respondents
Mean number of months between marriage and birth of first child	19.7	18.6	18.5	17.0	21.0	18.9
Mean number of months between first and second child	33.1	31.3	35.1	33.0	33.0	33.6

even longer, nearly three years. Differences between subgroups were minor. The Japanese first birth interval was longer than the average interval reported for most subgroups in the other VOC countries (see Arnold et al., 1975:35). When ideal and actual average intervals between marriage and the first birth are compared, we find that the actual interval was often shorter than the ideal given by most respondents (Table 5.10).

Table 5.10 Ideal and actual timing of first birth
(Percentage distribution of respondents)

Interval between marriage and first birth	Ideal spacing	Actual spacing
Less than 1 year	15	31
1–2 years	32	36
2–3 years	31	17
3–4 years	14	6
4–5 years	2	1
5 years or more	0	1
All intervals	94	92

NOTE: Percentages do not sum to 100 because of rounding and because data are unavailable for some respondents.

Discussion

To summarize the findings presented thus far on family size and attitudes toward birth control, the following points deserve emphasis:

First, desired family size ranged from 2.6 to 3.1 children per family among VOC respondents in Japan. Ideal family size was somewhat higher than desired family size, especially among lower-class and rural respondents, and in all SES subgroups was about three children. The findings from our sample thus accord with those on family-size norms obtained from larger national samples.

It should be understood that ideal family size refers to the number of children preferred given ideal living conditions. The total number of children desired refers to the number of children respondents wanted in their current situations. If ideal family size is greater than wanted family size, then wanted family size is suppressed because of economic or other considerations. If actual family size exceeds ideal family size, then children may have been produced for the sake of utility, but were later found to be a burden. Such was the case with many Japanese families prior to World War II, when economic conditions were difficult and utilitarian attitudes toward children predominated; couples of this type are now more likely to be found in pre-industrialized or developing countries. Our findings confirm that limiting family size is practiced by contemporary Japanese families at different socioeconomic levels, who experience many difficulties in coping with accelerating inflation and the dislocations caused by rapid industrialization.

Second, owing perhaps to the demands of modern life, VOC couples approved of contraception in general and in specific circumstances, the exception being to delay the birth of the first child. It is likely that they regarded the first child as a minimum requirement for the maintenance and enjoyment of marriage and the family.

Third, despite approving of contraception, most respondents disapproved of abortion in general, though large majorities approved of it in some situations. Disapproval may be based on the belief that termination of pregnancy is equivalent to homicide and that unwanted births can be avoided through the prevention of pregnancy—e.g., by using contraception. A moralistic attitude toward live births persisted, especially among wives, which may be rooted in oriental ways of thinking, such a guilt feelings and a sympathetic attitude toward the fetus. Thus, taken together with approval of abortion in specific situations, which is based on more or less modern pragmatic judgment, general attitudes toward abortion may still be in a stage of uncertainty: general disapproval coexists with specific approval, a situation that indicates the coexistence of traditional morals (sympathetic attitude toward live births) and modern, pragmatic thinking about abortion.

Fourth, the data on family planning indicate that respondents practiced it not only to control family size but also to regulate the spacing of their births, allowing sufficient time between births so as not to jeopardize their standard of living (although, as Table 5.10 indicates, the actual interval between marriage and first birth was shorter than the ideal one).

Prediction of family size and family planning

So far we have considered findings that assess important aspects of psychological values of children, economic costs and benefits, and family size and family planning variables. Our final task is to see how the value-of-children (VOC) variables, economic costs and benefits, and socio-demographic characteristics of respondents related to respondents' fertility and family planning behavior and whether they were good predictors of the fertility and family planning variables.

To place the results of this study in a broader perspective, we conducted multivariate analyses of the survey data. The analyses, derived from correlations between pairs of variables, show relationships among the various topics studied. Our primary purpose was to analyze the extent to which measurements of the value of children could predict family size and family planning, especially when various background characteristics of the respondents were held constant.

The particular method used was multiple regression analysis. A description of this method and its application to the present data may be found in the introductory volume of this series (Arnold et al., 1975: 115–29). That volume also shows selected results for Japan and the other countries in the VOC study in a comparative format. In general, we found that the levels of prediction in Japan were quite weak. This finding is probably due to the homogeneity of the Japanese sample and the clustering of the dependent variables within a narrow range. It may also be attributable to response sets or biases that were especially strong in Japan. Certain aspects of the results from Japan are of interest, however. I will present here only a summary table of the regression analysis and comment on selected findings.

Data for prediction of three family-size variables and three family planning variables are shown in Table 5.11. The predictors fall into three groups: socio-demographic characteristics of respondents, economic values of children, and psychological/social values of children. The items within each group, which are mainly self-explanatory, are derived from measures discussed earlier in this book. For further details about the measures, see Arnold et al. (1975:100–2).

Most of the figures within the table are beta weights, indicating the strength and the direction of the relationship between the predictor and the dependent variable, when the effects of other predictors are

Table 5.11 Prediction of selected family size and family planning measures as shown by normalized regression coefficients (betas) and proportion of variance explained (R^2)

	Dependent variables					
Predictors	Total number of children wanted	Ideal number of children	Number of additional children wanted	Number of contraceptive methods known	Situational birth control attitudes	Current use of contraceptive methods
Socio-demographic characteristics of respondents						
Parity and pregnancy	na	na	-.10*	na	na	na
R^2	na	na	.04*	na	na	na
Age	.13*	.10*	.06*	-.07*	-.04	.04†
Income	.03	-.04	-.05*	.10*	.10*	.14*
Education	.14*	.10*	.17*	.12*	.02	.19*
Urban experience	.15*	.11*	.18*	.14*	-.08*	-.21*
Media exposure	-.02	.05†	-.02	.14*	.06*	-.01
Marriage duration	-.06*	-.06*	-.10*	-.04	-.01	.04
R^2	.06*	.04*	.13*	.12*	.02*	.08*
Economic values of children						
Economic burden to educate children	.04†	.04	.03	.01	.11*	-.02
Financial ease/large family	.19*	.21*	.14*	-.01	.00	.02
Expected economic help	.15*	.14*	.08*	.03	-.07*	-.08*
Decreased utility of children	.02	.05†	.08*	.08*	-.02	.01
Economic benefits of large family	.05*	-.01	.04†	-.04†	.05*	.01
R^2	.10*	.09*	.16*	.13	.05†	.11*

Psychological/social values of children						
Continuity, tradition, security	-.13*	-.12*	-.11*	-.01	.00	-.14*
Parenthood satisfactions	.12*	.07*	.06*	-.06*	-.05	.03
Role motivations	-.10*	-.02	-.12*	-.02	-.01	-.07*
Happiness, affection	.08*	.07*	.05*	-.13*	-.01	.00
Goals, incentives from children	.12*	.02	.02	.01	.08*	.14*
Social status from children	-.06*	.02	-.06*	-.06*	-.11*	-.06*
External controls on childbearing	-.03	.01	-.02	.05*	-.07*	-.02
Cost of children	.05†	-.10*	.04	-.03	.13*	.05†
Decision-mindedness in childbearing	-.04	-.05†	-.01	.01	.14*	-.01
Reasons for wanting children	na	na	.30*	-.14*	-.04	-.16*
Reasons for not wanting children	na	na	-.14*	.03	.01	.16*
Benefits to children of large families	-.08*	-.03	.01	.00	-.02	-.08*
R^2	.14	.12	.25*	.19*	.10†	.18*

na—not applicable.

* Significant at the .01 level.

† Significant at the .05 level.

taken into account. For the rows labeled "R^2", however, the figures represent the proportion of variance accounted for by all of the variables above that particular row.

In the socio-demographic group, education and urban experience are found to be especially strong predictors of the family-size variables. Of particular interest is the direction of the relationship, which is positive. That is, respondents with more education or longer experience in cities tended to prefer larger numbers of children than respondents with less education or urban experience. This finding is contrary to the results from most other VOC countries and may indicate that parents with more favorable prospects, by virtue of their education, felt less constrained to limit their wanted and ideal family size. In this connection, it is of interest to note that current income shows essentially no relationship with family size. Age, on the other hand, has a positive relationship. This could reflect a generational influence, or perhaps be indicative of accumulation of wealth.

The prediction of contraceptive knowledge by socio-demographic factors is fairly strong and in the expected direction. Prediction of attitudes and behavior is not so clear, however. A peculiar finding is the negative relationship between urban experience and birth control attitudes and practice.

The overall level of prediction (R^2) for socio-demographic factors is highest for additional children wanted and contraceptive knowledge. These levels are still quite low, however, in relation to prediction in some other countries in the VOC study.

With respect to economic values, the variables predicting family size include the perception that it is financially easy to raise a large number of children, the expectation of economic help from children, and the belief that larger families are economically beneficial. Economic factors clearly play a part in family-size decisions, although the increments in prediction from this set of variables are not large. With respect to family planning, the most notable finding is the positive relationship between perception of the economic burden of educating children and favorability toward birth control.

The group of predictors labeled "psychological/social values of children" consists mainly of the VOC attitude scales, plus composite scores on reasons for wanting or not wanting another child and a score reflecting the belief that large families are beneficial to children. These measures, it should be noted, include items on perceptions of economic costs and benefits of children. For the attitude scales, the strongest and most consistent finding is the negative relationship between family-size variables and the scale on continuity, tradition, and security. It is noteworthy that this is in the opposite direction from what would normally be expected, apparently reflecting the preferences for larger families among the middle class, who were better educated and less prone to hold traditional values. The same pattern is shown for the scale on role motivations, which also reflects traditional values.

The highest level of prediction overall is shown for the dependent variable measuring the number of additional children wanted, which is also the variable that is most congruent with the VOC model, since it is indicative of fertility motivations at the time of the interview. The best predictors of this variable are parity and duration of marriage (negative); education and urban experience (positive); the perceived economic benefits of a large family and the financial ease of raising such a family (positive); the scales on role motivations and continuity, tradition, and security (negative); and the scores on reasons for wanting another child (positive) and reasons for not wanting another child (negative). The last two items are of course conceptually very close to the dependent variable, and for that reason they should be strong predictors.

For Japan, it is not surprising that prediction of fertility-related variables should be weak, given the relative homogeneity of the population and the fact that the dependent variables fall within a narrow range of values. The multivariate analysis has given some insights into the factors influencing Japanese fertility, but in general we believe that the descriptive findings on motivations, presented earlier, are of greater value. I will concentrate on those findings in the discussion in the final chapter, attempting to relate the findings to social-psychological theory, the Japanese cultural context, and population policies.

6

summary and conclusions

The purpose of this research, as stated in the introductory chapter, was to analyze the values attached to children by parents—assuming that children are valued according to the satisfactions they provide parents, weighed against the costs entailed in bringing them up. The fundamental assumption underlying the study is that parental satisfactions and costs—psycho-biological, sociocultural, economic—are essential components of motivations for childbearing that interact with culture and environment to influence family-size preference and fertility.

I have emphasized throughout this study the distinctions between reasons for wanting and not wanting children. Parents may want children for a variety of reasons that are not closely linked to personal motivation, such as deference to societal norms about family size and fatalistic or naturalistic orientations toward childbearing (see Rabin, 1965; Rabin and Greene, 1965). Parents may also want children for reasons that are intimately related to personal happiness and well-being—for example, the giving and receiving of love, fulfillment of the marital relationship, a sense of achievement connected with child-bearing, or the provision of economic and emotional security in old age. In this study, both types of reasons were assessed and their strength in connection with number of children wanted was investigated, in relation to various dimensions of the costs of children.

The following section summarizes the findings presented in each chapter and discusses some theoretical and hypothetical assumptions regarding values. Subsequent sections examine methodological problems encountered in the study, relevance of the findings to VOC theory, directions for future research, and issues related to population policy.

The findings

The study explored both positive and negative values that parents associated with children, then analyzed the relationship between these values and disvalues to determine how they operated in a hierarchy of child-related values. The open-ended questions revealed several important facets.

With regard to the advantages of children, emotional rewards for the parent (such as happiness, love, and companionship), childrearing satisfactions (pleasure from growth and development, children to carry out parents' hopes and aspirations), personal development of the parent (children representing incentives to succeed), and benefits to the family unit were more important to respondents than economic benefits and security or kin group benefits of children. When respondents were asked about the value of children as perceived by others in the community, their responses became more general and traditional, apparently in conformity to perceived normative values.

The question concerning why respondents did not want fewer than the desired number of children was aimed at establishing their threshold value for wanting children. In other words, failure to achieve the desired number of children (positive value) itself became a negative value.

Another interesting finding was that some of the benefits of children mentioned by respondents were benefits not to the parents themselves but to their other children or the family as a whole. An example was to provide companionship for existing children, which may be considered an instrumental value. Thus, children's influence on the family was recognized and valued.

With regard to sex preferences, affective values (companionship, personality) were generally more important than instrumental values (help with housework, economic contributions from children). The instrumental value of sons as heirs was quite salient, however.

When asked about disadvantages of having children, many respondents cited such instrumental disvalues as restrictions on alternative activities and financial costs. Psychological disvalues such as emotional strain, children's health problems, and noise and disorder were also salient and important to respondents.

Thus, with respect to the advantages and disadvantages of children, certain conclusions emerge. Advantages consisted for the most part of affective values (affection, love, companionship) but included instrumental values (children as incentives, helpers around the house, a bond between spouses). It is likely that when negative instrumental values predominate (restriction of activities, financial burden), then the potential positive values in having a child are suppressed.

In citing reasons for wanting and not wanting another child, most respondents ignored traditional reasons (e.g., to continue the family name, inherit property, perform religious duties) while stressing affective values such as love, companionship, and parental incentives for having children. Moreover, in giving reasons for not wanting another child, such as restrictions on their freedom, emotional strain, and the financial burden, Japanese respondents gave about equal importance to psychological and economic factors. However, the financial burden of another child was more important to the urban lower class than to middle-class and rural respondents, and restrictions on alternative activities were less important to the rural respondents than to the other groups.

Analysis of the Likert-type attitude items revealed that parental goals and incentives from children were very important. Somewhat less important value dimensions were role motivations, parenthood satisfactions, and happiness and affection. The dimensions of continuity, tradition, and security and of social status from children received relatively low scores.

A cost-benefit analysis of children was explored in relation to the economic and psychological costs of children to parents. We elicited subjective responses concerning the costs (or burdens) of raising certain numbers of children and compared the results with respondents' estimates of their expenditures on children. Results indicated that Japanese parents did not feel the financial burden of childrearing to be great, especially if they were raising two or three children. Estimated annual expenditures on children came to only 10 percent of total income for the whole sample, which may be due to the young ages of their children.

Utilitarian values of children (especially economic and psychological reliance upon children) were not very strong. In other words, parents were rearing children in the expectation of deriving happiness from them, but after bringing them up most parents did not intend to rely on them financially or emotionally. Their attitude appears to be typical of modern parents in Japan, who try to minimize the economic and psychic costs of children by limiting family size, and to maximize the pleasure they receive from their children as the children grow up. Thus the economic and psychological costs of children were not perceived in isolation from compensating benefits. Similarly, practical and financial help from children was not important to the VOC respondents, since modern Japanese parents rely increasingly on pensions, savings, and governmental services in their affluent industrial society.

Owing to such pragmatic attitudes toward children, respondents were controlling their family size—for the family's sake, not for the sake of society. They strongly approved of contraception, and even of abortion in certain circumstances. But their desires for children were not completely satisfied, for ideal family size exceeded the total number of children wanted, given present living conditions. Factors respondents mentioned as contributing to their desire for smaller families were the cost of rearing children, inadequate housing, pollution, and overcrowding. Nevertheless, few respondents thought that overpopulation influenced their family-size decisions.[1]

Japan's problems are not unique, nor is the demographic response. In other industrialized countries, couples have tended to reduce family size on pragmatic grounds, and not simply for economic reasons. The discrepancy between preferred family size and actual family size is one of the most crucial problems of the modern family in modern industrial societies. Its solution depends on social and population policies.

Another technique employed in the analysis was multiple regression using three sets of socio-demographic, economic, and social-psychological variables as independent variables. The purpose of this analysis was to predict fertility and family planning variables. The results were generally weak, but gave some useful insights about the patterns of fertility motivations in Japan. For example, in our sample higher education was found to be related to the desire for more children, with both economic and psychological values contributing to this desire.

The results of the regression analysis suggest that highly technical

---

1 The problems of pollution and overcrowding are widely recognized; 55 percent of the VOC respondents who replied to the country-specific survey said that they did not like raising children in such a polluted environment. But respondents de-emphasized overpopulation as a reason for not wanting children. For a discussion of this apparent contradiction, see page 42. Shortage of housing space, however, is an aspect of overcrowding that does seem to affect family size. The 13th Mainichi KAP survey conducted in 1975 found that more than 60 percent of the households sampled had only 49 square meters of living space and that in these circumstances respondents believed they could not raise more than three children (Mainichi Newspapers, 1976:317).

and complex methods do not always elucidate actual causes. Values operate very subtly in daily situations. They may be directly manifested when elicited by simple questions or a set of structured items, but they become confounded when treated with complex operational methods. Such a process does seem to be operating when we search for such mechanisms as values through the use of different methodologies.

Methodological problems

The interview schedule used in this study included 165 items on a variety of topics. Many of the items were similar in content, the purpose being to explore respondents' values and attitudes in detail. As a consequence, some respondents got a little frustrated during the interviews because questions seemed repetitious to them. Though the refusal rate was rather high (30 percent of the rural sample, 40 percent of the urban sample),[2] fair cooperation was obtained. Some respondents made accusations and expressed worries during the interviews. Other respondents, however, mentioned the fruitfulness of the study, saying they had learned a lot from the questionnaire about their child-rearing attitudes and practices.

Many respondents regarded the questionnaire as somewhat abstract since it included hypothetical questions and was inquisitive and provocative. Although the phrasing and sequencing of questions had been carefully considered, about one-third of the respondents thought some questions were abrupt or not directly related to their own experience. They found the opening paragraph for some questions to be lengthy and boring, and had difficulty responding to questions asking "why." When asked about personal matters like contraceptive practice, miscarriages and stillbirths, income, and ownership of modern consumer durables in a face-to-face interview, respondents seemed somewhat embarassed (especially when the interviewer was of the opposite sex), though they usually answered each question. Such probing questions could not be avoided, but they might have been made more consonant with the everyday experience of Japanese couples so that the respondents could participate more fully in the interviews, revealing more of their subjective experiences. Owing to the cross-cultural design of the study and to problems of translation, it would not have been possible

---

2   The refusal rate may have been lower in the rural areas because local health personnel there arranged interviews after project personnel sent letters to eligible couples requesting their cooperation. In the case of urban respondents, such a follow-up procedure was not possible.

to eliminate all of the respondents' objections. An effort was made to elicit culturally relevant data from the Japanese sample by including a number of country-specific questions (see Appendix).

As a consequence of the abstraction and inquisitiveness of the core questionnaire, questions remain as to whether respondents gave accurate responses based on their experience. Doubt could be cast on the rate of abortion experience and statements of income, expenditures, and savings, as well as on responses to some of the attitude items. This shortcoming is characteristic of all interview techniques, however, and one cannot blame only the present study. Still, greater efforts to elicit sincere responses from such surveys must be made.

Finally, some problems of translation from the original English questionnaire should be mentioned. Although we carried out pretests in Japan and performed forward translation (of the original questionnaire into Japanese) and backward translation (of the Japanese version back into English), the Japanese wording still presented difficulties to our respondents, especially the attitude items. "Act of virtue," "up to fate or god," "for most people it is inevitable to have children," "the family with children is all that is good in our society"—these statements in particular sounded alien to most of the Japanese respondents. Although the questionnaire was constructed collaboratively by researchers from six countries, a Western sociocultural context quite different from our own may have predominated. The Japanese respondents did not have the experiential equivalence of the meaning of some terms, in contrast to respondents of other countries. This is a crucial problem of cross-cultural research, although in our research the problem was relatively small. The validity of the instrument of any cross-cultural research must be seriously pre-examined. If a research instrument designed in the context of one society tries to find universality in human behavior without reference to the sociocultural context of other countries, the results may be misleading. The validity of the research technique should therefore be considered in connection with the purpose of the proposed cross-cultural research and the criteria that are used to uncover universality of human behavior. These matters should be carefully weighed before an empirical investigation is undertaken—especially for cross-national research on population.

Theoretical relevance

We now turn to a discussion of the findings in the context of theoretical assumptions regarding the value of children. In the introductory chapter value was defined as one's personal regard for certain objects, persons, or events. The valued object can be concrete or abstract. It can be either a goal-object or an instrumental means. It can exist in one's consciousness and manifest itself or recede depending on the environmental context, a change within the value holder's system of organizational hierarchies, or new relational dependencies: an object liked at one time may be disliked at another time. Values defined in this fashion can be measured in a variety of ways. First, we can assign a high or low degree, or great or small quality, to the value we attach to a particular object. A pen can be of greater importance than a pencil or of less importance than a watch. An eraser and a pencil can be of equal value as writing implements. Thus, "greater than" or "less than" should be an important category for measurement. There are at least four major scaling systems for measuring value in objects: nominal scale, which clusters objects in certain ways; ordinal scale, which orders objects according to their importance; rating or interval scale, which rates the degree of importance along a continuum from most important to least important, or vice versa; and ratio scale, which has a fixed zero point and thus permits comparison of ratings in absolute terms. By such means, the components of values can be classified by their qualities, which are then decomposed into quantitative terms, leading to an increasingly refined technique of measurement. It is thus possible to see how values of objects are extracted from such measurement, how they are intertwined, isolated, and coherently organized into a system of values, and how such systems differ from one person to another.

In this study we considered the values assigned to children by parents. Children may be liked at one time, but disliked at other times, depending upon parents' experiences or situational constraints (environment). We paid particular attention to the relationship between parents and children that exists as a consequence of their continuing biological linkage, not just in the external relation of social objects. At this point, it would be worthwhile to look at some existing theories of value that emphasize motivational orientation toward objects. I shall mention only a few of these theories, in particular those proposed by Charles Morris and Talcott Parsons.

In his pioneering study on the varieties of human value, Morris (1956) distinguished three types of value: object value, conceived value, and operative value. Object value is concerned with what is preferable (or desirable) in objects, persons, or events. In other words, it refers to an ideal conception of value in objects and individuals. Conceived value refers to preferential behavior directed by anticipation or foresight toward the outcome of such behavior. For example, a person anticipates that his or her action will have a desired effect on an object before taking that action, the outcome of which, however, may be quite different from the desired outcome because of circumstances beyond the person's control. Operative value refers to the actual direction of preferential behavior toward one object rather than another. That is, it refers to an individual's chosen behavior toward a set of alternative valued objects regardless of whether the person thinks the behavior is preferable or attainable in its outcome.[3]

In an attempt to integrate a model of motivational orientation into a theory of social action, Parsons postulated a theory of value that emphasizes three aspects of value: cognitive, cathectic, and evaluative (Parsons and Shils, 1962). According to his terminology, cognitive mode refers to one's cognitive attitude toward an object, in which one perceives it in relation to a system of dispositional hierarchics. Cathectic mode involves the process by which an individual invests an object with affective significance; it includes positive or negative cathexes upon objects by their gratification or derivational significance with respect to the individual's need dispositions. Evaluative mode refers to the process by which an individual distributes energy with respect to various cathected objects in an attempt to optimize gratification. It includes, according to Parsons's terminology, "the processes by which an actor organizes his cognitive and cathectic orientations into intelligent plans" (Parsons and Shils, 1962:59).

Comparing these two theories, one finds some striking similarities, though their phraseology appears to be different:

1. Both theories rest on cognitive-action concepts encompassing the process of situation (inner and outer situation of an individual) in which an individual acts toward objects.
2. Both theories admit some kind of selective behavior—Morris's operative value roughly corresponding to Parsons's evaluative modes—in a final decision or judgment of the situation.
3. Both theories refer to some kind of resolution resulting from the conflict between object and conceived value (Morris) or between cognitive and cathectic modes (Parsons). Morris's object value is very close to Parsons's cathectic (affective) mode, while conceived value roughly corresponds to cognitive mode.

In summary, the value theory based on the individual's motivational orientation to a situation assumes some kind of choice resulting from

---

3 A similar definition is given by Smith (1969).

an organized solution of the conflict between ideal value and conceived value or between cathectic and cognitive values toward a specific object or event, within a system of valued objects and behavioral
dispositions toward them. Such theories, derived mainly from psychological explanations, are based on an assumption of values operating
within a hypothetical individual in a society, and they cannot easily
be used to explain the status of a real individual at a particular place
and time.

A group model is needed to explain people's motivations *en masse*
and the values of a society or class with its own cultural and historical
traditions. What kind of model would serve as a conceptual framework
for the present investigation? Lois and Martin Hoffman have developed a schematic postulate concerning the components of values of
children to parents which is applicable to any group of parents resid-
ing in different regions of a society, country, or culture.

Based on a survey of literature on attitudes and motivations of parents for raising children, Hoffman and Hoffman (1973) came up with
nine categories of values: (1) adult status and social identity; (2) expansion of the self; (3) morality: religion, altruism, good of the group;
(4) primary group ties, affiliation; (5) stimulation, novelty, fun; (6)
creativity, accomplishment, competence; (7) power, influence; (8) social comparison, competition; (9) economic utility. The nine value
categories were also seen as part of a larger context, with five major
components: (1) value of children; (2) alternative source of value;
(3) costs; (4) barriers; and (5) facilitators. Clearly, these factors are
not only the inherent value of children per se but are the combined
results of the VOC dimensions in relation to external factors that influence the attitudes of individual parents. The categories deal with
the positive and negative factors influencing the values. However,
Hoffman and Hoffman do not fully explain how the components are
related to one another in such as way as to influence the value of
children.

It is possible that the nine categories of values can be regrouped
into more basic components. Take, for example, adult status and social identity (first dimension) and stimulation, novelty, fun (fifth
dimension). Both dimensions view children as agents, but they cannot
be ordered in the same group of categories. Adult status and social
identity can be classified as a sociocultural value emphasizing the adult
role acquired through one's society and culture after having children,
whereas the dimension of stimulation, novelty, and fun can be classified as a cathectic (affective) value inherent in psycho-biological char-

acteristics derived from interacting with children. In this fashion, the other dimensions of value might be reformulated and grouped into quite different categories.

According to this reclassification, dimensions 1 (adult status) and 3 (morality) seem to belong to the same category in the sense that they emphasize sociocultural roles. Dimensions 4 (primary group ties) and 5 (stimulation, novelty, fun) belong to the affective or psychological value dimension. Dimensions 2 (expansion of self), 6 (achievement, competence), 7 (power, influence), 8 (social comparison, competition), and 9 (economic utility) may be regarded as social-psychological values gained through children. As is clear from such a classification, values regarding children could be ordered according to different schemes, and a systematic integration of concepts is necessary if they are to be used as basic assumptions for empirical testing.

By taking advantage of the foregoing classification of concepts, one can distinguish two kinds of values, those gained directly from watching and interacting with children (psycho-biological in nature) and those gained indirectly as reflection and expansion of self (feedback). In this sense, it would be useful to distinguish between values regarded as inherent characteristics of children (related to parental drives or instincts) and those acquired from society whereby children serve as the instruments of their formation. Thus some of the values of children may be considered as biological or instinctive parental feelings,[4] and other values may be considered as mainly derived from sociocultural norms. The former are likely to be called "intrinsic values of children"; the latter may be called "extrinsic values." These values are intimately related to perceptions and conceptions of children in the manner of hierarchical systems within individual value systems.

It might be argued that in this study we have discovered the contents and functions of these two values. That is to say, we have found, within a general system of values of parents, the range of these two values and how they interact with each other. These two values have positive or negative aspects (like or dislike, approval or disapproval), and they also have strong and weak aspects (how much parents like or dislike, approve or disapprove). In other words, we studied the qualitative as well as the quantitative aspects of these values. Another, related

---

4 Biological value is defined here as biologically endowed instinctive feelings and motivations that result from intrinsic characteristics—for example, contact with children accompanied by feelings of maternity or paternity, often enhanced by mating and reproductive behavior (cf. Kestenberg, 1956; Rheingold, 1963).

feature of these values is their hierarchical organization by a parent or group of parents. The two values may coexist in balance, sustained by positive and negative qualities as well as strong and weak qualities.

Our first approach was to identify intrinsic and extrinsic values of children by assessing respondents' perceptions of the advantages and disadvantages of children by means of open-ended questions. The method used was a nominal scale. The second approach was to assess the relative importance of reasons for wanting and not wanting children by means of structured questions. This was performed with an ordinal scale. The third approach, the attitude measurement, used a rating scale to measure the quantitative dimensions of values that were itemized in hierarchical clusters. Factor analysis revealed how the items were correlated with each other and clustered in the framework of the VOC dimensions.

Structured questions on costs and benefits of children explored the positive and negative qualities of values. The questions on family size and family planning assessed respondents' efforts to balance positive and negative qualities, when confronted with situational constraints, by reducing the number of children, though sometimes desiring more than that number. Thus the questions measured different modal relations of values. The results, though as yet exploratory, are quite consistent and shed a good deal of light on childbearing and childrearing behavior. The values we obtained can be classified as intrinsic versus extrinsic, positive versus negative, and strong versus weak. In general, respondents exhibited intrinsic values of children more strongly than extrinsic qualities, which were more widely spread and displayed more variety. Furthermore, respondents perceived positive values of children more strongly than negative values. However, in the total framework of respondents' childbearing decision-making the values and disvalues existed in interactive relationships. Thus the values of children did emerge as psychological concerns of parents. If negative values prevailed over positive ones in certain situations, then parents would not want more children. The varieties and intensity of these values may differ from parent to parent, from group to group, and from culture to culture. Assessment of these values for each child would depend on the context. The issues we focused on were measuring how the state, or modal relations, of values—expressed as intrinsic and extrinsic values, positive and negative values (advantages and disadvantages), and intensity dimensions (strong-weak relations, frequencies, correlations)—exist in balance or change in different situations.

Such relationships may be more easily seen with the help of a model

Figure 6.1 Psychological structure of VOC variables among Japanese respondents

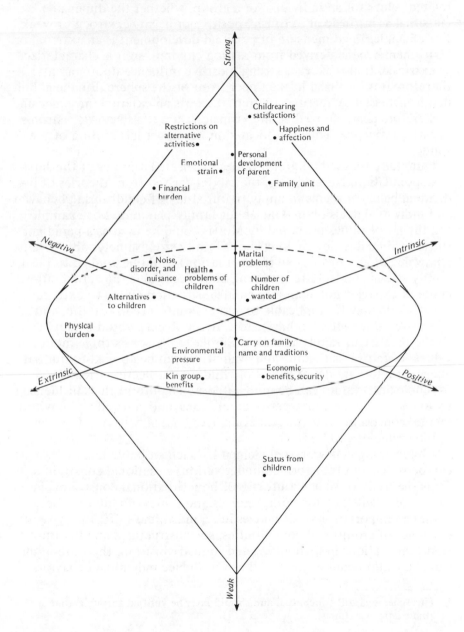

(Figure 6.1).[5] Each dimension of values obtained from our study can be localized on a three-dimensional axis showing the sphere of child-related values for an individual or a group, whether the dimension is classified as intrinsic or extrinsic, positive or negative, strong or weak. For example, the dimension of personal development is an external or instrumental value derived from rearing children, so it is characterized as extrinsic. It also exerts a strong, positive influence upon parents; therefore it is localized in the upper front of the sphere. Financial burden is increased by rearing children; it exerts an external influence and is therefore characterized as an extrinsic value. It also exerts a strong negative influence. Thus it is located in the upper left section of the sphere.

Our study focused on group values in selected samples of the Japanese population. Nevertheless, the model derived from theories of individual behavior seems to apply to our study of childbearing behavior and individual decision-making about family planning. For example, the theory of values proposed by Morris could be used as a paradigm for individual decision-making about family size. Namely, object value (the value of an object in an ideal situation) could be applied to ideal family size in an ideal life situation, conceived value (an actual outcome of behavior not achieving an ideal situation owing to extrenal constraints) may be applicable to actual family size in real life, and operative value (actual behavior toward an object) would be applicable to the practice of family planning. Similarly, Parsons's three modes of values (cognitive, cathectic, and evaluative) can be applied to our balanced structure model of values of children. Cathectic (affective-psychological) values can be moderated by cognitive values influenced by external pressure, interpersonal relations, and cultural and environmental constraints—creating an evaluative (actual behavioral or conscious) value of children.

Childbearing behavior as explained by such an individual model can be varied and transformed under various situational constraints. Thus the study of social contexts—of how situational constraints influence individual childbearing choices and values of children—becomes an important issue. Changes in an individual's life, the state of existence of groups and communities, social structures and institutions, innovations in technology and industrialization, the state of culture, education, and folklore—all can influence individual behavior.

---

5 This scheme is still conceptual and should later be verified through some quantitative treatment.

Earlier we considered some of these influences: respondents' socioeconomic background, education, modernity, and exposure to mass
media. But the exploration of these variables during the interview
stage was rather meager, and we inferred the meaning of these variables after collecting the data. The influence on an individual's life
of certain dramatic events (the Arab oil embargo of 1973, for instance)
can be crucial, as is the impact of industrialization, long-term economic trends (e.g., growth and inflation), congestion, and changes in
urban life. Such external constraints have always influenced individual
fertility behavior by altering the values attached to children. Although
we cannot provide convincing evidence from our cross-sectional data
on the impact of such long-term trends, we can still attempt to understand how changes of values regarding children reflect, in the long run,
changes in society as a whole.

The following section discusses some problems and issues we were
unable to explore in the present study and suggests some new approaches to this relatively unexplored yet important area of research.

Future directions for research

One of the most important findings of the VOC Study was the somewhat different structures of attitudes exhibited by the three socioeconomic groups (urban middle class, urban lower class, and rural) selected
for study, although differences were less pronounced than in other
VOC countries. The urban middle-class group showed a structure combining intrinsic (affective-psychological) and extrinsic values (particularly utilities and benefits for the sake of children). The urban lower-
class group favored a structure centered on extrinsic values (influenced
by external situations like income, costs, and burdens, showing pragmatic and modern attitudes). The rural group exhibited a structure
combining intrinsic (psychological-affective) and extrinsic values (particularly sociocultural tradition, continuity, or kin group).

Future research should investigate whether such patterns persist or
are subject to change according to socioeconomic status. Change in
fertility coincident with change in socioeconomic status is well recognized by demographers: higher fertility accompanies poverty and the
preindustrialized stage of a society, but tends to fall with the advent
of economic growth and technological innovation. One question for
future research is whether a marked change of values would accompany
such a fertility transition. How would values of children change if Japanese society, for example, further developed industrially and economically? If the middle-class group were to become upper-class by

sociocultural transformation and occupational mobility, would their values remain those of the middle class? If the rural group were transformed into the urban middle class, would the rural pattern of values persist or would it be changed into the pattern of the middle-class group?

Another task of research will be to compare the attitudes toward children that parents of different ages hold and to relate those attitudes to prevailing social and economic conditions during the parents' child-rearing years. In a country like Japan, where drastic social change has taken place in a short period, one would expect to observe different attitudes toward children, for example, among parents born in the 1880s, 1930s, 1940s, and 1950s. It is important not only to correlate changes in attitudes toward children with different periods but also to discover how the society in each period influences the values of each generation. (See Iritani, 1972, for a discussion of this matter.) The coexistence of these generations in a rapidly changing society is likely to create generational conflicts regarding childbearing and childrearing practices. It is important to observe which values have permanence and which reflect the society of a given period.

Another question for future research is how values of children change when young children grow older and parents have more children. At the time of marriage and the conception of a first child, for example, a couple's parental motivations may be strongest. After a number of difficult and unexpected situations, their attitudes toward children may change (see Wyatt, 1967). The present study focused on relatively young couples who had at least one child. A longitudinal study with a small sample should shed light on changing perceptions of children and changes in the interaction of biological-instinctive motives and socioculturally influenced motivations.

Closely connected with this question is the value of children viewed through parent-child relationships. The value of children can be regarded as a dual relationship, or bond, between parents and children—consisting not only of the view parents have of children, but also of the view children have of parents. Such reciprocity in the relationship between parents and children can influence attitudes toward children.

The family and the parent-child relationship are often threatened by the social impacts of a computerized, capitalistic society. Unable to obtain stability, meaning, and creativity from life, people seek material compensations. Competition for these compensations often destroys creative and meaningful life for a family, leading to family tensions. Children become disrespectful toward parents and unmanageable.

Abnormal behavior of both parents and children is commonly reported nowadays—for example, the killing of unwanted children by parents and assaults against hostile parents by their children.

Why does the priceless value of children to parents change into such hostility and hatred? The bond between parent and child, as found in the present study, is based on affective feelings that may have biological roots. Such irrational and emotionally involved relations, however, easily collapse under external pressures unless supported by firm cognitive and intellectual control, mutual understandings, and respect. The disequilibrium caused by parental and child goal-seeking creates a loss of security at home, which in turn becomes the agent of family crises: parents tend to deny their children and children tend to deny their parents, destroying mutual respect and affection.

This study has focused only on one side of the parent-child relationship—namely, parents' perceptions of children—and under specified and normal conditions. We overlooked children's perceptions of parents. Thus the reciprocal influence of parent-child perceptions, particularly in stressful family situations, is an important area of psychological research awaiting further attention.

The study of the substitutive value of children should be of major concern in view of the emphasis on costs and benefits in modern capitalistic society. Children can be replaced with other objects and a balance between children and alternative sources of satisfaction may be considered appropriate for the standard of living in the modern family. Are children indispensable to a couple's standard of living? What substitutes for them can be considered? Modern people exhibit substitutive behaviors in buying something for money to establish their status and authority. In the VOC survey, some questions were concerned with alternatives to children and the process of decision-making (trade-offs). The questions we posed were somewhat abstract, however, and did not establish many meaningful relationships. Thus one task of future research will be to determine how trade-offs between children and other "goods" operate in the minds of modern parents in the actual process of raising children.

Issues related to population policy

It will be recalled that one purpose of this investigation was to assess values attached to children by Japanese parents of different socioeconomic backgrounds, on the assumption that the three SES groups chosen represented varying degrees of modernity—from least modern (rural) to most modern (urban middle class). Thus, although the study

was not longitudinal, by enabling us to compare the values held by less
and more modern parents it would, we believed, suggest emerging
trends in such values in contemporary Japan. Our findings bore out
the assumption that lower SES, or less modern, parents would have
more traditional values than higher SES (or more modern) parents, although differences between the SES groups were less pronounced than
in the other countries surveyed.

With the acceleration in population growth in developing countries
and increasing urbanization in most countries of the world since World
War II, there has been a growing awareness on the part of government
officials and the public at large of problems related to population.
Awareness has been heightened by mass communication campaigns
sponsored by governments and private organizations. These educational efforts culminated in the declaration of 1974 as World Population Year and the United Nations-sponsored World Population Conference held in Bucharest in August of that year. Topics discussed at
the conference included consumption aspects of population, such as
the relationship between population on one hand and natural resources, food supply, and the environment on the other, and the social and economic impacts of rapid population growth, at the individual as well as the societal level.

In July 1974, a month before the Bucharest conference took place,
a population conference sponsored by several civic organizations was
held in Tokyo, providing an opportunity for Japanese population
specialists to exchange views on many of these issues. The conference,
which was well publicized in Japan, aroused considerable interest. (For
details of the proceedings, see Secretariat, First Japan Population Conference, 1974.) Nevertheless, public attitudes toward family size and
population, particularly as it relates to broader social and economic
issues, do not appear to have been influenced by the innovative ideas
put forth both at the conference and in other forums.

For example, the Study Committee of Population Problems, an ad-
visory organ for the government on population policy, asserted at the
General Assembly of April 1974 the necessity of attaining a zero rate
of population growth in Japan. Participants of the First Japan Population Conference recommended that the Japanese nation take a stance
on human reproduction that would lead to a stabilization or reduction
in population size in the future—specifically, that the number of children per couple be two, rather than three. This recommendation was
based on demographic studies forecasting Japan's future population.[6]

6 Okazaki (1973), using Japan's 1970 population of 103.7 million as a baseline

Such statements should not be viewed as explicit proposals for Japanese governmental policy, but as the consensus of population specialists, critics, and informed laymen. The Japanese public tends to think that Japan's recent population growth has placed a burden on their daily lives, according to several recent surveys.[7] Therefore, those who are concerned about the continued growth of Japan's population are not limited to the population specialists. It will be difficult, however, and will take some time, for the public to learn the relationship between general social problems, the present growth rate of the population, and their current childbearing—that is, to become fully aware of the population problem and reduce their fertility because of it.

If policies limiting families to two children were to be launched in the future, what might be the outcome? Obviously, there would be many advantages as well as disadvantages. Material resources would be conserved to a great extent, such as staple products for living, and fewer financial resources would be devoted to raising children. As for psychological benefits, attention would be focused on each individual of a family and the emphasis would be on a better quality of living. On the other hand, with social policy directed toward small family size, social welfare would be oriented toward the construction of small housing units, and recreation and other public facilities would be geared to small families. As a result, there would be pressure on couples to conform to a stereotyped, nuclear family of two children. In my opinion, rigid conformity to such a family stereotype is not conducive to the future prosperity of this nation, for social and racial reasons. One disadvantage is that the small family would foster strong individualism

and different assumptions about average family size, projected a population of 121.2 million in the year 2015 if the average number of children per couple were two, i.e., if the net reproduction rate (NRR) of 1.0 were maintained into the future. His projections for a hypothetical three-child average family size showed a population of 132.8 million in 2015. Frejka (1973:142–43), using a somewhat different methodology, projected the population to be 136.0 million in the period 2010–2015, if the NRR of 1.0 continued, and showed that under this condition the population would stabilize after 2040 at about 138 million.

7   In response to our own optional country-specific survey, which was administered after the main VOC questionnaire, 90 percent of the respondents said that Japan's current population was too large and 58 percent agreed with the statement that "a decrease of population is desirable." Sixty-one percent agreed that birth control should be encouraged as a future orientation of Japanese policy. Because of the small proportion of respondents who answered this portion of the questionnaire (59 percent of the urban and 21 percent of the rural), the results were not reported in the main body of the report.

in children, in contrast with the large family, where mutual help, co-operation, and sociability are emphasized. The second disadvantage is that planning for small families throughout the country—which is limited in area and densely populated—would be likely to influence personality formation by encouraging the trait of insularism, already a major disvalued aspect of our national character.

The ideal public policy is the one that offers equal opportunity to families of different sizes to live in happiness and satisfaction. The social policy of the future should ensure that all citizens, regardless of family size and background, enjoy their lives without being forced to limit their family size to two or three children. In the absence of demographic regimentation, some families would have four or five children while other families would have one child or none at all. The result would likely be an average of two or three children. The principle of freedom to determine family size would ensure the fulfillment of individual needs and protect individual rights.

On the other hand, as our findings indicate, there is still a great reluctance on the part of many Japanese to consider the impact of their actions on society at large. Childbearing is regarded solely as one's private concern; societal problems and individual decisions exist separately. Population specialists consider it a dilemma that the fertility rate depends entirely on individual decision-making. They warn that if parents continue to bear more than the two children needed for replacement, there will be greater population pressure within the next 30 years than there is today, the result of which could be catastrophic. (See, for example, the projections for Japan cited above from Okazaki, 1973.)

Contrary to such opinions, however, many top policymakers are pronatalist. They contend that the average life span is increasing because of new medical technology. They also fear that, as a result of the fertility decline since the 1960s, there will be a shortage of labor within the next two or three decades. Faced with a declining proportion of population in the younger age groups, they believe that encouragement of fertility is desirable.

As is clear from the preceding statements, attitudes toward fertility—the values of childbearing—are quite varied. With such divergent opinions, a crucial issue for the Japanese is reaching a consensus, one that resolves the essential problem of population policy.

In my opinion, it is useless to make recommendations for changing people's behavior, given the existence of such a cleavage. It is necessary to wait. In this age of freedom and respect for individual rights, it is not desirable to alter demographic behavior by imposing a stringent policy to limit family size directly or to influence it indirectly, for example by taxing large families at higher rates than small families. Such policies would not work. On the contrary, they would arouse opposition from the general public.

What would succeed are educating the public about population and environmental conditions and then waiting for individual action. Just as the people of this country practiced birth control methods without waiting for the government to endorse family planning, when they see that limiting family size is related to their own welfare, they will probably have the wisdom to continue controlling family size so that the population problem does not become critical.

At the present stage, while people are individualistic and the connection between individuals and society is not widely recognized as having bearing on the population problem, it is premature to expect people to control family size for societal reasons. However, it is likely that with the present nationwide campaign to warn people about the population crisis and with abundant information and educational media, the time will come when all people will have to consider their individual lives in relation to future population. In this way, the population problem will ultimately be reflected in the attitudes and opinions of each individual, for reasons reaching beyond their immediate family situation. One can say that as human beings develop, enriching their wisdom through education, the imposition of a specific population policy will not be necessary. If Japan should succeed in this approach, she will certainly become a model for the world in controlling population growth via individual knowledge and free will. This step will definitely take some time, however, both for motivating the individual action and for influencing the change of population growth.

But this does not mean that policies aimed at fostering demographic change are unnecessary. It is essential to create an atmosphere in which people initiate their own action by referring to the condition of society or the status of population. What policies are needed to facilitate individual action toward solution of population problems?

In the first place, further welfare-oriented policies are urgently required to take care of children in day-care facilities. Shortages of such facilities are still recognized in Japan today. Such physical facilities are necessary before people can undertake individual action: facilities for rearing children as well as for taking care of the aged after their children have left home. Provision of such facilities would remove anxiety and make individual decision-making much easier. In the second place, improvement of the living conditions in every household should be considered. Inflation, poor housing, disruption of surroundings through traffic, pollution, and other public nuisances—people have suffered to a great extent trying to maintain a decent standard of living while supporting their families. Under such circumstances, children cannot be brought up to be valued by parents and appreciated by society, and no one can afford to consider individual childrearing and its relation to social problems. Thus, to initiate a compromise between individual interests and social involvement, improvements of living conditions through public policy are essential.

A serious problem related to population growth in this country is the high concentration of population in urban areas. Owing to Japan's rapid economic expansion and industrialization, urban growth has far exceeded growth in rural areas, causing a host of difficulties: congestion, noise, air pollution, and various social and economic dislocations. In response to our country-specific survey, 74 percent of the sample said the solution of unequal population distribution is the responsibility of the government. Policies aimed at reducing the high concentrations of population in the major urban centers, in my opinion, deserve urgent attention.

To conclude, after a better living standard is achieved, individuals are likely to turn their eyes toward public affairs. Individual concern for family planning is likely to become social concern for population. Until then, social policy should encourage the people to turn their eyes to social problems. At that stage, the value of children can be regarded from a fresh point of view—namely, through a convergence of individual problems and social concerns and with a consensus of laymen, specialists, and policymakers.

appendix and appendix table

Appendix   Country-specific questionnaire (Japan)

A number of country-specific questions were administered after the completion of the major interview survey. Completion of this portion of the questionnaire was optional. The country-specific items were self-administered and the questionnaire was to be returned by mail. Because of the small number of respondents who answered the country-specific questions, a tabulation of results is omitted and instead only a description and a translation of the questions are presented here.

Themes of the country-specific questions

1. Views about the present population in Japan in relation to having and educating children
   a. Perception of the population of Tokyo, of the other districts surveyed, and of the country as a whole
   b. Opinions about raising children in a polluted environment

2. Changes in attitudes after having children
   a. Change of conjugal affection between spouses
   b. Anxieties about raising children

3. Opinions about educating children in contemporary society
   a. Change in parental authority
   b. Feelings of parental protectiveness toward children resulting from competition and struggle up the "educational ladder"
   c. Opinion regarding sexual emancipation and childbearing
   d. Opinion regarding sex education of children

Actual questions

The following questions are specifically concerned with our country; please fill them in when you have time. Consultation with your husband or wife is possible, but certain questions will be asked of each of you separately, so please pay attention to that. When you have completed the questionnaire, please mail it to the address written on the enclosed envelope.

Address: _____ (Ward/District)
Name of husband: _____
Name of wife: _____

General impression of the major survey

Please write your frank impressions of the survey you have just completed.

Attitude toward population problems

I am going to ask you several questions concerning population problems. Circle the appropriate number.

1. Do you think the present population of Japan is too large?
   1. Too large.
   2. A little large.
   3. Appropriate.
   4. A little small.
   5. Too small.

2. Do you think that the population of Japan will continue to increase in the future?
   1. Continue to increase.
   2. Increase and then decrease.
   3. Same as at present.
   4. Continue to decrease.

3. Which of the following opinions do you agree with?
   1. Population is the basis of national power; therefore an increase of population is favorable.
   2. It gets harder to live when population increases; therefore a decrease of population is desirable.

4. What do you think of urban density and rural sparsity?
   1. It is the natural consequence of the development of civilization and industry.
   2. A political solution should be sought.
   3. I don't think that present-day Japan is worried about the density-sparsity problem of the country.

5. Which way do you think Japan's population policy should be oriented?
   1. Encouragement of childbirth.
   2. Control of childbirth.
   3. Population policy is not necessary.

6. What do you think of the increase in the population of the aged?
   1. The increase of the aged population results from the diffusion of technology of medical care and other welfare policies in advanced countries and therefore is not undesirable.
   2. One should bear more children to moderate the population of the elderly.
   3. I don't think that the present age structure of the population is too old.

7. Do you think that the metropolitan city of Tokyo and its vicinity are over-crowded?
   1. Too crowded.
   2. A little crowded.
   3. Moderately populated.
   4. A little underpopulated.
   5. Very underpopulated.

8. [*For those who answered "crowded" in Question 7.*]
   What do you think is the appropriate size of a population?
   1. 20–30 percent less than the present population.
   2. 50 percent less than the present population.
   3. One-third of the present population.

9. Do you think that the population of Tokyo (or your local district) and its vicinity will continue to increase (decrease)?[1]
   1. Increase (decrease) sharply.
   2. Increase and then decrease (decrease gradually).
   3. Same as at present.
   4. Continue to decrease (increase gradually).
   5. (Increase sharply—local survey).

10. [*For urban respondents only.*]
    Density of the urban population has produced many harmful effects. Please circle the items whose effects you think are strong. Write additional items if you think they are necessary.
    1. Shortage of housing
    2. Narrowness of house
    3. Noise
    4. Garbage disposal
    5. Air pollution
    6. Traffic accidents
    7. Traffic density
    8. Loss of sunshine in the house
    9. Fear of disaster
    10. River and sea pollution
    11. Shortage of green areas and parks
    12. Loss of contact with nature
    13. Increase of commuting time to work place
    14. Increase of psychological stress
    15. Crime
    16. Unconcern for others
    17. Egoism
    18. Feeling of loneliness
    19. Decrease of morality

Attitude toward Tokyo

[*For urban respondents only.*]
I am going to ask you about the city of Tokyo. Do you want to continue living in Tokyo?
1. Continue to live in Tokyo.
   1. Going to stay in the present residence.
   2. Want to stay in Tokyo, but somewhere other than here.
2. Do not want to live in Tokyo.
   1. Want to move to a local area as soon as possible.
   2. Want to move to a local area after getting old.
   3. Want to move to a local area if the following things are satisfied (circle the numbers you think are appropriate):
      1. Occupation.

---

1   Phrases in parentheses apply to rural sample. "Local district" refers to rural district of sample.

    2. Education of children
    3. Benefit from culture.
    4. Living conditions.

Change of conjugal affections

I am going to ask you several questions about parent-child relationships.

1. Did you experience any change in conjugal relations after having a child?
    1. Conjugal affection became deeper because of having a child.
    2. No change of affection.
    3. Affection toward children became deeper and conjugal affection lessened.

2. Objectively considered, do you think of yourselves as overprotective parents?
    1. More or less overprotective.   3. "Laissez-faire" parents.
    2. Just moderately protective.

3. Are you confident about bringing up your children?
    1. Confident.
    2. Not very confident.
    3. Should bring them up regardless of having confidence or not.

4. With which items do you agree concerning the relationship between one's sex life and bearing children?
    1. One's sex life and bearing children are two different matters. People should please themselves with their sex life.
    2. It is a mistake to think separately of one's sex life and bearing children. Sex exists for procreation.
    3. The pleasure of one's sex life and the duty of procreation can coexist.

5. The following items concern fears and anxieties for children. Please circle the number which indicates the degree of fear and anxiety you feel.

	Very anxious	A little anxious	Medium	A little less anxious	Not anxious at all
1. Child's health	+2	+1	0	−1	−2
2. Cost of raising children	+2	+1	0	−1	−2
3. Discipline for children	+2	+1	0	−1	−2
4. Accident of children	+2	+1	0	−1	−2
5. Matters concerned with children's friends	+2	+1	0	−1	−2
6. Matters concerned with children's play	+2	+1	0	−1	−2
7. Abilities of children	+2	+1	0	−1	−2
8. Sex education of children	+2	+1	0	−1	−2

6. Husband and wife please answer these questions about parental authority separately.

Opinion of husband:
1. Authority of husband
   1. Has become stronger.
   2. Has become weaker.
   3. Has not changed.
2. Authority of wife
   1. Has become stronger.
   2. Has become weaker.
   3. Has not changed.

Opinion of wife:
1. Authority of husband
   1. Has become stronger.
   2. Has become weaker.
   3. Has not changed.
2. Authority of wife
   1. Has become stronger.
   2. Has become weaker.
   3. Has not changed.

Sex education

1. Which subject is the most desirable regarding sex education for the child?
   1. Sexual morality.
   2. Scientific knowledge about sex.
   3. Dignity of life.
   4. Sex education not necessary.

2. Who is responsible for sex education?
   1. Parents.
   2. School.
   3. Mass media.
   4. Leave as it is.

Pollution

An opinion exists among young people today that they do not want to bear children in such a polluted environment. What do you think about this opinion?
   1. Completely agree.
   2. Understandable to some extent.
   3. Not always true.
   4. Cannot understand at all.

That is all. Thank you very much for your cooperation.

Appendix Table   Factor structures of 45 attitude items after varimax rotation
(Analysis based on Japanese data only)

Item	Factor						Commu-nality	Mean score
	I	II	III	IV	V	VI		
36 One of the best things about having children is that you are never lonely	.58	.04	.05	.08	-.23	.20	.46	6.5
14 Having children around makes a stronger bond between husband and wife	.55	.17	.03	-.03	.01	-.10	.35	6.2
15 One of the highest purposes of life is to have children	.54	.36	-.07	-.04	-.01	.11	.45	5.8
20 Life for most people would be pretty dull without children	.50	.02	.03	.04	-.04	-.00	.27	6.2
8 It is only natural that a man should want children	.49	.25	.01	.08	.04	.23	.38	5.9
13 All the efforts a parent makes for his children are worthwhile in the long run	.48	-.02	-.03	.13	.25	-.19	.36	6.2
40 The really important things in life can be learned only from the experience of raising children	.48	.24	.01	.28	.09	.25	.45	5.5
6 Having children gives a person a special incentive to succeed in life	.47	.03	-.00	-.00	.06	.25	.30	6.7
22 After becoming a parent, a person is less likely to behave immorally	.45	-.08	.15	.13	.27	-.09	.34	6.1
31 The family with children is the basis for all that is good in our society	.45	.23	-.13	.26	.28	-.04	.44	5.8
29 Just the feeling a parent gets of being needed is enough to make having children worthwhile	.43	.20	.05	.09	.16	.38	.42	5.6
18 Having children is the most important function of marriage	.43	.46	.08	.18	-.03	-.04	.45	5.2

Item								Mean
5 Most married couples would be happier if they did not have any children	**.42**	-.12	-.25	-.06	-.07	.07	.27	6.6
16 A girl becomes a woman only after she is a mother	**.41**	.25	.13	.33	-.22	.25	.46	5.4
7 It is important to have children so that the family traditions will live on	.09	**.71**	.00	.04	.03	-.01	.53	4.7
34 A man has a duty to have children to continue the family name	.15	**.68**	.10	.20	-.08	.00	.54	4.0
2 A good reason for having children is that they can help when parents are too old to work	-.02	**.66**	.13	-.02	-.04	.10	.48	2.7
25 One of the best things about having children is the true loyalty they show to their parents	.03	**.51**	-.00	.19	.09	.31	.41	4.1
12 It is a person's duty to society to have children	.18	**.48**	.08	.04	.31	-.31	.48	4.3
35 A person can feel that part of him lives on after death if he has children	.25	**.45**	.04	.08	.12	.16	.32	4.8
44 A person who has no children can never really be happy	.06	**.43**	-.07	.48	-.04	.06	.43	3.6
43 The family with children is the only place in the modern world where a person can feel comfortable and happy	-.09	**.42**	-.06	.51	-.00	.18	.49	2.9
19 Children limit you in what you want to do and where you want to go	.04	-.09	**.70**	.09	-.01	-.14	.54	4.5
39 When you have children, you have to give up a lot of other things that you enjoy	.09	-.09	**.65**	.13	.00	-.07	.48	4.3
10 Always having children around is a great mental strain	.02	-.05	**.63**	-.11	.08	.00	.43	3.4
37 Raising children is a heavy financial burden for most people	.03	-.06	**.51**	.08	.18	-.03	.33	4.8
32 Before having a child, a couple should consider whether they would rather use their money for something else	.05	.13	**.49**	.05	.08	-.01	.28	2.5

Appendix Table (continued)

Item	Factor I	II	III	IV	V	VI	Communality	Mean score
1 Caring for children is a tedious and boring job	-.11	.11	.41	-.03	-.07	.10	.22	2.7
21 A young couple is not fully accepted in the community until they have children	.09	.00	.14	.60	-.12	.03	.41	2.5
27 A person with children is looked up to in the community more than a person without children	.02	.13	.04	.55	.05	.34	.45	3.0
17 It is the parents' fault if their children are not successful in life	.02	.03	.12	.49	.08	-.07	.27	3.8
45 A boy becomes a man only after he is a father	.27	.34	.17	.45	-.03	.10	.44	4.4
23 The first thing a couple should think about when deciding to have children is whether or not they can afford it	.03	.10	.14	.00	.64	.03	.45	5.1
9 A couple ought to think seriously about the inconveniences caused by children before they have any	-.03	-.04	.08	.04	.59	.09	.38	5.8
41 Before having a child, a couple should consider whether it would interfere with the wife's work or not	-.09	.10	.23	-.09	.48	.25	.38	5.4
33 One of the best things about being a parent is the chance to teach children what they should do and what they should not do	.17	.19	-.09	.11	.26	.57	.49	4.2
4 It is only with a child that a person can feel completely free to express his love and affection	.18	-.02	-.03	.08	.03	.46	.26	5.8
28 It is only natural that a woman should want children	.39	.15	.01	.23	-.04	.11	.25	6.0

3 Raising children is an act of virtue	.31	.37	-.01	.04	.07	.23	.30	5.0
42 Having children is a sign of blessing on a marriage	.23	.38	-.03	.18	.16	-.17	.30	4.6
30 A person who has been a good parent can feel completely satisfied with his achievements in life	.26	.06	-.12	.29	.32	.17	.31	5.5
38 It isn't right for a couple to interfere with nature by deciding to limit the number of children they will have	.23	-.08	-.00	.38	.23	-.16	.30	5.1
11 Considering the pressures from family and friends, a person really doesn't have much choice whether or not to have children	.03	.28	.31	-.06	.02	.21	.24	2.8
26 Having children causes many disagreements and problems between husband and wife	.08	-.09	-.33	-.08	-.09	-.16	.17	3.0
24 For most people, it is inevitable to have children	.12	.11	-.09	.24	.14	.11	.13	4.8
Eigenvalue	7.27	2.45	2.20	1.70	1.60	1.41	16.63	

references

Arnold, Fred, and James T. Fawcett

1975   *Hawaii.* Vol. 3, The Value of Children: A Cross-National Study. Honolulu: East-West Population Institute, East-West Center.

Arnold, Fred, et al.

1975   *Introduction and Comparative Analysis.* Vol. 1, The Value of Children: A Cross-National Study. Honolulu: East-West Population Institute, East-West Center.

Fawcett, James T.

1970   *Psychology and Population: Behavioral Research Issues in Fertility and Family Planning.* New York: Population Council.

Fawcett, James T., ed.

1972   *The Satisfactions and Costs of Children: Theories, Concepts, Methods.* Honolulu: East-West Population Institute, East-West Center.

Frejka, Tomas

1973   *Reference Tables to the Future of Population Growth.* New York: Population Council.

Hoffman, Lois W., and Martin L. Hoffman

1973   The value of children to parents. In James T. Fawcett, ed., *Psychological Perspectives on Population,* pp. 19–76. New York: Basic Books.

Iritani, Toshio

1972   Values of children in contemporary Japan. In James T. Fawcett,
            ed., *The Satisfactions and Costs of Children: Theories, Concepts,
            Methods*, pp. 311–24. Honolulu: East-West Population Institute,
            East-West Center.

Kestenberg, Judith

1956   On the development of maternal feelings in early childhood.
            Psychoanalytic Study of the Child 11:257–91.

Mainichi Newspapers, Population Problems Research Council, ed.

1976   *Japanese Population Problems*. Tokyo: Shiseido.

Matsubara, J.

1964   *Modern Family*. Tokyo: Nikkei Newspaper Press.

Morris, Charles

1956   *The Varieties of Human Value*. Chicago: University of Chicago
            Press.

Okazaki, Yoichi

1973   The forecasting of population in Japan. *Mainichi Shinbun*,
            June 16, evening edition.

Office of the Prime Minister, Statistics Division

1959   *White Paper on Population*. Tokyo: Printing Office, Japanese
            Ministry of Finance.

Parsons, Talcott, and E.A. Shils, eds.

1962   *Toward a General Theory of Action*. New York: Harper Torch
            Books.

Rabin, A.I.

1965   Motivation for parenthood. *Journal of Projective Techniques and
            Personality Assessment* 29:405–11.

Rabin, A.I., and Robert J. Greene

1968   Assessing motivation for parenthood. *Journal of Psychology*
            69:39–46.

Rheingold, H.R., ed.

1963   *Maternal Behavior in Mammals*. New York: John Wiley.

Secretariat, First Japan Population Conference, ed.

1974   *Proceedings of the First Japan Population Conference.* Tokyo.

Smith, M. Brewster

1969   *Social Psychology and Human Values.* Chicago: Aldine.

Spranger, Eduard

1928   *Types of Men: The Psychology & Ethics of Personality.* New York: Stechert.

Stephan, Frederick F.

1962   Possibilities and pitfalls in the measurement of attitudes and opinions on family planning. In Clyde V. Kiser, ed., *Research in Family Planning,* pp. 423–31. Princeton: Princeton University Press.

Tietze, Christopher, and Marjorie Cooper Murstein

1975   *Induced Abortion: 1975 Factbook.* Reports on Population/Family Planning, no. 14 (2nd. ed.). New York: Population Council.

Wyatt, Frederick

1967   Clinical notes on the motives of reproduction. *Journal of Social Issues* 23:29–56.